IMAGES
of America

CYNTHIANA

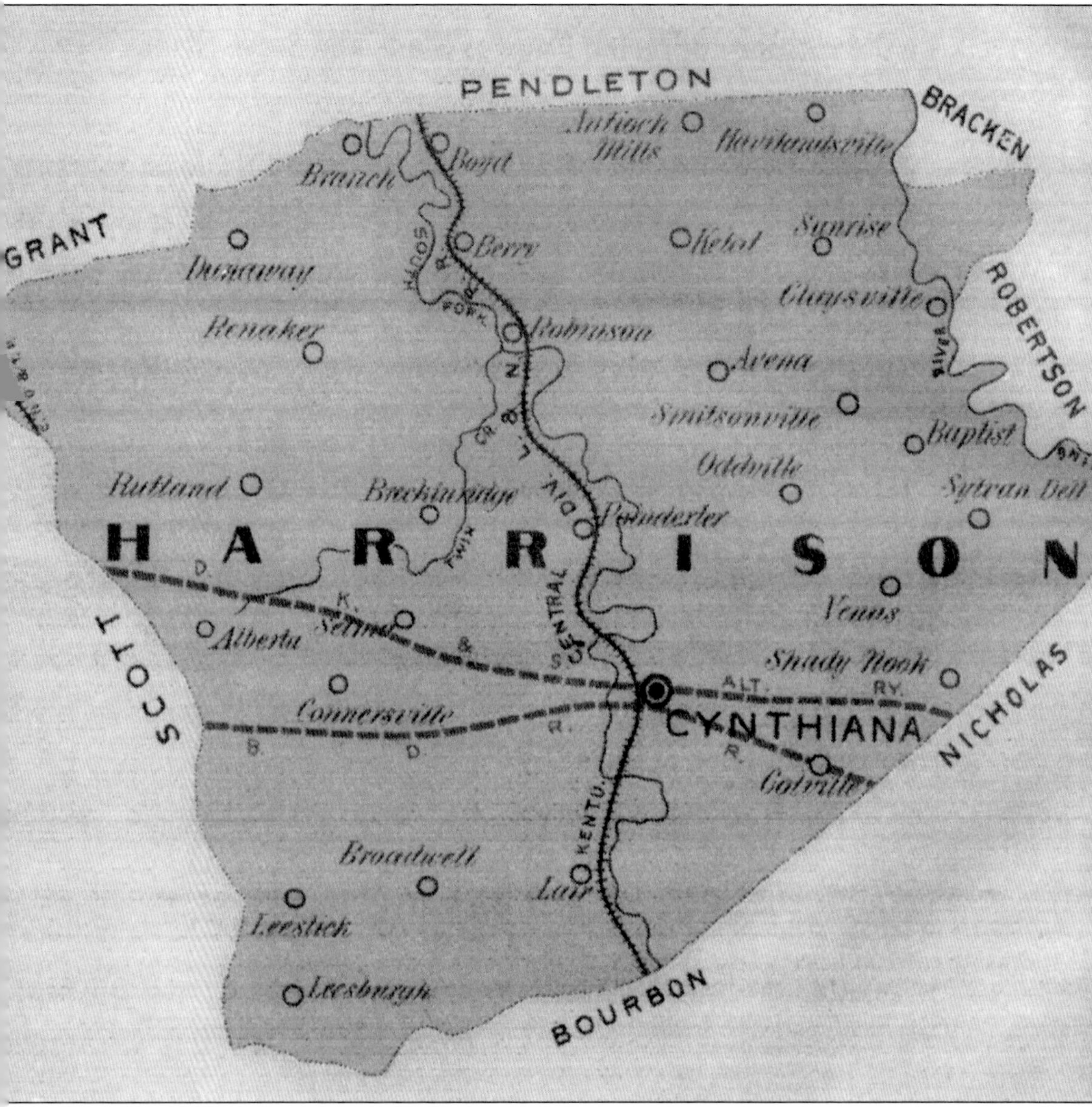

An 1897 map of Harrison County shows existing and proposed railroads, along with the names of the local communities served by those railroads. The proposed railroads, denoted by dotted lines, were never built. (Courtesy of the Cynthiana–Harrison County Museum.)

ON THE COVER: Members of the 1913 Cynthiana High School football team pose for a photograph on the hill where the school once stood facing Bridge Street. (Courtesy of the Cynthiana–Harrison County Museum.)

IMAGES
of America

CYNTHIANA

M. Britt Kennerly

ARCADIA
PUBLISHING

ISBN 978-0-7385-6652-8

Published by Arcadia Publishing
Charleston, South Carolina

Printed in the United States of America

Library of Congress Control Number: 2009931086

For all general information contact Arcadia Publishing at:
Telephone 843-853-2070
Fax 843-853-0044
E-mail sales@arcadiapublishing.com
For customer service and orders:
Toll-Free 1-888-313-2665

Visit us on the Internet at www.arcadiapublishing.com

To the loving family who assured me that my writing mattered: Robert W. and Helen Harney, Bessie Perkins Barnes, Godfrey Barnes, and Douglas Steed Kennerly.

Contents

Acknowledgments 6

Introduction 7

1. Grounded in the Past 9
2. We Know Them Well 23
3. Familiar Places and Faces 39
4. Halls of Learning 49
5. Faith of Our Families 69
6. Down to Business 77
7. The Sports Pages 109
8. Good Neighbors 121

Acknowledgments

In a photograph taken on Christmas Day, 1971, I am shown clutching Rod Stewart's *Every Picture Tells a Story* album. I am thrilled and honored to share, through vintage views, the story of my hometown—"the Maiden City"—better known as Cynthiana, Kentucky.

This book would not and could not have happened without the help, patience, and records of the dedicated, delightful heroes who volunteer at the Cynthiana–Harrison County Museum, along with the members of the Harrison County Historical Society. These historians' years-long mission to preserve all things Cynthiana has resulted in an impressive written and physical guide to days gone by and a wonderful outpouring of local interest in the same.

I am especially grateful to Dorothy and Harold Slade, whose passion for preserving the treasures of their hometown brought them out at odd hours and on days the museum was closed to help in my quest for photographs. I am indebted, too, to William A. "Bill" Penn, whose grasp of Cynthiana's importance in central Kentucky history is inspirational. Others who provided sorely needed information, photographs, support, and good humor include Pat Barnes and Terry Harris of the Cynthiana–Harrison County Public Library; Rose Chasteen; Flossie Gasser; Helen McNees; Sarah Kinney; Meg and Bob Ammerman; Marilyn David Wash; Jeanine Webber Lulich; Dean Peak; Linda H. Moore; Patsy Palmer Hampton; the folks at the *Cynthiana Democrat*; Katharine Smith; and the staff of the Student Technology Resources Center in the University of Cincinnati's Langsam Library.

It bears mentioning, too, that many Cynthiana-based family photographs were lost to the flood of March 1997, and my heart goes out to those who lost precious glimpses into their pasts. Finally, I would like to thank Luke Cunningham and Amy Perryman of Arcadia Publishing, who encouraged my efforts from book concept to final draft. Labors of love are still, well, laborious—but the love, I find, always wins out.

INTRODUCTION

In a fast-moving, ever-evolving global community, some places are destined never to be a destination, the subject of exploration, or even a gasoline stop. Cynthiana, Kentucky, is not one of those places.

Credit for assuring Cynthiana's well-deserved place in history books and hearts alike rests now, as it has since the city's founding, with its people—those who live Cynthiana's stories and those who tell them. Those people—from the earliest pioneers to volunteers at the Cynthiana–Harrison County Museum to local writers—are more than the keepers and makers of dates. They are the weavers of a warm and comforting tapestry of time, and *Cynthiana* celebrates them.

Lying about 35 miles north of Lexington and 60 miles south of Cincinnati, Cynthiana is many things to numerous people traveling U.S. Route 27, U.S. Route 62, and Kentucky Highway 36, the highways that serve it. For history buffs, this county seat was the home of two Civil War battles. For lovers of nature, Cynthiana is the Licking River and numerous, well-cast fishing spots. For older travelers who hit the road pre–fast food, it was a good place to stop and eat, where Groucho Marx stopped at McKnight's Restaurant for home cooking and Pine Villa was a solid choice as one headed to Cincinnati.

For all who love it and those who have called it home, this city of about 6,200 people is one of those "good to grow up in" places, full of faces, spaces, and seemingly ordinary times that, in hindsight and in Cynthiana, truly matter.

There are the groundbreaking dates, like December 10, 1793, when Cynthiana was chartered as a town, followed 11 days later by the formation of Harrison County by the state's general assembly. The oldest brick house in Cynthiana, next to the Cynthiana Presbyterian Church until 1936, was built in 1805 on the northwest corner of Main and Pleasant Streets. Schools, churches, and growth blossomed, with the eye-catching county courthouse erected on Main Street in 1853 and a clock installed in the structure three years later.

The railroad thundered into town, bringing jobs and then riders—the Covington-to-Lexington railroad was completed to the town limits on May 16, 1854, and the first passenger train from Covington to Cynthiana ran the rails on May 22, 1854. In the 1850s, agriculture and manufacturing were king. One hundred years later, factories, said *Cynthiana Democrat* writer Thelma Taylor, "sprouted like dandelions around the perimeter of Cynthiana again." *Cynthiana* visits some of those dates, viewing days gone by through the photographs and snippets of written history from those who were there.

There are the people whose very names spark an instant smile of recognition–people like the quotable, colorful "Judge Mac" Swinford, the long-serving federal judge from Cynthiana who told his own story in his book *Kentucky Lawyer*, and Joe B. Hall, the former University of Kentucky basketball coach who graduated from Cynthiana High School in 1947 but needs no introduction to hoops fans of all ages.

There are the businesses locals still treasure—Biancke's Restaurant, which opened in 1894 and fills its walls today with photographs from the city's past—and the ones long-loved but now gone, like M. Goldberg and Sons clothing store. *Cynthiana* drops in for a visit with Biancke's and other downtown, down-home friends.

And luckily, at every milestone along the way since the 1800s, there have been the storytellers—those whose love for their city and county has pushed them to record the passage of time.

William H. Perrin penned *History of Bourbon, Scott, Harrison, and Nicholas Counties, Kentucky* in 1882; a few years later, Cynthiana transplant Lucinda Rogers Boyd—wife of Judge J. Strother Boyd—crafted unforgettable tales in her flowery, commentary-rich 1894 book, *Chronicles of Cynthiana.* Decades later, Cynthiana children whose grandparents grew up reading the chronicles were still hearing one of Boyd's tales—that of the innocent David Sheely's 1847 hanging for the murder of his wife, Nancy, a gory tale gussied up by Boyd's ghostly description of David Sheely's specter.

In the early 20th century, John M. Cromwell, a banker and Cynthiana mayor who lived from 1862 to 1951, spun the saga of the city in style. A history buff, he started writing articles in the local newspaper, then called the *Log Cabin*, in the late 1920s.

In the latter part of the 20th century, those who enjoy reading about and keeping up with Cynthiana's people and progress have been kept informed by writers including the late George Slade, one of the founders of the Cynthiana–Harrison County Museum and the author of a weekly *Cynthiana Democrat* column called "Museum Musings." A "Cromwell's Comments" fan, Slade dug into the past but never stopped looking ahead. Thelma Taylor of the *Cynthiana Democrat* looked to the past for modern-day cues, too. Her conversational style was as inviting as an open front door. In 1983, for example, Taylor described Harrison County's 197,000 acres of land as "shaped like a warm Hershey's chocolate—almost, but not quite, square" and explained how the Main Licking and South Licking Rivers "wiggle through Harrison County." The Licking Rivers splash into *Cynthiana* too.

Another Cynthiana native, William A. "Bill" Penn, has been an avid historian and photographer since his days at Cynthiana High School. The author of *Rattling Spurs and Broad-Brimmed Hats: The Civil War in Cynthiana and Harrison County, Kentucky* and longtime editor of the Harrison County Historical Society's monthly newsletter, he offered written and photographic vantage points for *Cynthiana.*

Almost 150 years after the war that inspired *Rattling Spurs*, road names and residents have changed in the Maiden City. One must look only as far, however, as Lucinda Rogers Boyd's *Chronicles of Cynthiana* to see the good that comes from a sense of wonder, an interest in history and community. Boyd wrote,

> If Abram Crossdale, who died and was buried in the old cemetery, in 1812, could rise from the dead and sit on his moss-grown tombstone, how would he be surprised to see the cars thunder past his resting-place! And if he might interrogate 'Young American' (he wouldn't be afraid of the 'Old Ghost,' not he), he might learn that since he fell asleep, eighty years ago, steamboats and steamships have been made to sail all the rivers and seas, and that they and steam cars had brought all the wonders of once unknown lands to our very doors; that a man in Cynthiana can reprove, by word of mouth, his son who is in Cincinnati; that a woman can scold her husband, through the telephone, from Boston to New York! And, equally strange, that telegraph wires belt the globe, and that by lightning we send messages to the uttermost parts of the earth.

If Boyd could rise from the dead, she would surely be pleased to see change in a city she loved. There is little doubt she would explore it. She would write about it. She would, as does *Cynthiana*, embrace everything about that change—and look ahead.

One

GROUNDED IN THE PAST

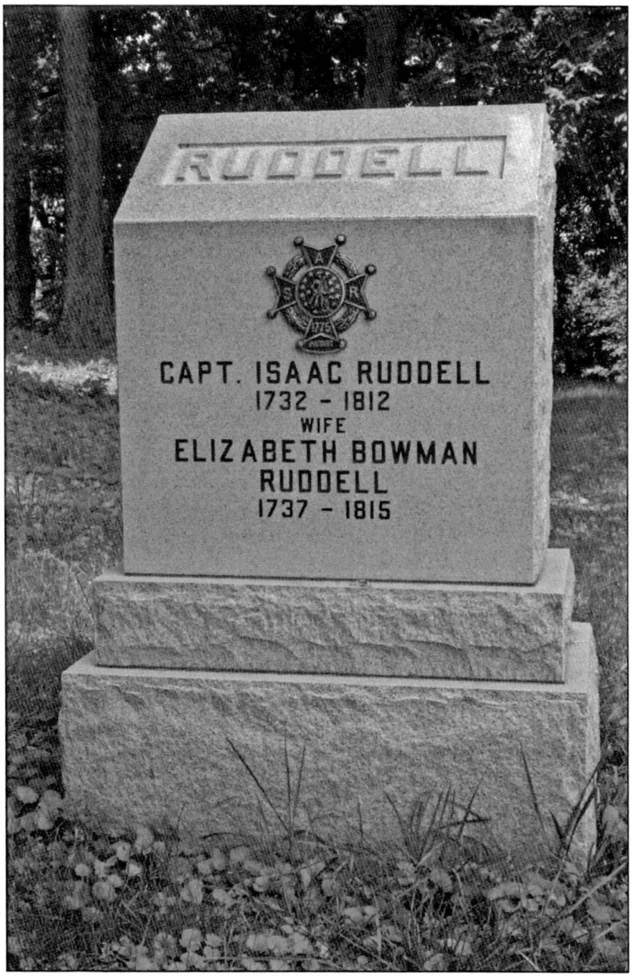

A simple, dignified marker in Stonermouth Presbyterian Cemetery at Ruddell's Mills commemorates the life of Capt. Isaac and Elizabeth Ruddell, who are among the area's memorable pioneers. Capt. John Hinkson and 15 others from Pennsylvania were the first settlers in the Cynthiana area in 1775, abandoning the site on the south fork of the Licking River a year later. In 1779, Isaac Ruddell led another group to the site just south of what is now Cynthiana, lending the name Ruddell's Station to the pioneer settlement. British and Native American troops led by Capt. Henry Byrd attacked the site in 1780, killing about 20 people and forcing the Ruddells and other survivors to march to Detroit as prisoners. After their release, Isaac and Elizabeth returned to Kentucky. Captain Ruddell died in 1812, and his wife died three years later. (Courtesy of Linda H. Moore.)

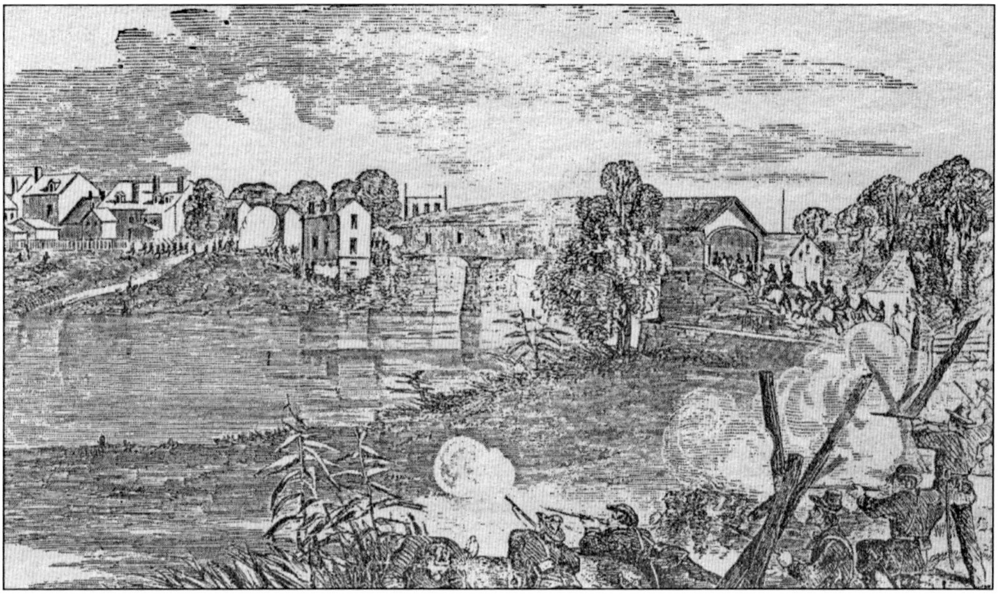

Two Civil War battles were waged in Cynthiana, which sent native sons to fight for both the Union and the Confederacy. The first battle of Cynthiana, on July 17, 1862, brought Gen. John Hunt Morgan to town with 816 men. They battled with the Federal forces led by Col. John J. Landrum and drove them back at the old covered bridge on Main Street. Eight Union soldiers died that day. Morgan returned to Cynthiana on Saturday, June 11, 1864, along with 1,200 soldiers. Three battles—the last Civil War battles fought in Cynthiana—ensued that weekend. Just a few years later, the grove where fighting took place east of town on Millersburg Pike on June 12, 1864, was named Battle Grove Cemetery. (Both courtesy of the Harrison County Historical Society.)

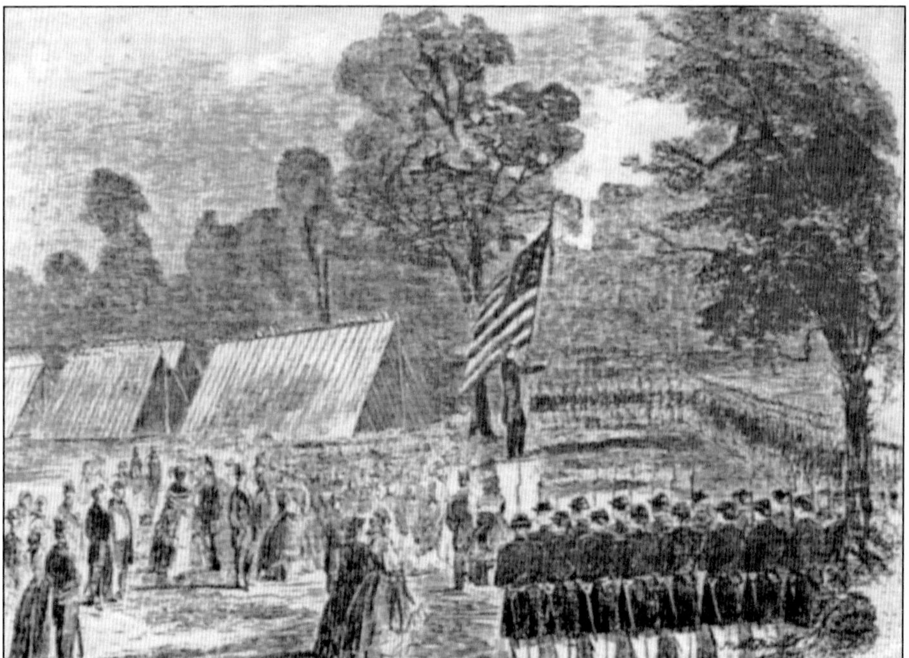

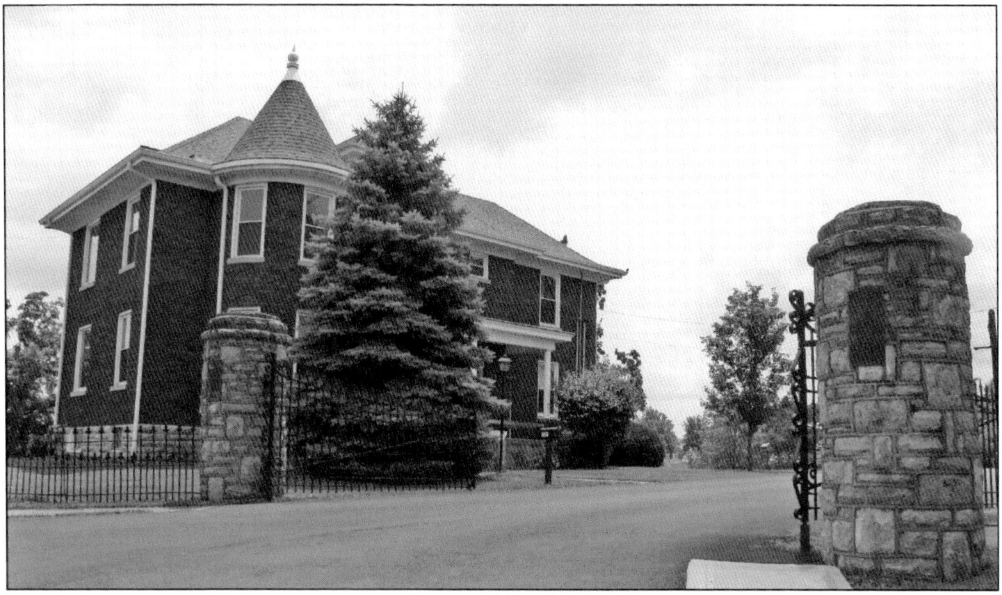

Battle Grove Cemetery, the site of the last Battle of Cynthiana, was dedicated on November 4, 1868. For 75 years before Battle Grove Cemetery was founded via a Masonic order, the Old City Cemetery on North Main Street was the city's only burial spot. (Courtesy of Linda H. Moore.)

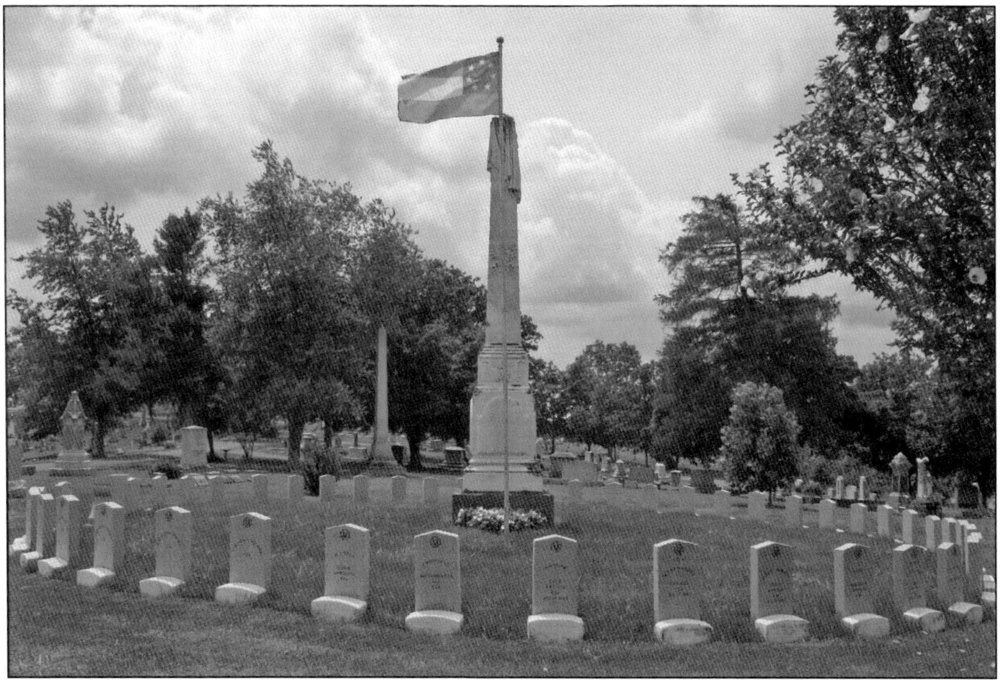

The Confederate monument at Battle Grove Cemetery is surrounded by 48 graves, the final resting spot for soldiers who died in battle on June 12, 1864. (Courtesy of Linda H. Moore.)

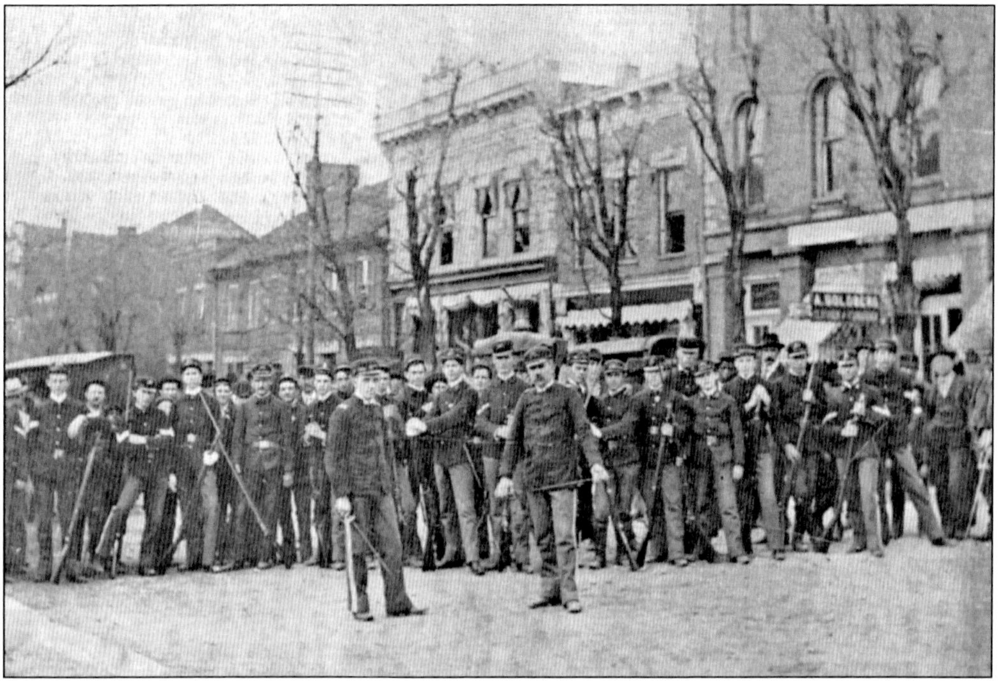
Veterans returning from the Spanish-American War are pictured in the late 1800s. (Courtesy of the Cynthiana–Harrison County Museum.)

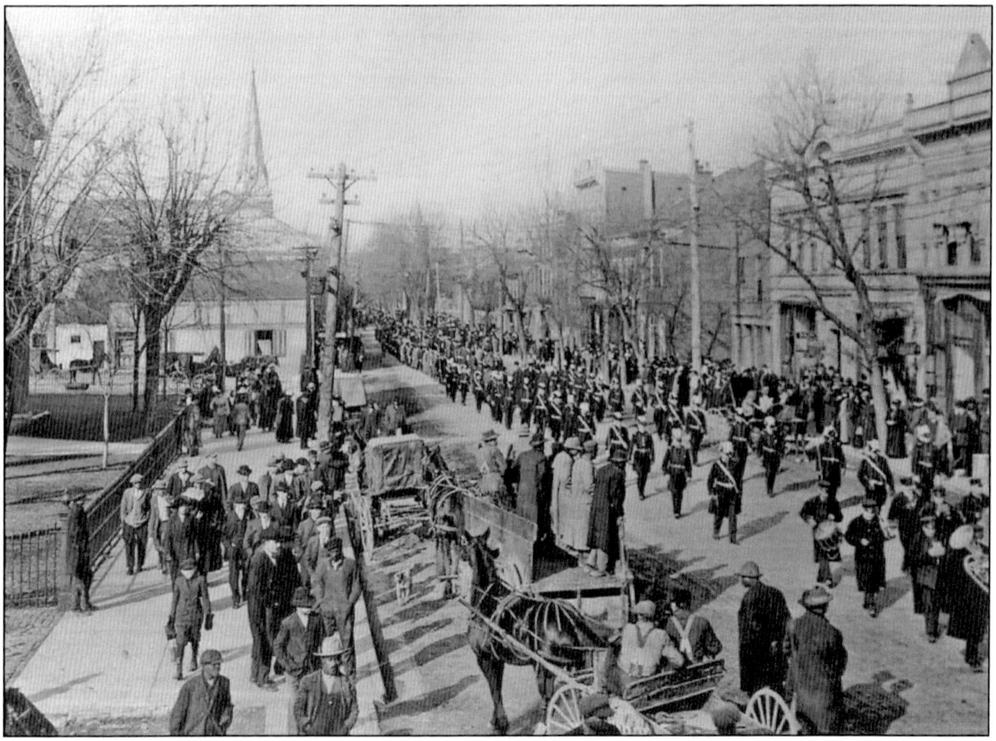
A funeral procession for attorney Harry Bailey, who was murdered in downtown Cynthiana on January 27, 1913, heads down Main Street. (Courtesy of the Cynthiana–Harrison County Museum.)

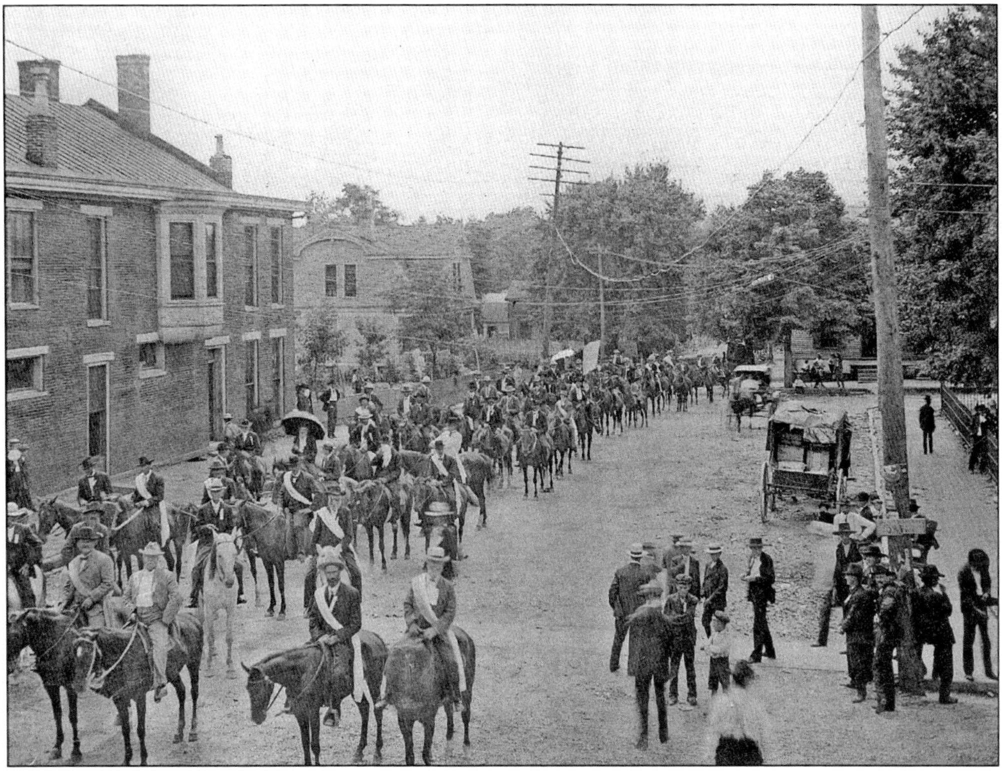

In 1897, an election was held to determine if Harrison County would serve alcohol or remain a dry county. Residents are shown on Cynthiana's Main Street the day of the vote—the courthouse fence is visible at right. The result: Harrison County remained dry. (Courtesy of the Cynthiana–Harrison County Museum.)

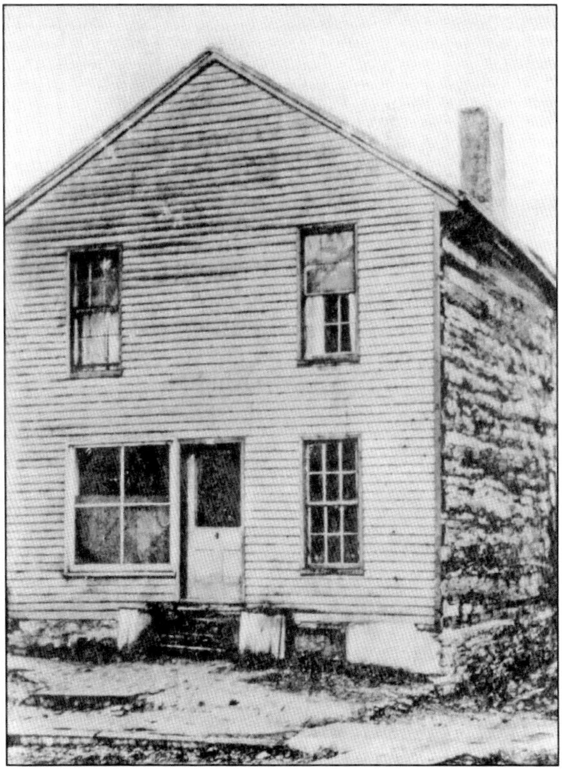

While it was commonly thought for years that this building on Court Street was the original Harrison County Courthouse—it was touted as such on postcards—members of the Harrison County Historical Society cannot find evidence that court was ever held there. The house later became popularly known as the Old Log Cabin, serving in a variety of roles detailed on page 40. The house was built in 1790 by Dr. James McPheeters and was later the home of Dave Rees. (Courtesy of the Harrison County Historical Society.)

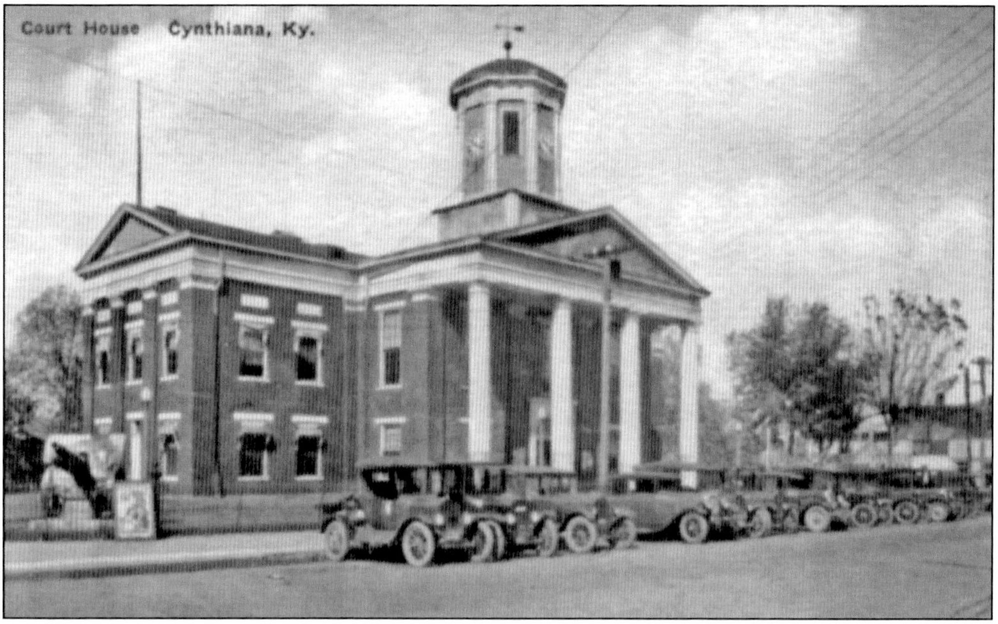

Postcard views of the Harrison County Courthouse have been popular for decades. The major change in the building's look came when it was painted white in the 20th century. (Courtesy of the Cynthiana–Harrison County Museum.)

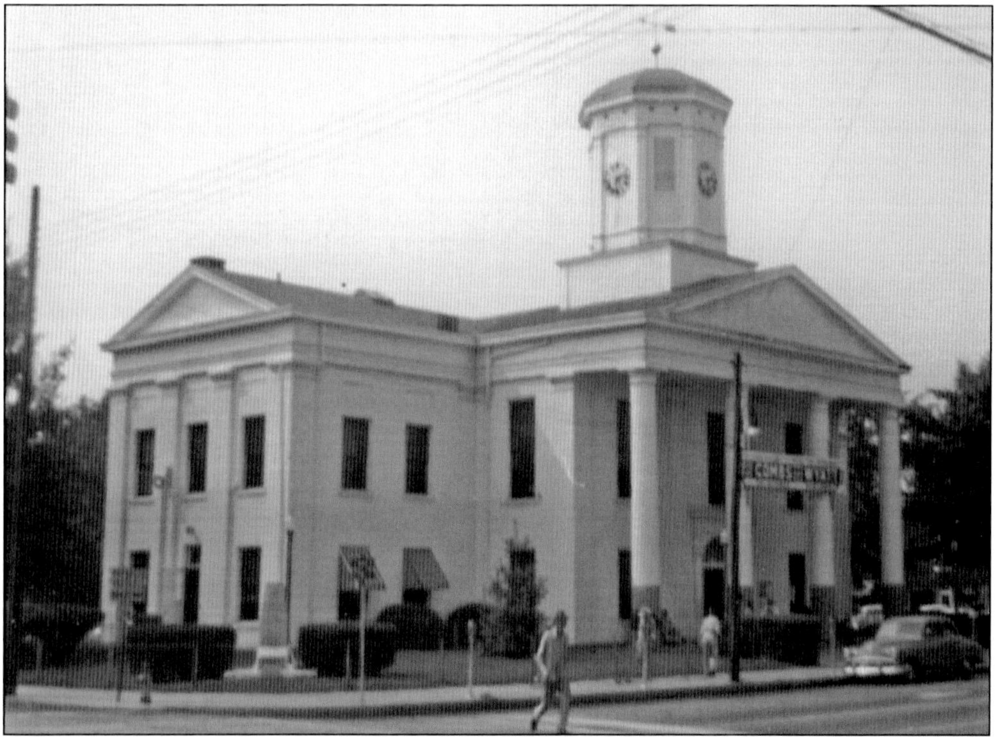

William A. "Bill" Penn's love of history and photography took him to the streets of Cynthiana during his high school days. He took many pictures of the downtown area, from special events to beloved sites, including the county courthouse. (Courtesy of William A. Penn.)

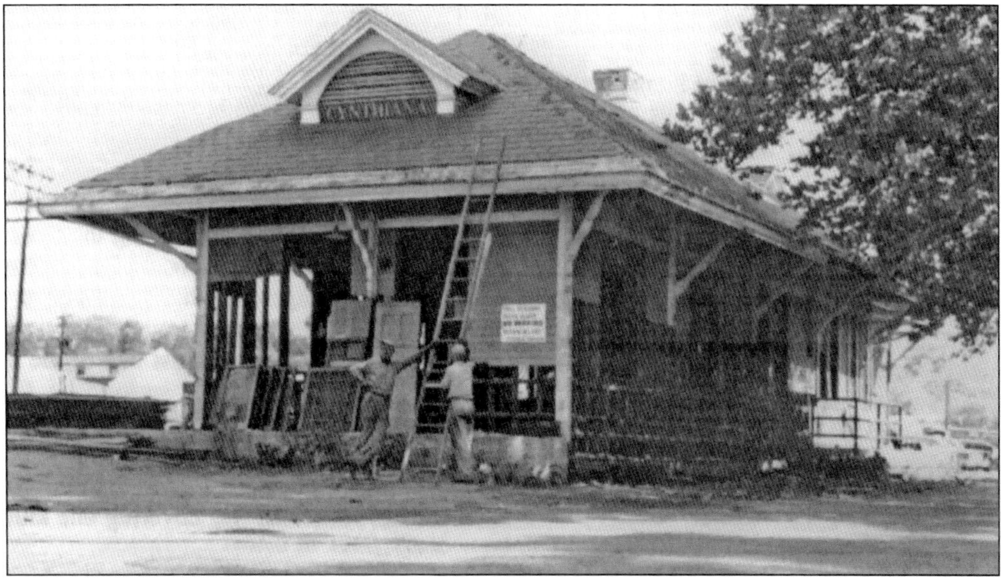

The Louisville and Nashville Railroad Depot stood between Bridge Street and the home of Southern States. The passenger depot was built in 1892 and remodeled in 1912. (Courtesy of the Cynthiana–Harrison County Museum.)

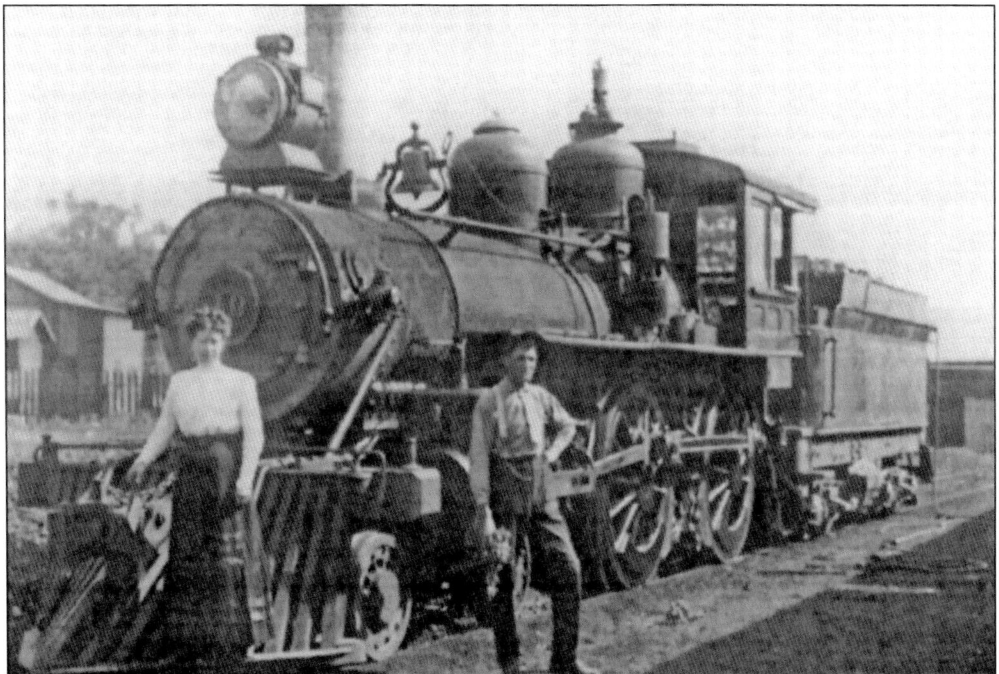

Railroad worker Obe Terry and his wife, Anna, of Cynthiana stand near the tracks around 1900. (Courtesy of the Cynthiana–Harrison County Museum.)

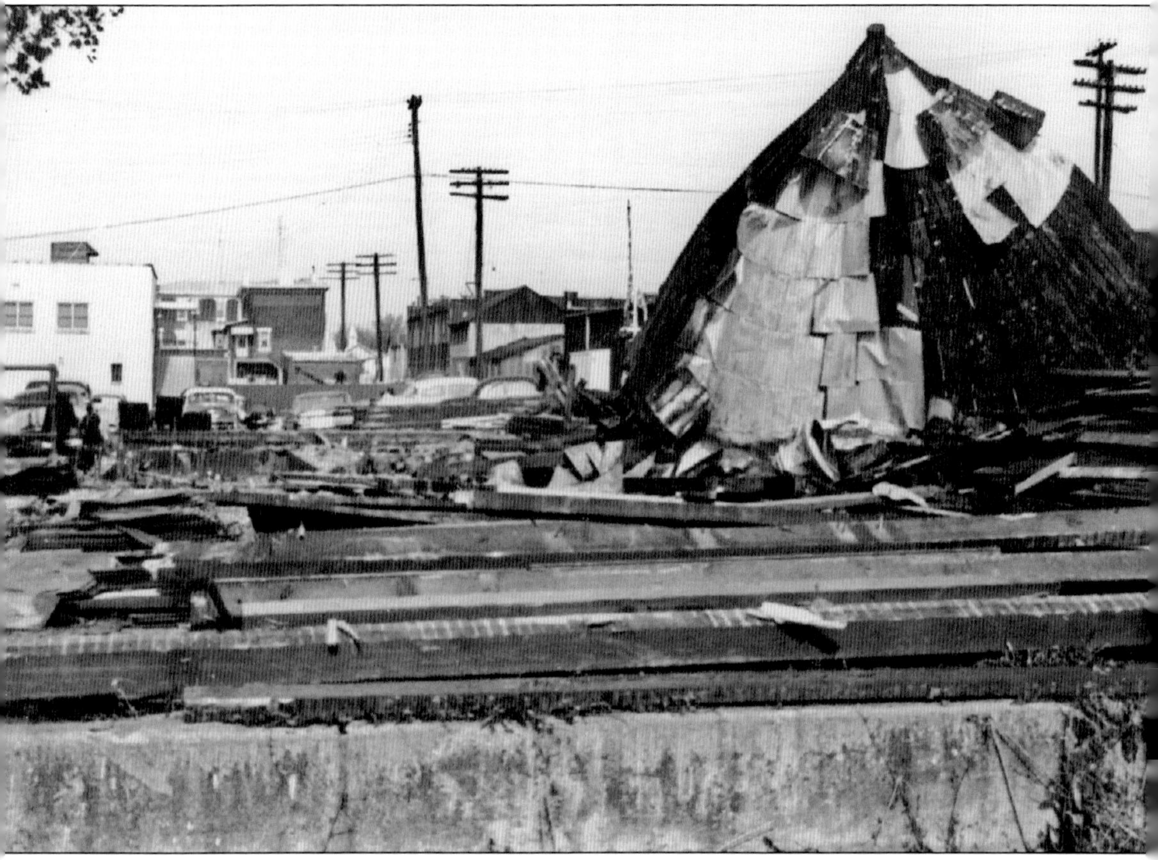

Bill Penn, a 1961 graduate of Cynthiana High School, witnessed the razing of the Louisville and Nashville depot that year. The freight depot, on the southeast corner of Bridge Street and the railroad tracks, was demolished 15 years later. (Courtesy of William A. Penn.)

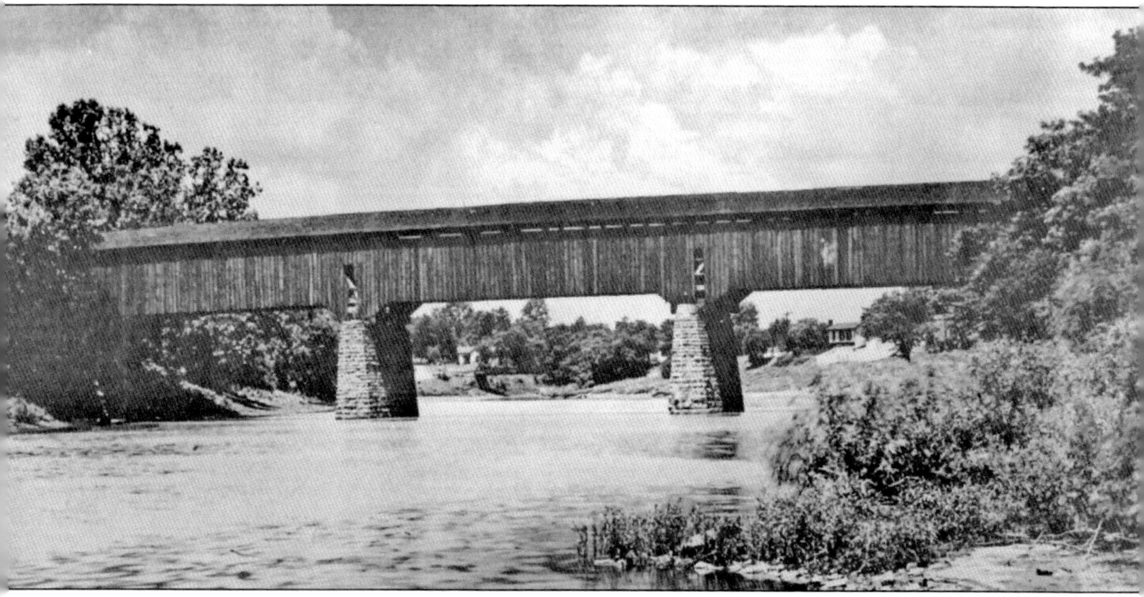

In 1837, a covered bridge was built over the Licking River on Main Street leading into downtown Cynthiana. The bridge, designed by Lewis Wernwag and built by Greenup Remington, closed 107 years later, in June 1944. Four people drowned when a car went through the floorless skeleton of the bridge on December 18, 1946. The remains of the bridge were pushed into the river in December 1948, and on October 8, 1949, the John Hunt Morgan Bridge opened in the old covered bridge's place. (Courtesy of the Cynthiana–Harrison County Public Library's James Saunders Whaley Collection.)

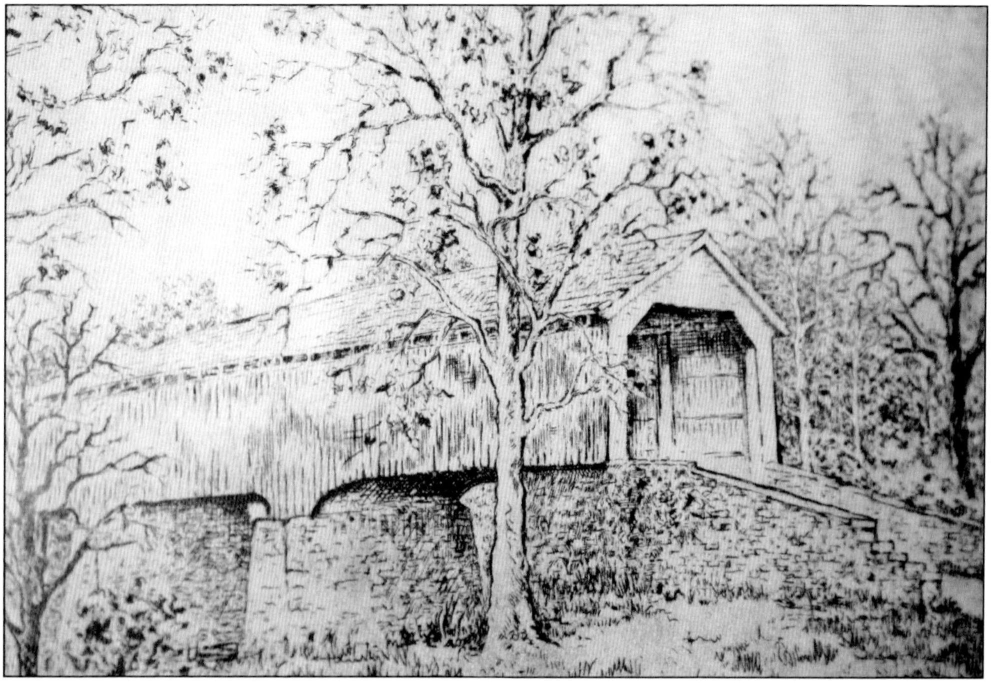

The bridges of Cynthiana are a vital part of travel into and out of the city. And drought or downpour, the Licking River's ups and downs bear daily impact on life in Harrison County. One devastating example of flooding occurred in March 1997, when more than 12 inches of rain fell during a three-day period and swelled the Licking's waters to a cresting point of 8 feet above flood stage. Hundreds of people had to be rescued from their homes, with residences and businesses alike left underwater. (Both courtesy of the Cynthiana–Harrison County Museum.)

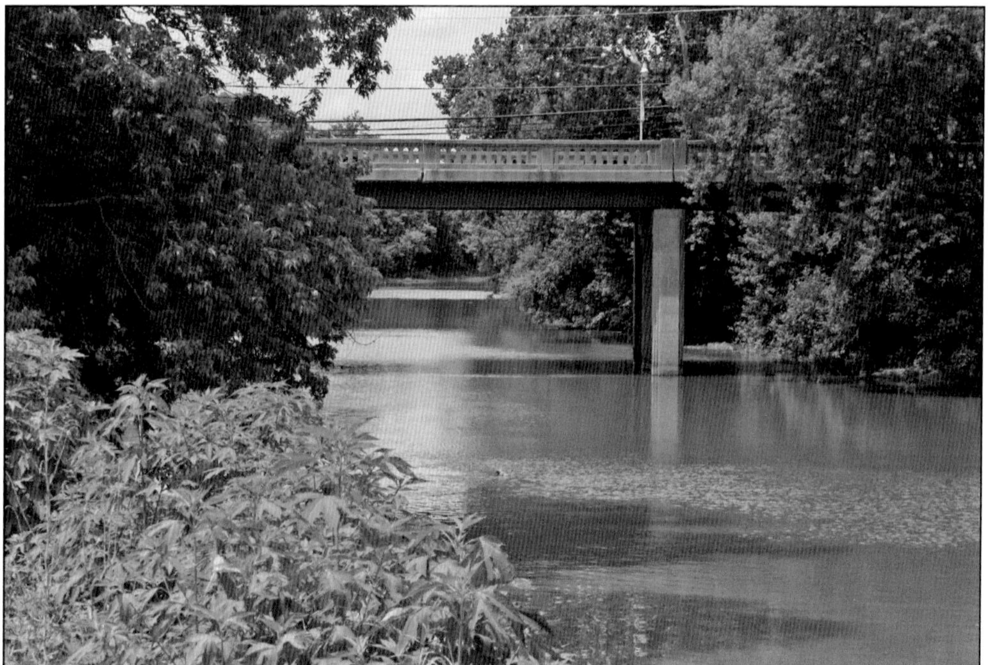

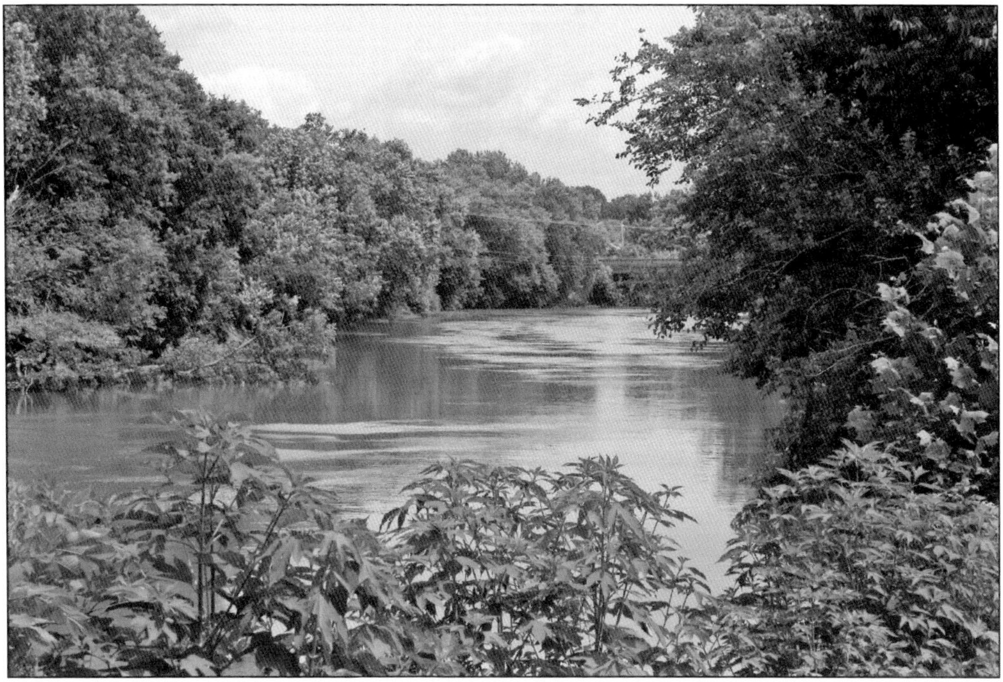

The modern-day Licking River is shown to the north from the Pleasant Street bridge. An older view shows the effects of a 1948 flood that brought the waters of the Licking River into downtown homes and businesses. Flooded buildings included the Dr Pepper bottling plant at Pike and Poplar Streets. (Above courtesy of Linda H. Moore; below courtesy of Helen Harney.)

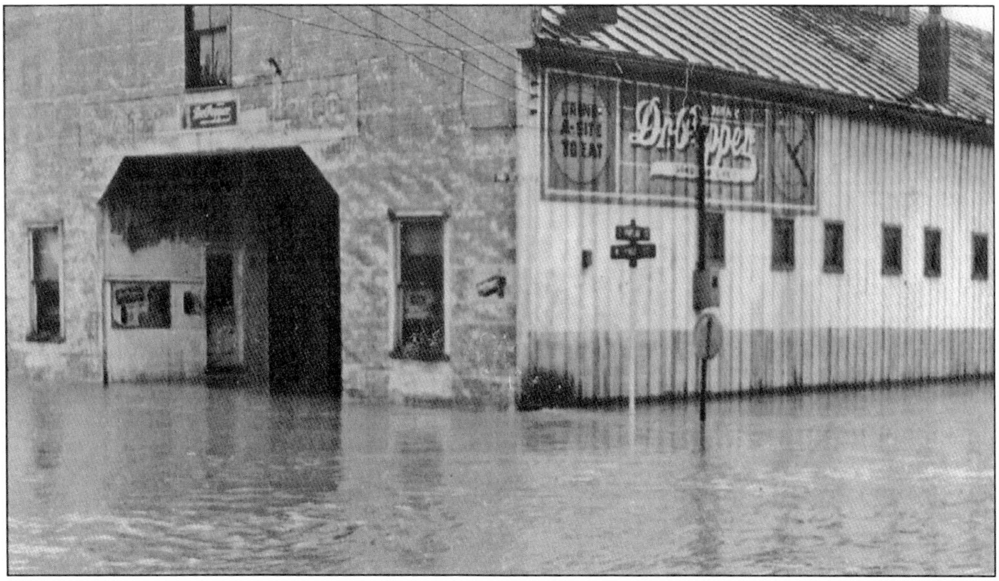

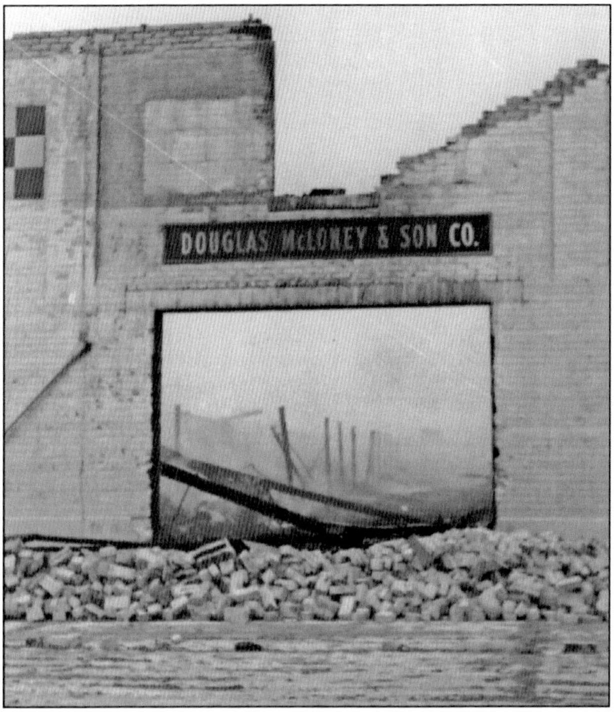

On July 10, 1960, the McLoney Warehouse burned in the 300 block of South Church Street, leaving damages estimated at more than $750,000. Several businesses were located in the warehouse, including Douglas McLoney and Son, a feed and seed operation, and a hardware and farm store owned by Nelson McLoney. Other notable fires in Cynthiana over the years include an 1845 blaze that destroyed the Methodist church at Pike and Church Streets; the January 21, 1918, fire at Cynthiana High School; the December 30, 1965, blaze at St. Edward Church; the July 8, 1985, inferno at the Monticello mansion; and a February 1, 1994, blaze at Webber's Sausage. (Both courtesy of William A. Penn.)

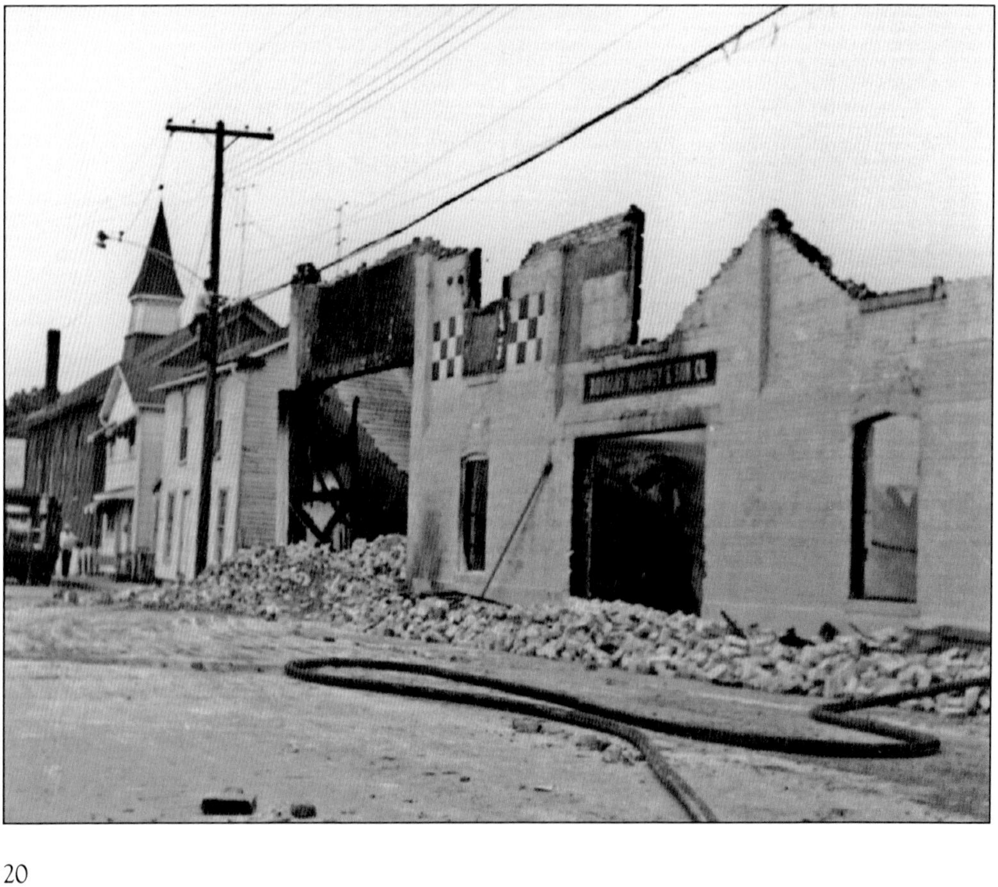

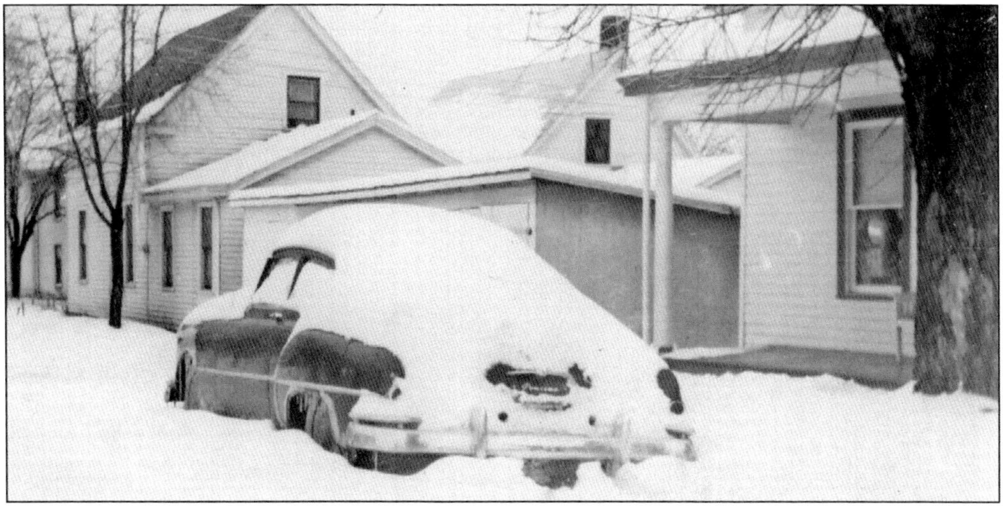

Rain, sleet, snow, sun—Cynthiana has seen it all over the years, and sometimes rain and snow in great amounts. Pictured is the aftermath of a typical snowfall in the 1950s. The annual average precipitation in Cynthiana, according to the National Weather Service, is 43.48 inches. (Courtesy of Helen Harney.)

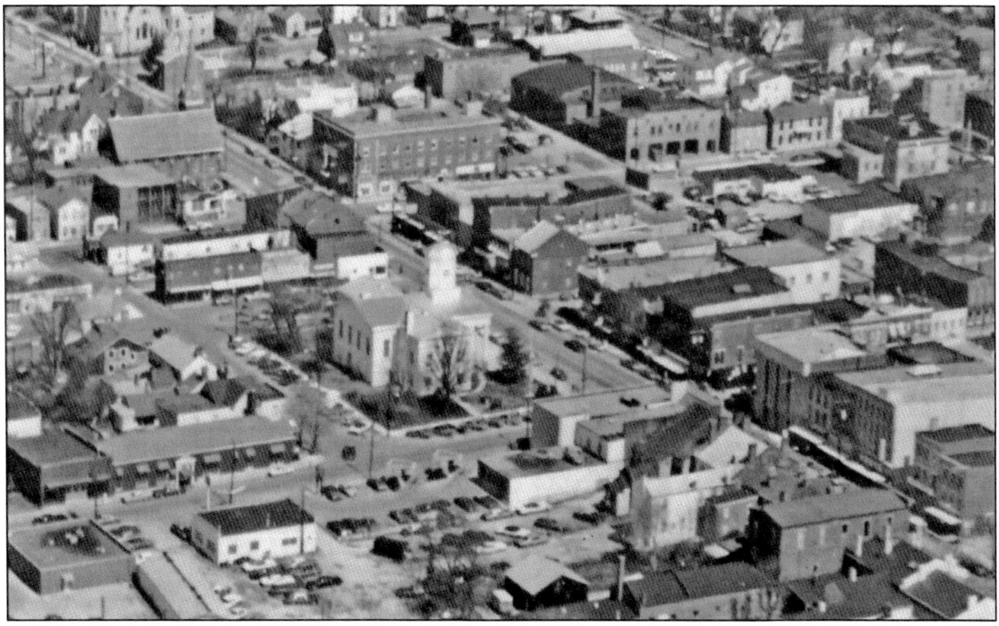

An aerial view of the city from the 1960s shows the heart of Cynthiana, the downtown area surrounding the county courthouse. (Courtesy of the Cynthiana–Harrison County Museum.)

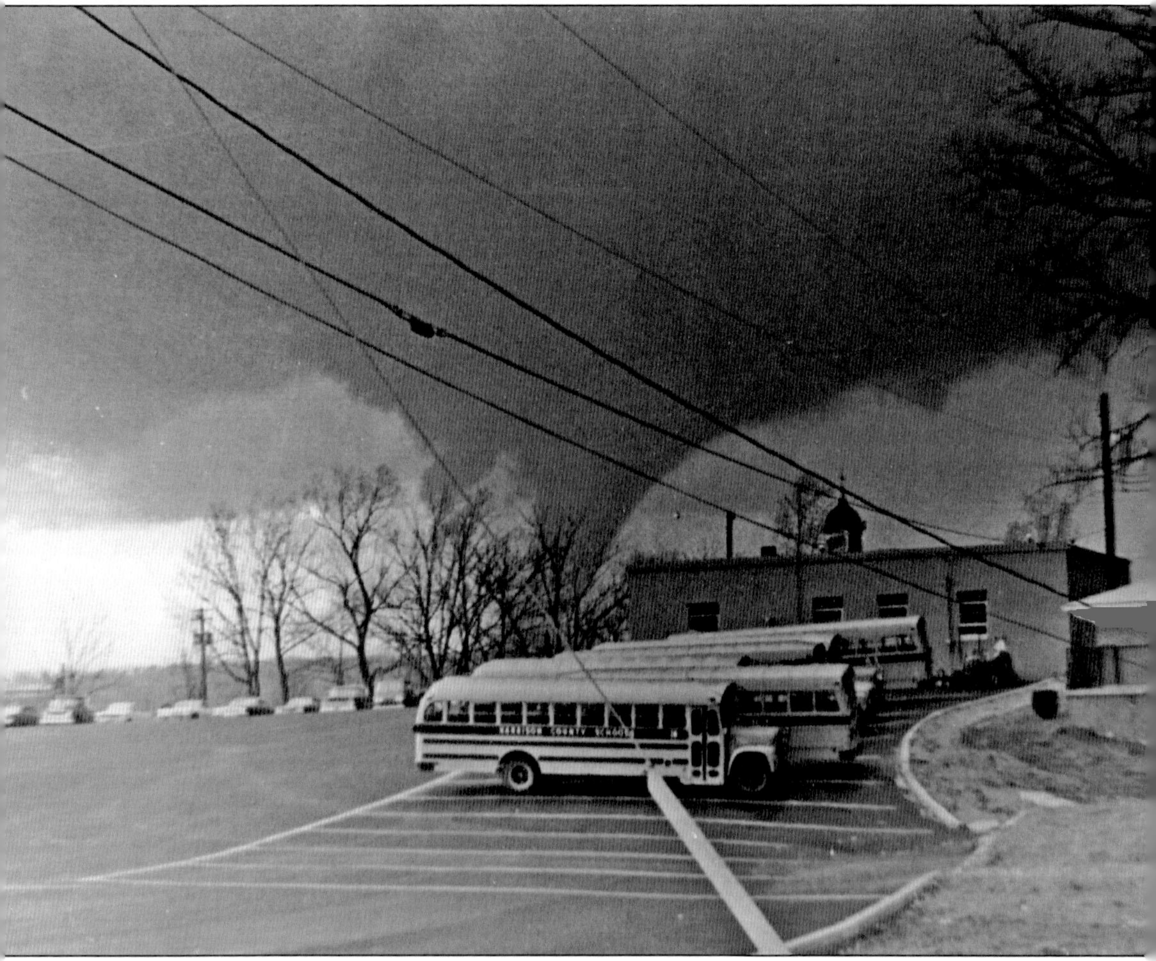

This terrifying yet exciting shot of an April 3, 1974, tornado was taken from the "hilltop," the home of Harrison County High School on Webster Avenue. Senior John LaBore, who was one month away from graduation at the high school at the time of the twister, took the widely circulated photograph that captured the intensity and immense size of the near-F4 storm. National Weather Service accounts of the storm stated that the tornado hit around 6:55 p.m. and "moved northeast from Lee's Lick to west of Cynthiana, east of Poindexter, ending near Claysville." Thankfully, no deaths or major injuries were suffered locally, but 40 homes and 75 barns were destroyed, with more than $6 million in real estate damage and more than $1 million in farm machinery and livestock losses reported. The storm was one of 148 twisters touching down in 13 states over April 3–4, 1974, part of what the National Oceanic and Atmospheric Administration called a "super tornado outbreak." It was, NOAA reported, the worst tornado outbreak in U.S. history, killing 330 people and injuring 5,484 in a path covering more than 2,500 miles. (Photograph by John LaBore, courtesy of the Cynthiana–Harrison County Museum.)

Two

We Know Them Well

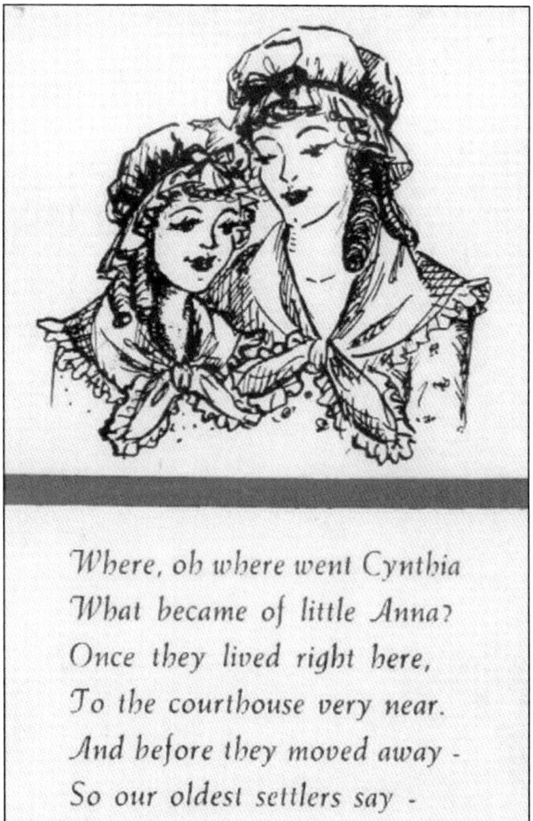

This winsome postcard tells the tale of Cynthia and Anna Harrison, whose father, Robert Harrison, donated the land on which Cynthiana was established in 1793. The girls' names formed the basis for the city's moniker. The county, however, is named after Col. Benjamin Harrison, once the sheriff of nearby Bourbon County and a framer of Kentucky's first constitution. (Courtesy of the Harrison County Historical Society.)

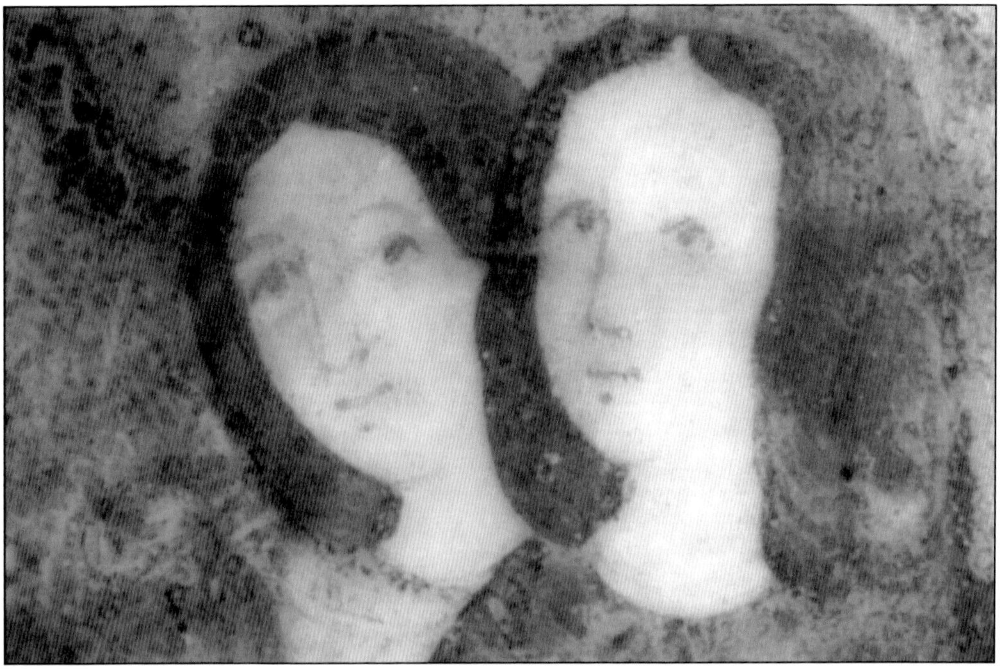

In 1894, writer Lucinda Rogers Boyd's *Chronicles of Cynthiana* shared this story about the Harrison family, from whom the city of Cynthiana got its name: "Tradition relates that Robert Harrison was a gay, healthy, rollicking son of the wilderness, just the man for the times; and that his blooming young daughters, not then grown, were the favorites of all their father's customers and neighbors. The name Cynthiana of course gave general satisfaction. But Robert Harrison soon sold out his rights to the soil here, for his farm was already, in 1793, laid out into convenient streets and alleys, and, before Cynthia and Anna had reached womanhood, he removed to Portsmouth, Ohio. This picture was on a pin given by Betty Biancke to the Cynthiana–Harrison County Museum. (Courtesy of the Cynthiana–Harrison County Museum.)

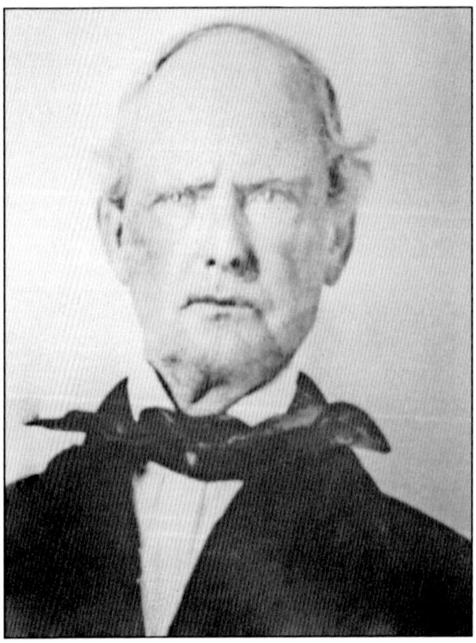

Cynthiana businessman and contractor Greenup Remington (1804–1891) built the old covered bridge over the Licking River on Main Street, a span used from 1837 until 1944. He also crafted the front doors of the Cynthiana Presbyterian Church. (Courtesy of the Cynthiana–Harrison County Museum.)

Samuel Farrow January, the first mayor of Cynthiana, was the eighth child of Samuel and Elizabeth Marshall January. Born March 26, 1809, in Cynthiana, he was married to Josephine B. Stevens in 1848. The Januarys had two children, Martha and James. Farrow, who was elected mayor in 1860, died on August 3, 1900, in Paris, Kentucky. (Courtesy of Cynthiana City Hall.)

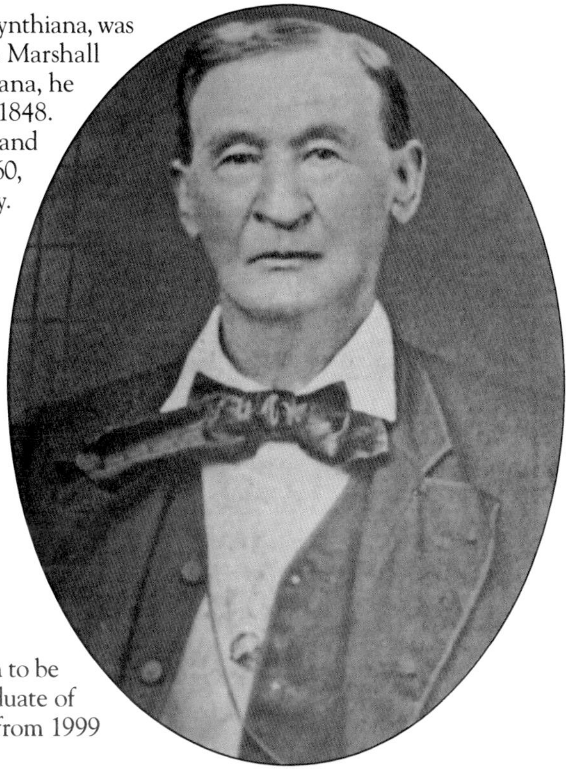

Virgie Florence Wells was the first woman to be elected mayor of Cynthiana. A 1954 graduate of Cynthiana High School, she held office from 1999 to 2006. (Courtesy of Virgie Wells.)

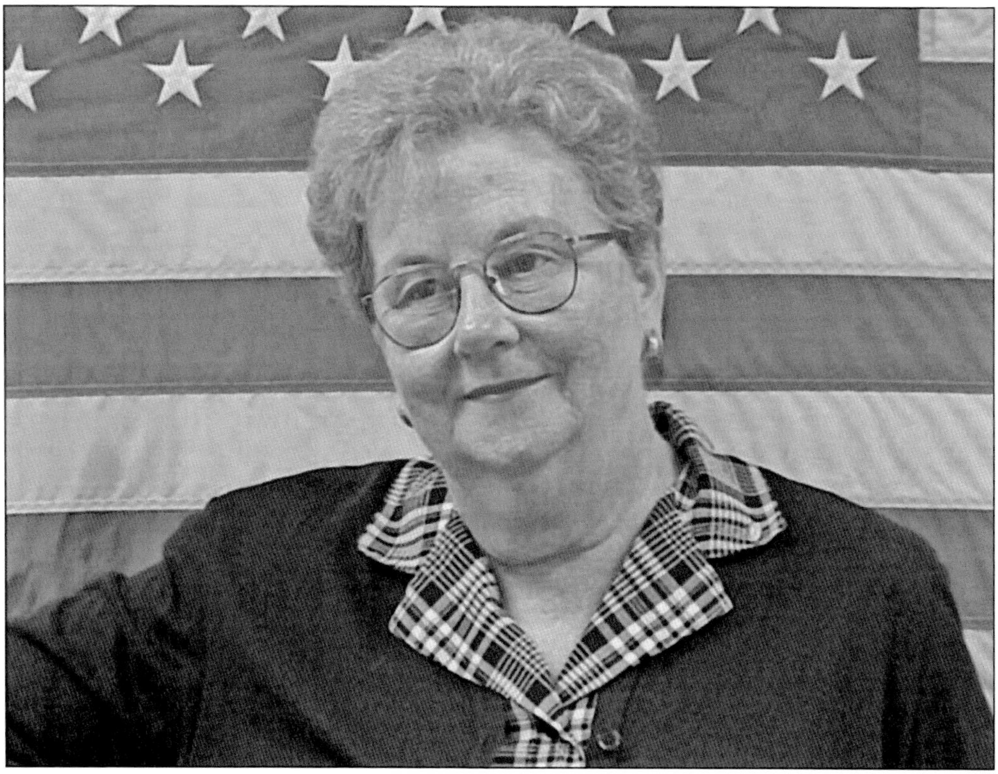

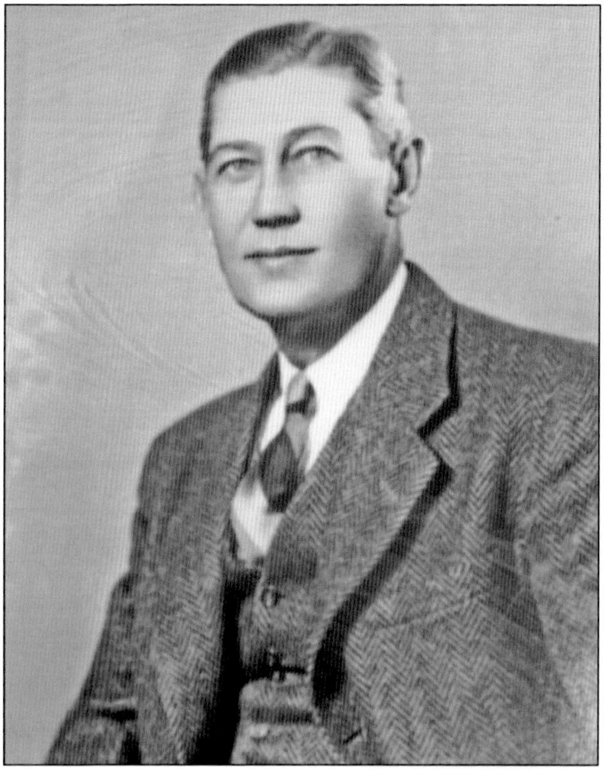

Sterling Owen Jr. served as mayor from 1934 to 1937. His son, Sterling Owen III, followed in his father's footsteps as a Cynthiana leader. (Courtesy of Cynthiana City Hall.)

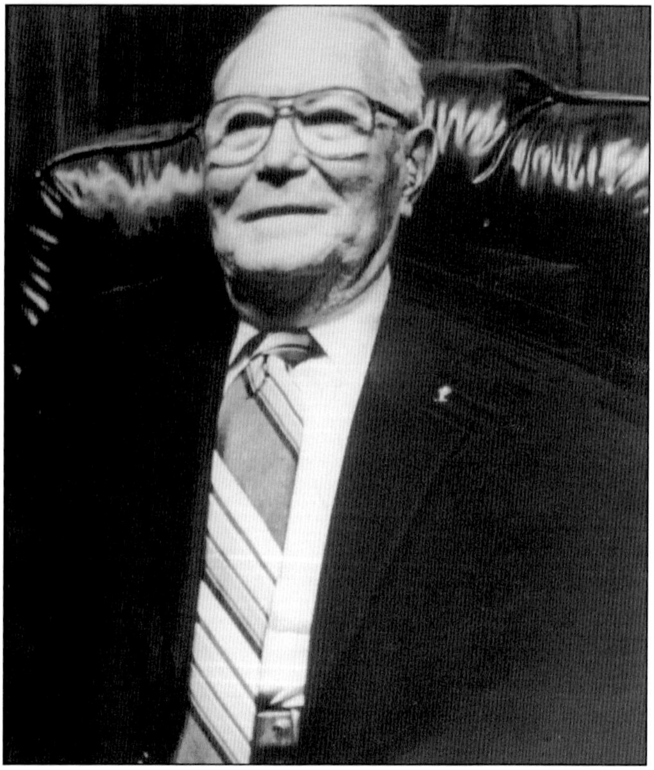

Auctioneer John Cummins led Cynthiana through the post–World War II years, from 1946 until 1953, and was elected again in 1958. He remained in the mayoral post until 1965. (Courtesy of Cynthiana City Hall.)

Sterling Owen III was Cynthiana's mayor from 1954 to 1957. In 2004, his son, Sterling Owen IV, was appointed police chief in Knoxville, Tennessee, a post he still held in 2009. (Courtesy of Cynthiana City Hall.)

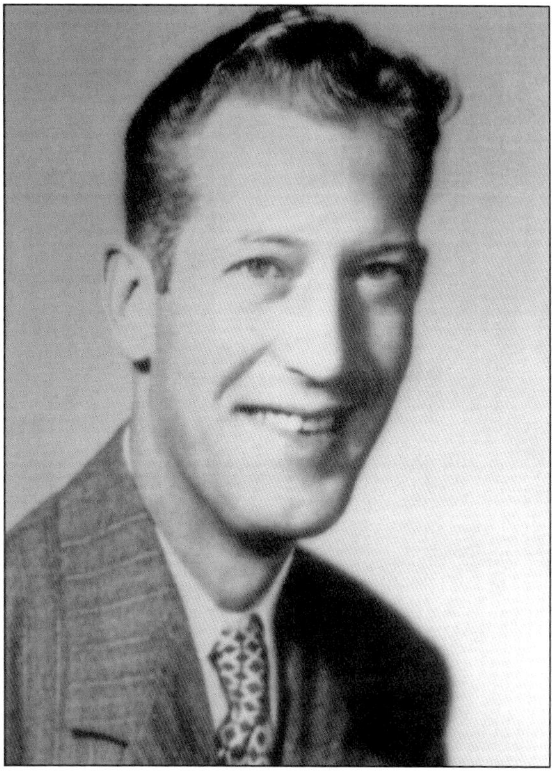

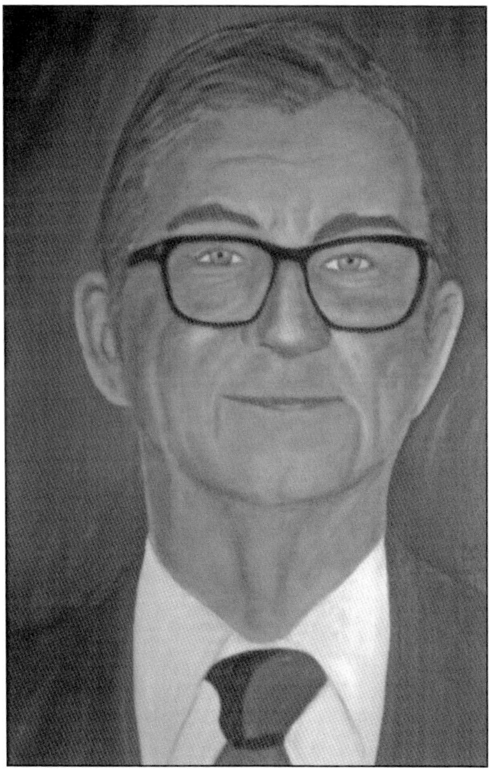

Mayor Marshall Bell's term of office ran from 1966 to 1968. (Courtesy of Cynthiana City Hall.)

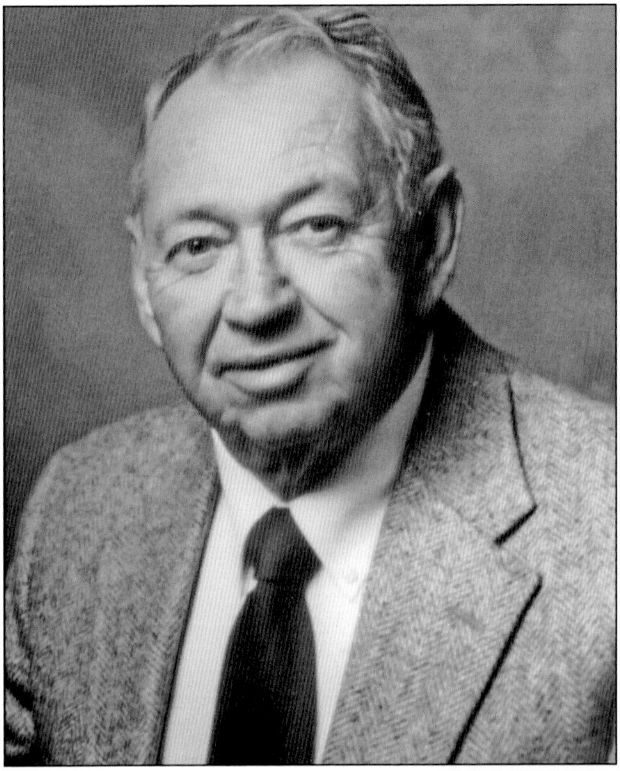

Melvin Hampton was Cynthiana's longest-serving mayor as of 2009, filling the role from 1970 until 1993. His son, Bruce Hampton, a former Cynthiana police officer, was elected sheriff of Harrison County in 1990 and was still in office as of 2009. (Courtesy of Cynthiana City Hall.)

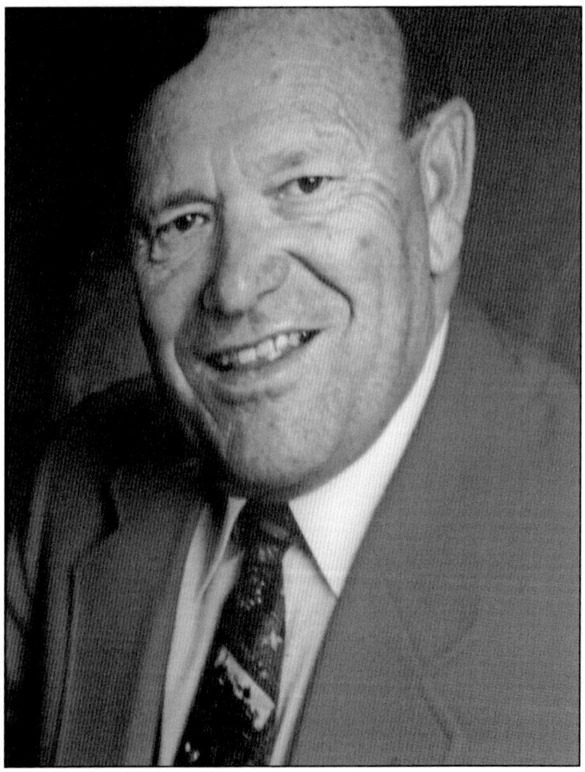

Cynthiana residents first elected James "Jim" Brown to the mayor's seat in 1994; he was in office until 1999. He was reelected in 2007 but stepped down in 2009 due to illness. (Courtesy of Cynthiana City Hall.)

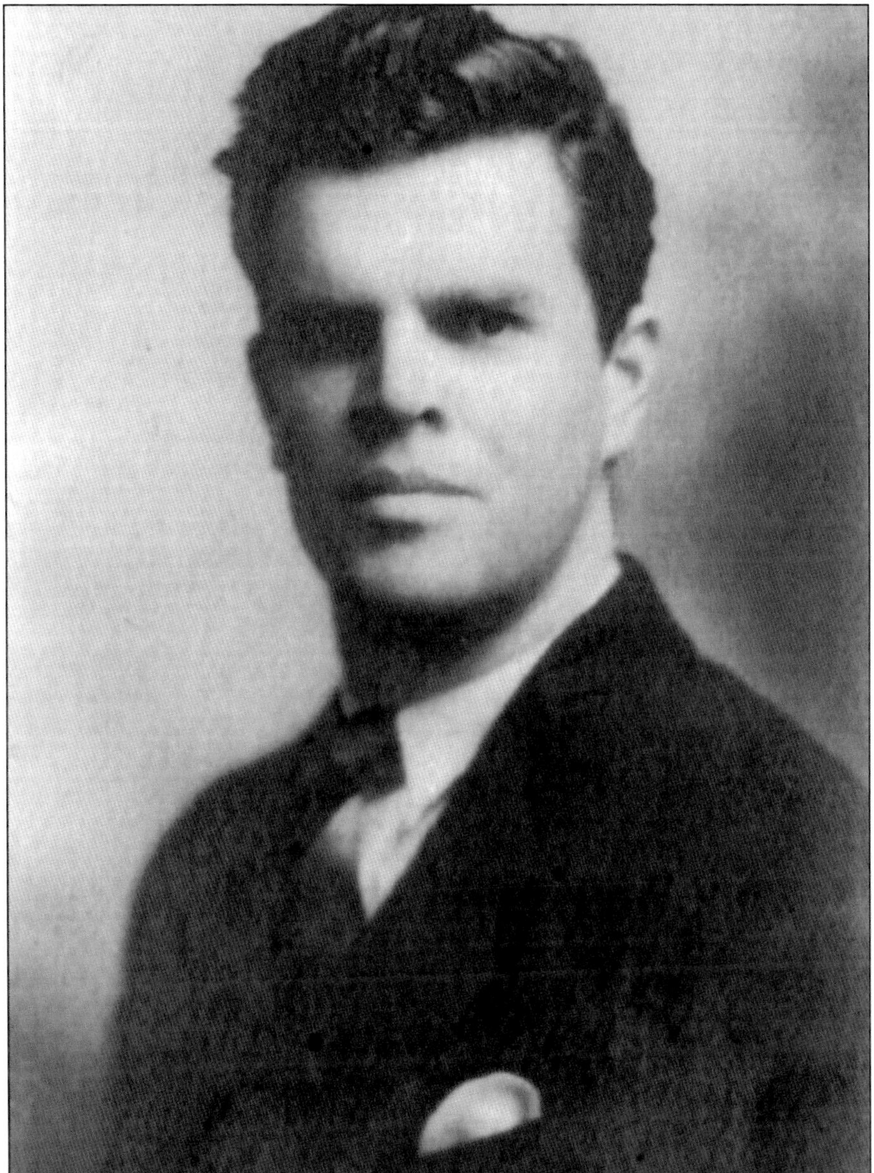

"Those bearing the name of lawyer are by their profession, like plumed knights, committed to its preservation and defense in the finest sense," said Mac Swinford in his 1963 book, *Kentucky Lawyer.* Swinford was born in 1899, lived his entire life on Pike Street in Cynthiana, and was known simply as "Judge Mac" to his local admirers. Yet Mac Swinford's name was well known in legal circles that looped far beyond the city and state of Kentucky, and his sense of duty and reasoned legal decisions touched lives countless miles from his hometown. The son of M. C. and Allie McKee Swinford, he graduated from Cynthiana High School and earned his law degree at the University of Virginia. A former Kentucky state representative, he became U.S. attorney for the Eastern District of Kentucky in 1933. In 1937, Pres. Franklin D. Roosevelt named Swinford the U.S. district judge for the Eastern and Western District of Kentucky. Judge Mac died in 1975—after a day in court. (Courtesy of Sarah Kinney.)

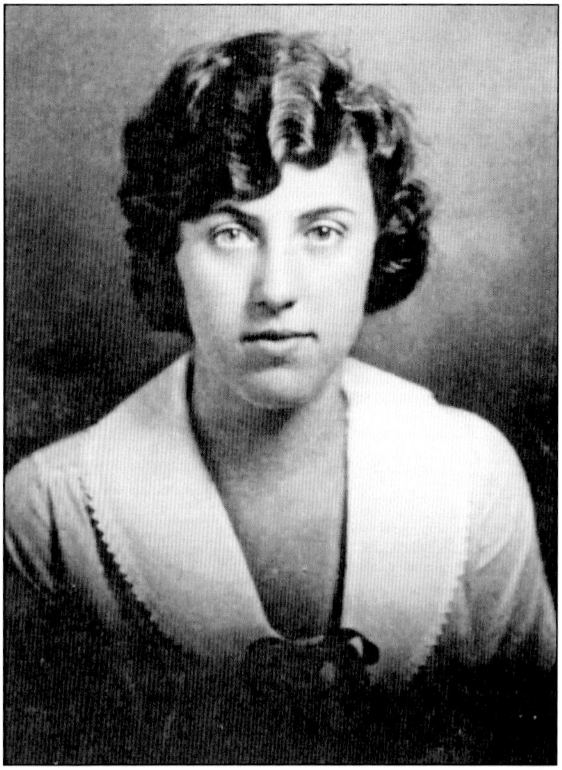

Cynthiana native Minnie Benton Peterson, the city's only female attorney for many years, was born in 1901 to attorney Hanson Peterson and Mary Jouett Peterson. After graduation from the University of Kentucky, where she was a member of the Mortar Board and Kappa Kappa Gamma, she practiced law with her father for two years in Cynthiana. She married Mac Swinford in 1927, and the couple had five children: Mary Jouett Reed, John Swinford, Sarah Kinney, Alice Kolbe, and Ann Gregg Dunn. Minnie was the first woman elected to the Cynthiana School Board and the Harrison County School Board. She was a leader in the drive to merge city and county schools and to integrate the local school system. Minnie died in 1995. (Courtesy of Sarah Kinney.)

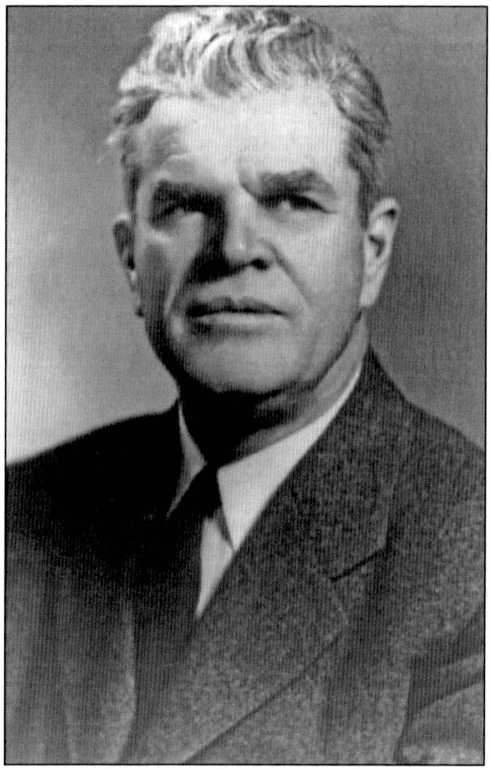

Judge Mac Swinford's record of support for civil liberties spanned several decades. Several of his decisions as a federal district judge, including integration of lower grades in Fayette County, are mentioned in an article in *The Register* of the Kentucky Historical Society (Vol. 101, No. 3). The article shares that in 1970, "he overturned the suspension of a long-haired student that had not met a school's rigid standards." Swinford wrote the opinion in the nation's first post–*Brown v. Board of Education* desegregation case in 1955, "ordering Adair County to allow black students to enroll in its white schools." The article also states that in April 1963, "he ordered the Bowling Green school system to do the same" and that Swinford "condemned the Kentucky High School Athletic Association for following racist policies." The article concludes, "We can only speculate when the vestiges of the old system (of segregation) would have disappeared had the (Jefferson) plaintiffs not brought the matter to court and had Swinford ruled differently in this historic decision." (Courtesy of Sarah Kinney.)

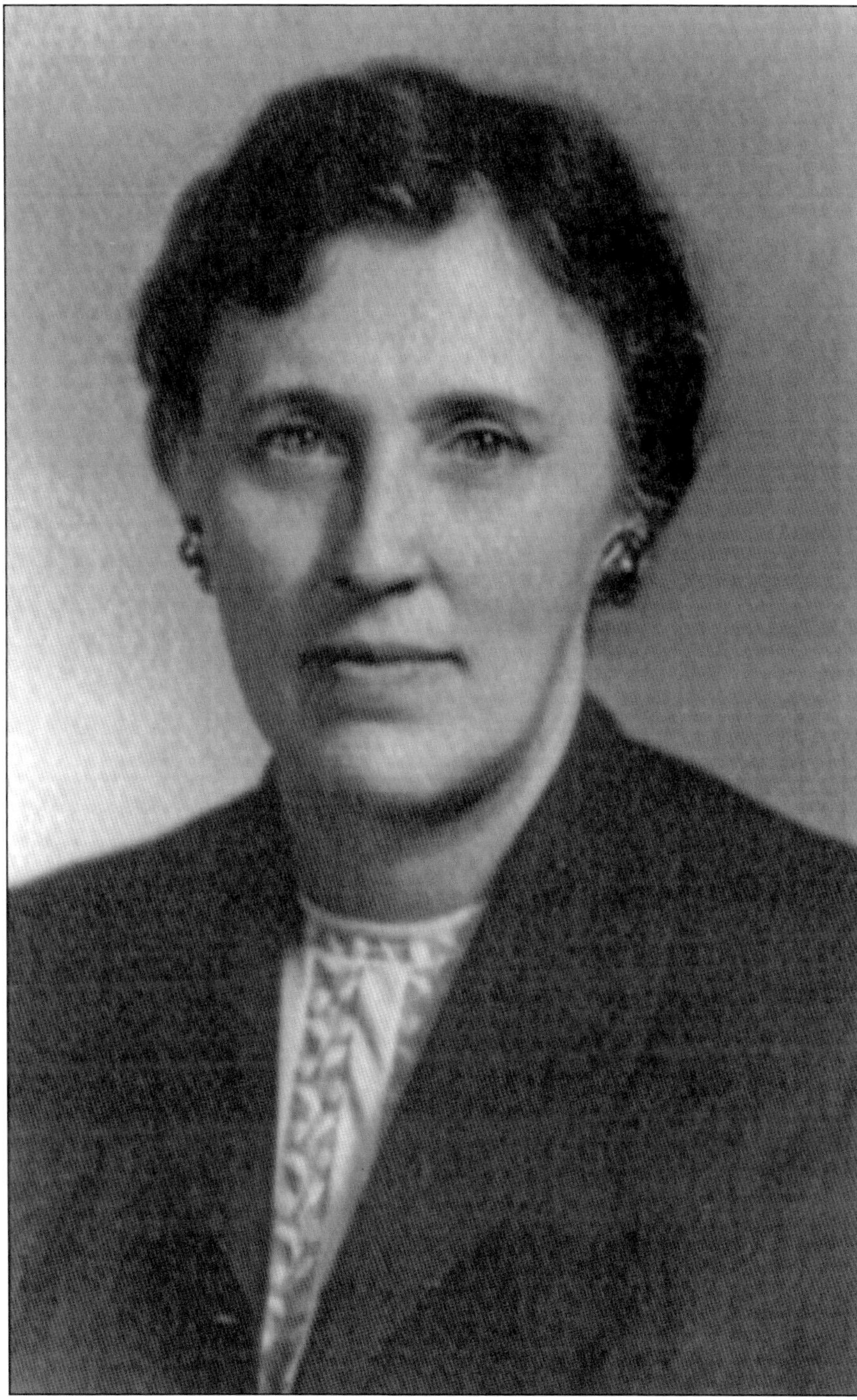

In 1968, the Woman's Club of Harrison County nominated Minnie Swinford for the state's Mother of the Year title. She certainly had the credentials. The mother of five, she was a past president of the Parent Teachers Association, the Woman's Club of Harrison County, Women of the Church in the Presbyterian church, and the local Democratic Woman's Club. Her other passions included volunteer work for the Red Cross and March of Dimes. (Courtesy of Sarah Kinney.)

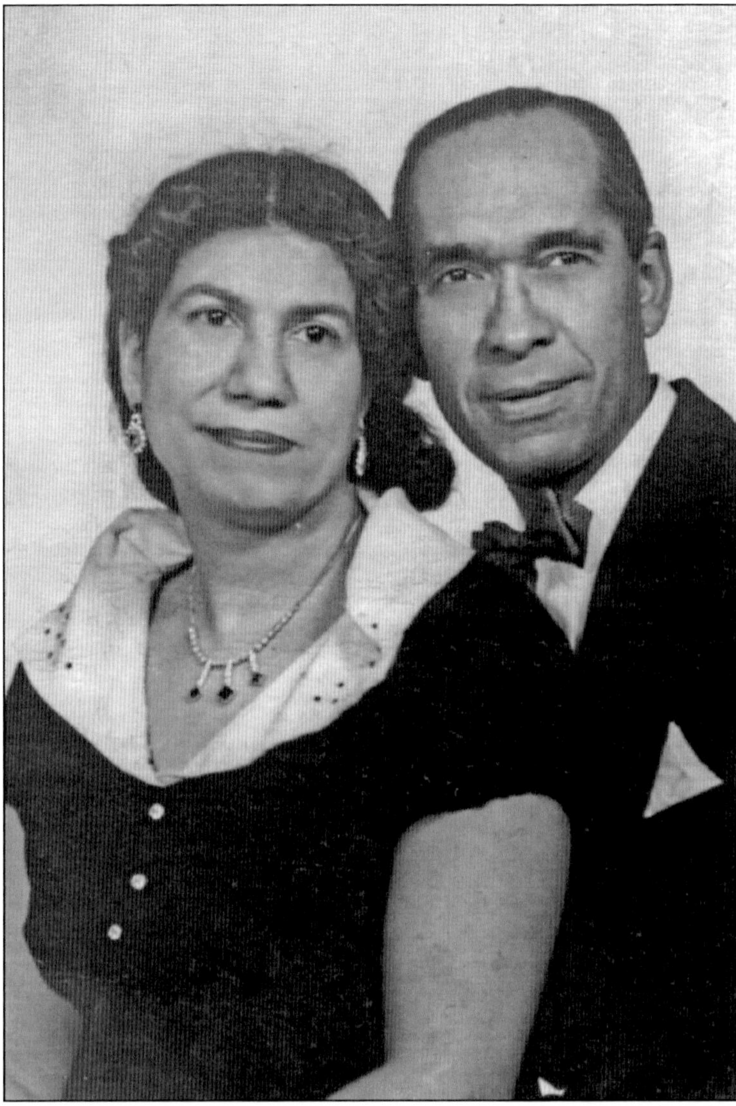

E. O. and Vivian David were instrumental in the quest to provide quality education for African American students in Cynthiana. E. O. was born in Cynthiana and graduated from Wilberforce University and the University of Cincinnati. He came to Banneker School in 1930 as a coach and science teacher, taking over the reins as principal after the retirement of principal W. E. Newsom in 1941. When Banneker closed in 1963, E. O. moved to the local junior high school. In 1974, the Davids' daughter Marilyn wrote that her father "spent the remainder of his life teaching science and developing a curriculum for education, and stressed physical education as developing the storehouse for man's knowledge." He was, she says, a "truly devoted teacher, thinking only of his students and how he could help them. Many have been able to go to college through his efforts to obtain scholarships and financial aid for them." Vivian F. David, a native of Urbana, Ohio, met E. O. David as a student at Wilberforce. A graduate of Central State University and the University of Kentucky, she was a full-time teacher at Banneker from 1946 until the school's closure in 1963. She developed the music department and taught choral music, speech, and dramatics. The couple had three children: Teresa Moore, Baldwin David, and Marilyn David Wash. (Courtesy of Marilyn David Wash.)

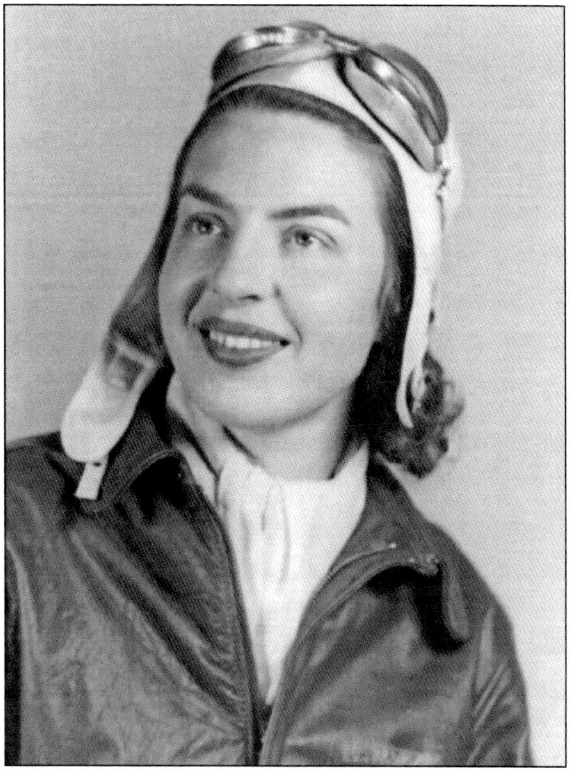

Cynthiana's most famous female pilot was Esther Lucille Mueller Ammerman, a Nebraska native who was her home state's first licensed female parachute rigger. A Women's Air Force Service Pilot (WASP) during World War II, she ferried bombs and towed targets for aerial gunnery practice from 1943 to 1945. She married Joe L. Ammerman of Cynthiana in 1946. In 2003, this woman on the wing was inducted into the Kentucky Aviation Hall of Fame. Her local affiliations included membership in the Covenant Presbyterian Church, the Fannie Zoller Church Circle, Thursday Club, Harrison County Homemakers, and the Harrison Memorial Hospital Auxiliary. Ammerman died in 2007. (Both courtesy of Bob and Meg Ammerman.)

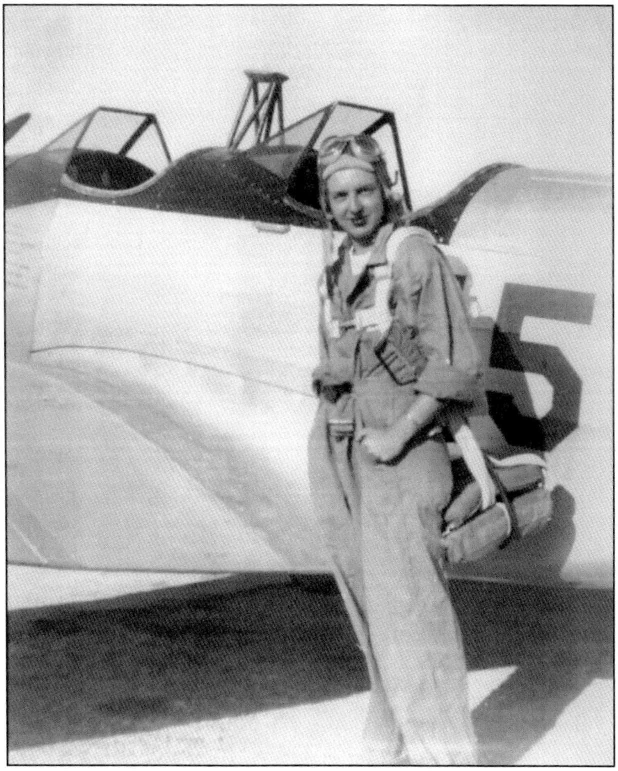

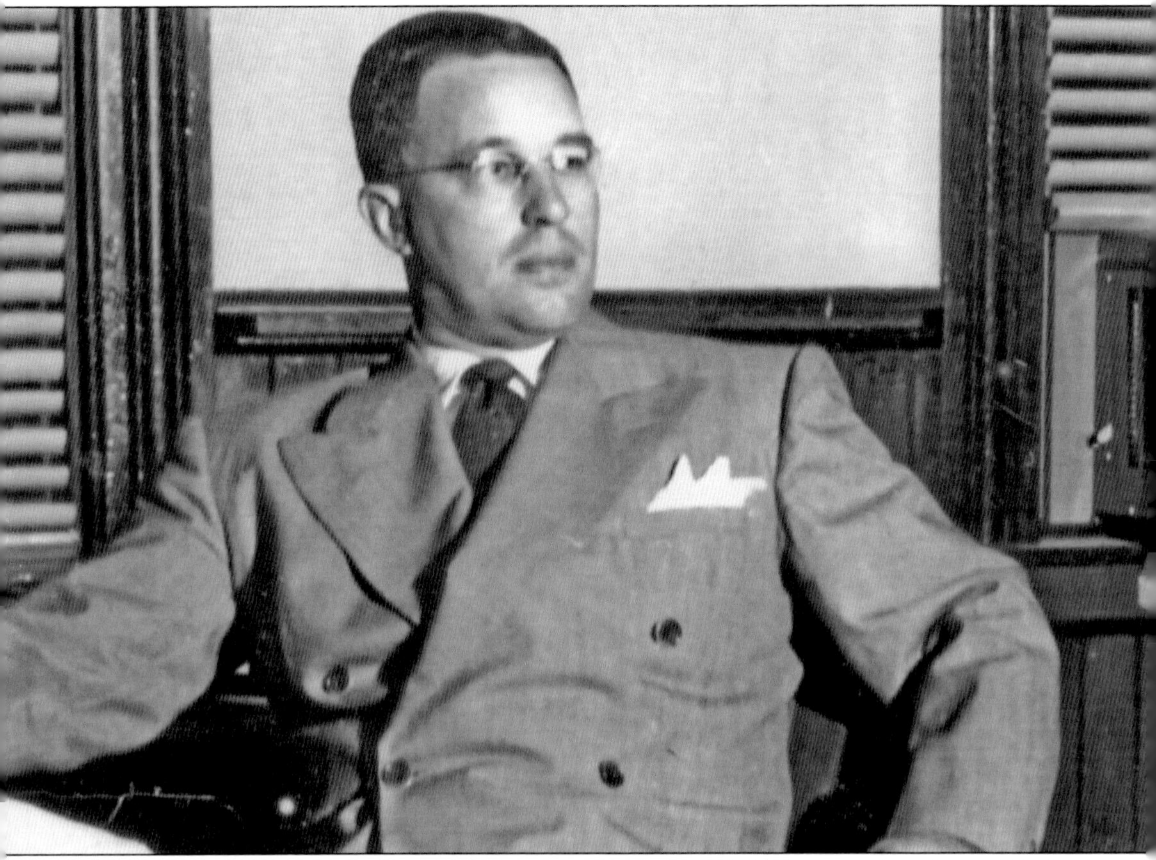

John Prentiss Lair was born in Cynthiana in 1906. As a child, he attended Marshall School, where he became friends with H. Tod Smiser (who became a doctor). The two, who graduated from Cynthiana High School in 1924, remained friends into adulthood. After graduating from the University of Kentucky Law School, Lair became an FBI agent and was stationed in Miami, Florida, during World War II. He is pictured here in the early 1950s. (Courtesy of John Lair.)

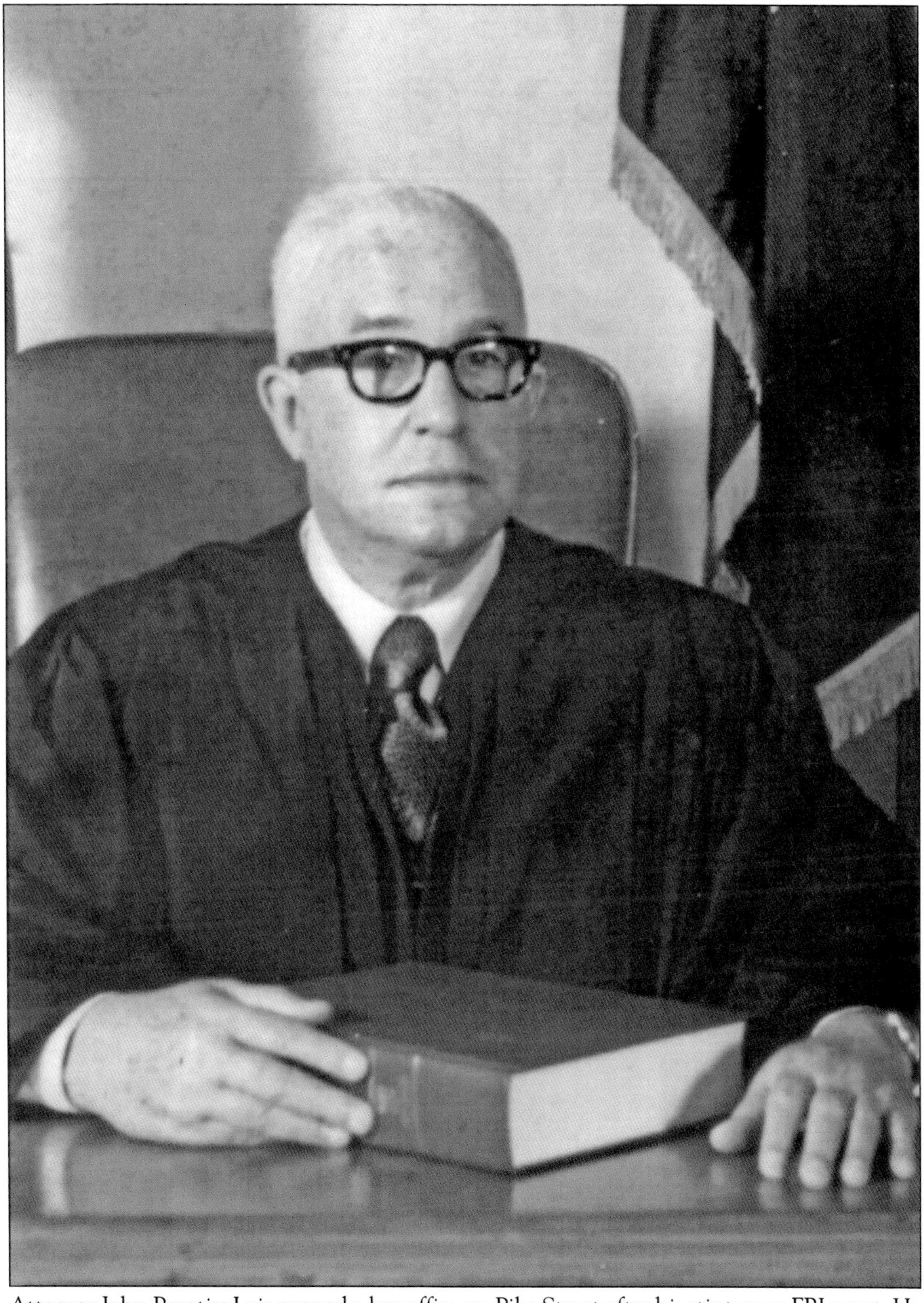

Attorney John Prentiss Lair opened a law office on Pike Street after his stint as an FBI agent. He became a circuit judge in 1961 serving Harrison, Pendleton, Nicholas, and Robertson Counties in that role for more than 20 years. In his spare time, he enjoyed hunting, fishing, and skeet shooting. A longtime trustee at the Cynthiana Christian Church, Lair died in 1988. Lair's son, attorney John Lair, also opened a law office on Pike Street in Cynthiana. (Courtesy of John Lair.)

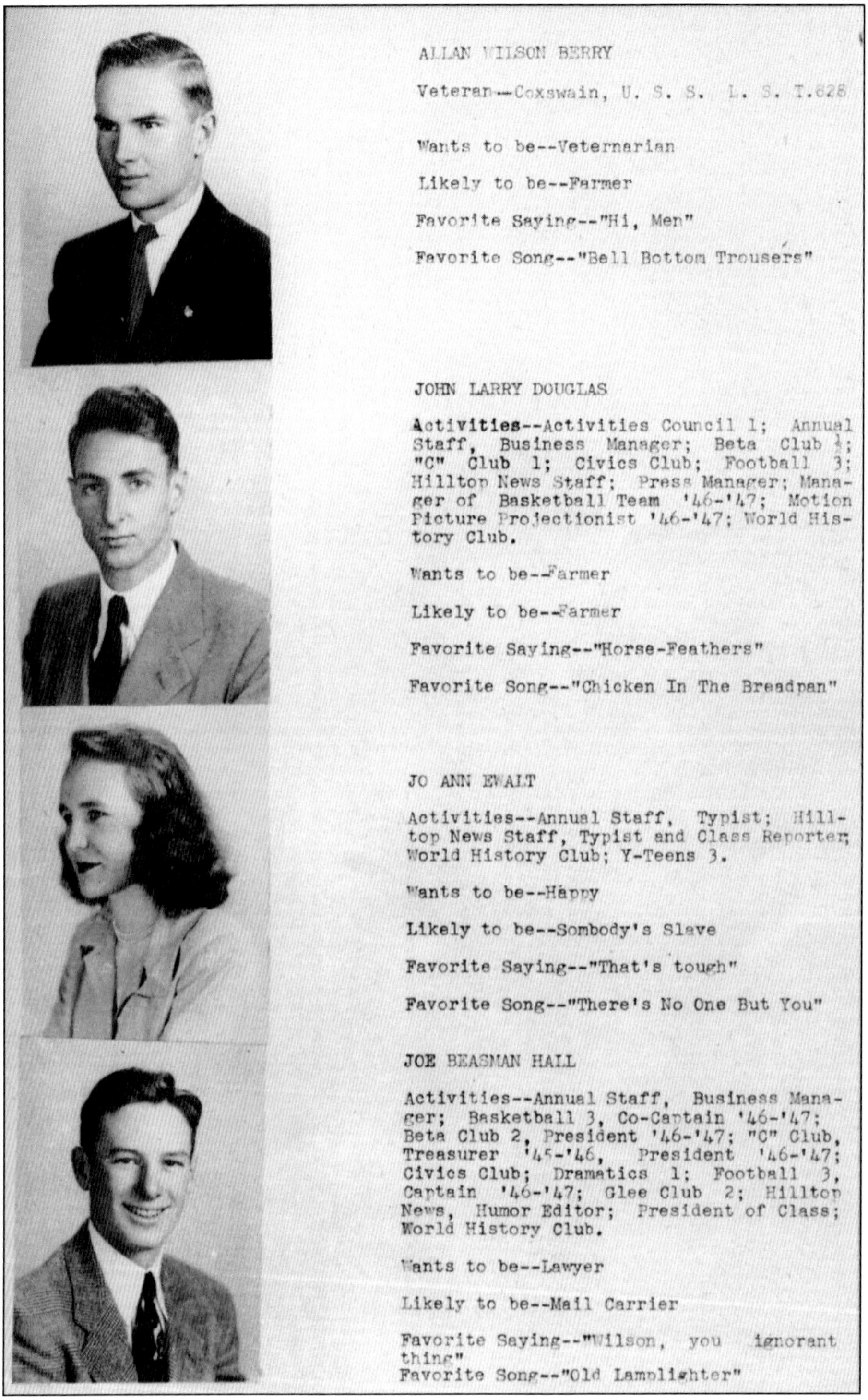

ALLAN WILSON BERRY

Veteran—Coxswain, U. S. S. L. S. T.628

Wants to be--Veternarian

Likely to be--Farmer

Favorite Saying--"Hi, Men"

Favorite Song--"Bell Bottom Trousers"

JOHN LARRY DOUGLAS

Activities--Activities Council 1; Annual Staff, Business Manager; Beta Club ½; "C" Club 1; Civics Club; Football 3; Hilltop News Staff; Press Manager; Manager of Basketball Team '46-'47; Motion Picture Projectionist '46-'47; World History Club.

Wants to be--Farmer

Likely to be--Farmer

Favorite Saying--"Horse-Feathers"

Favorite Song--"Chicken In The Breadpan"

JO ANN EWALT

Activities--Annual Staff, Typist; Hilltop News Staff, Typist and Class Reporter; World History Club; Y-Teens 3.

Wants to be--Happy

Likely to be--Sombody's Slave

Favorite Saying--"That's tough"

Favorite Song--"There's No One But You"

JOE BEASMAN HALL

Activities--Annual Staff, Business Manager; Basketball 3, Co-Captain '46-'47; Beta Club 2, President '46-'47; "C" Club, Treasurer '45-'46, President '46-'47; Civics Club; Dramatics 1; Football 3, Captain '46-'47; Glee Club 2; Hilltop News, Humor Editor; President of Class; World History Club.

Wants to be--Lawyer

Likely to be--Mail Carrier

Favorite Saying--"Wilson, you ignorant thing"

Favorite Song--"Old Lamplighter"

One of Cynthiana's most famous sons, former University of Kentucky basketball coach Joe B. Hall, is seen in this page from the 1947 *Cynthian* yearbook. Hall was born in 1928, the son of Bill and Ruth Harney Hall. (Courtesy of the Cynthiana High School Alumni Association.)

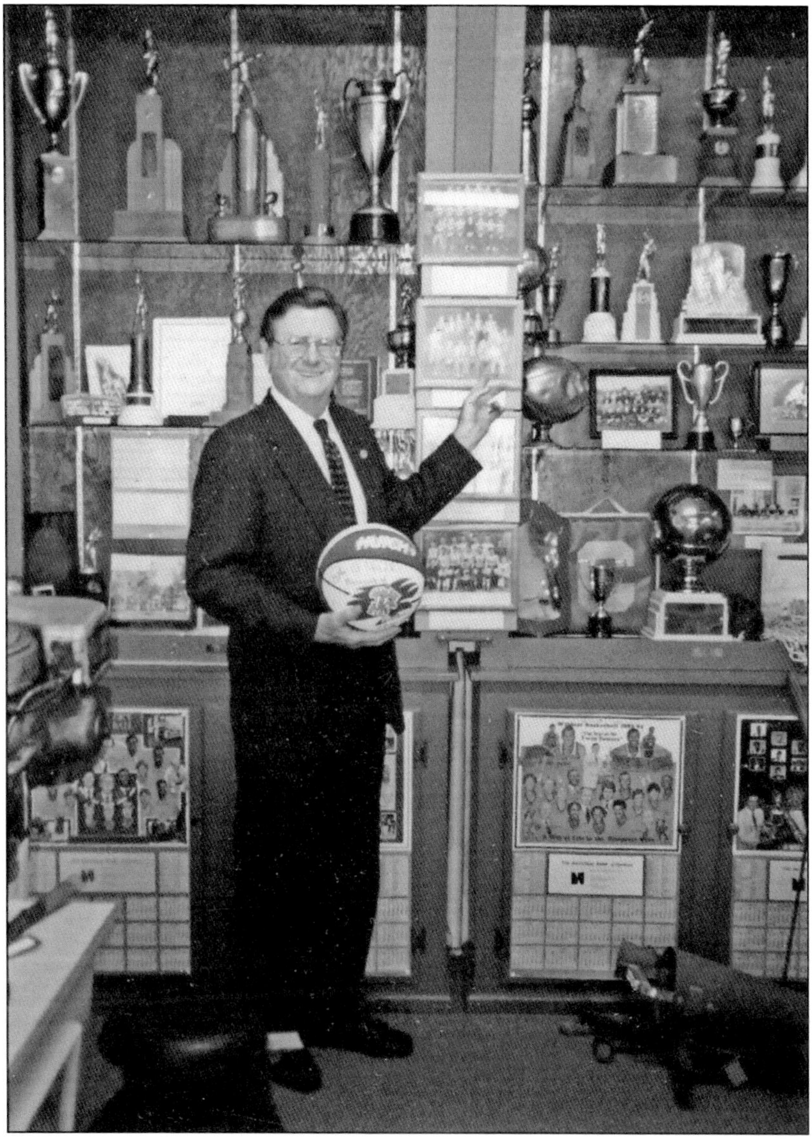

Joe B. Hall, pictured at the Cynthiana–Harrison County Museum, eyed a legal career as a student at Cynthiana High School, but the standout athlete and president of his senior class headed for a court of an entirely different and athletic nature. After playing basketball for the University of Kentucky and coach Adolph Rupp during the "Fabulous Five" era, he transferred to the University of the South in Sewanee, Tennessee, and finished his eligibility there before touring with the Harlem Globetrotters in 1951. Then it was back to the University of Kentucky, where he graduated in 1955, and a move to a high school—Shepherdsville High School—and college—Regis College in Denver and Central Missouri State—coaching career. Again, Hall headed home to the bluegrass and the University of Kentucky. This time, he served as assistant to coach Adolph Rupp. When Rupp was forced to retire at 70, Hall was named head coach of the Wildcats. He coached three teams to the Final Four, and the Wildcats won the 1978 NCAA championship—the school's fifth—under his leadership. Hall was named National Coach of the Year in 1978. And no, the "B" in Joe B. Hall does not stand for basketball: Hall's middle name is Beasman. (Courtesy of the Cynthiana–Harrison County Museum.)

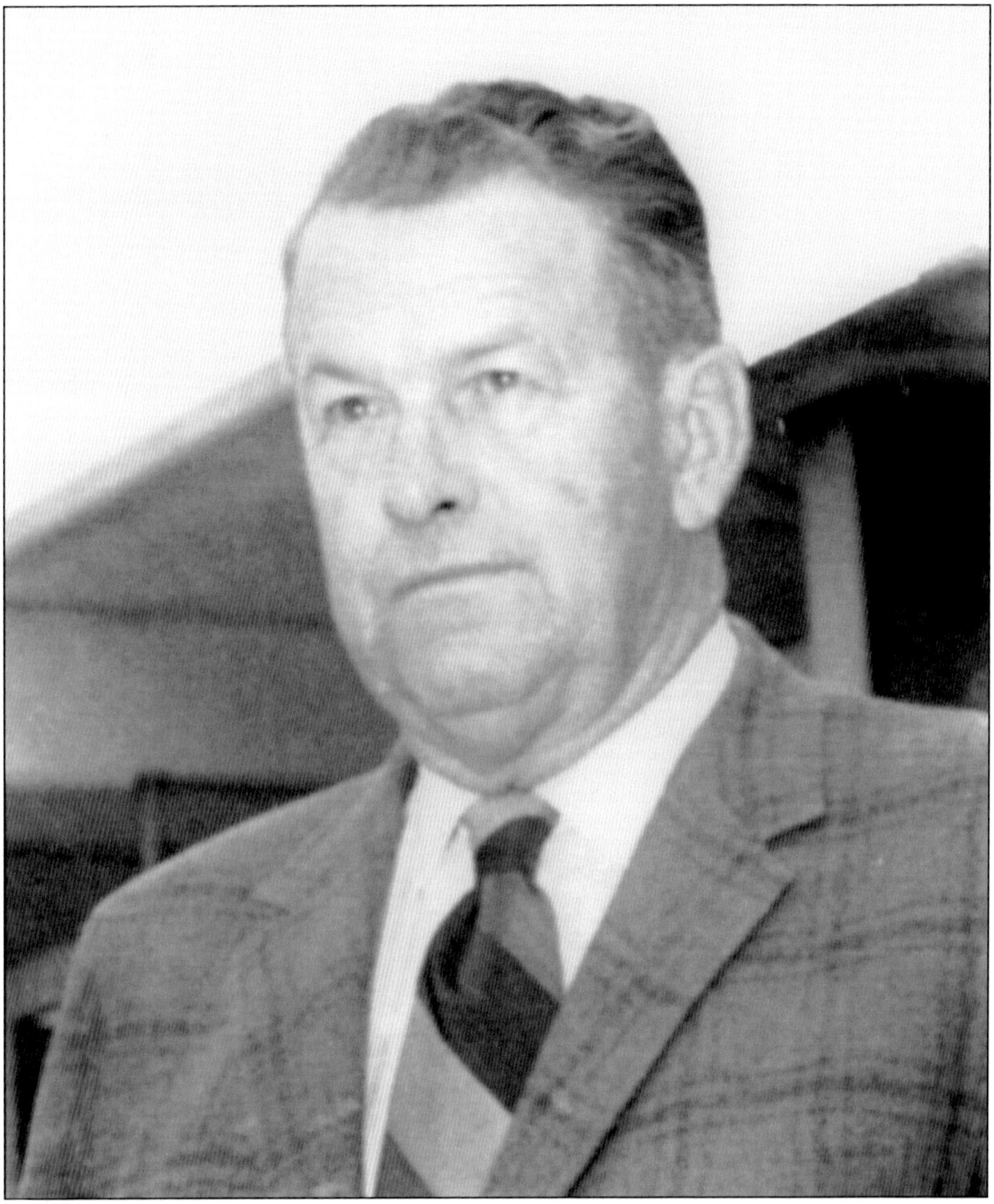

The popular and personable Everett Wilson Palmer—better known as Wilson—served as a state senator for the 30th Senatorial District from 1961 to 1973. A farmer from Buena Vista, he also was familiar to locals as a realtor and insurance agent with Palmer-Hampton Agency in Cynthiana. He wore many hats over the years, serving as a director of Fifth Third Bank and Harrison Electric Cooperative, a member of the Eastern Kentucky University board of regents and as a board member of Harrison Memorial Hospital and East Kentucky Power Cooperative. Eastern Kentucky University's Palmer Hall, built in 1966, is named in his honor. Palmer married Emma Jean Marsh on February 23, 1939. The couple had five daughters. Palmer died at the age of 84 in 2002, exactly four weeks after his wife's passing. (Courtesy of the Palmer family.)

Three

Familiar Places and Faces

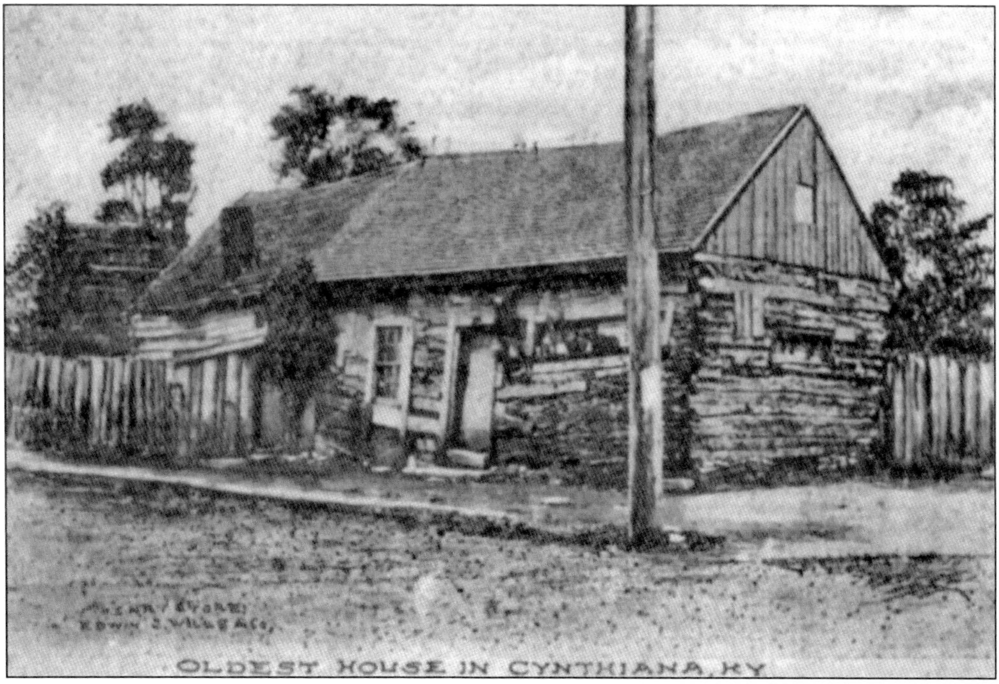

Once known as the oldest house in Cynthiana, this home at the corner of Pike and Poplar Streets is pictured in the early 1900s. On December 18, 1909, Cynthiana resident Mandy Lee burned to death when the house caught fire. The site later became the home of the Kentucky Utilities building, now the home of the Harrison County sheriff's office. (Courtesy of the Cynthiana–Harrison County Museum.)

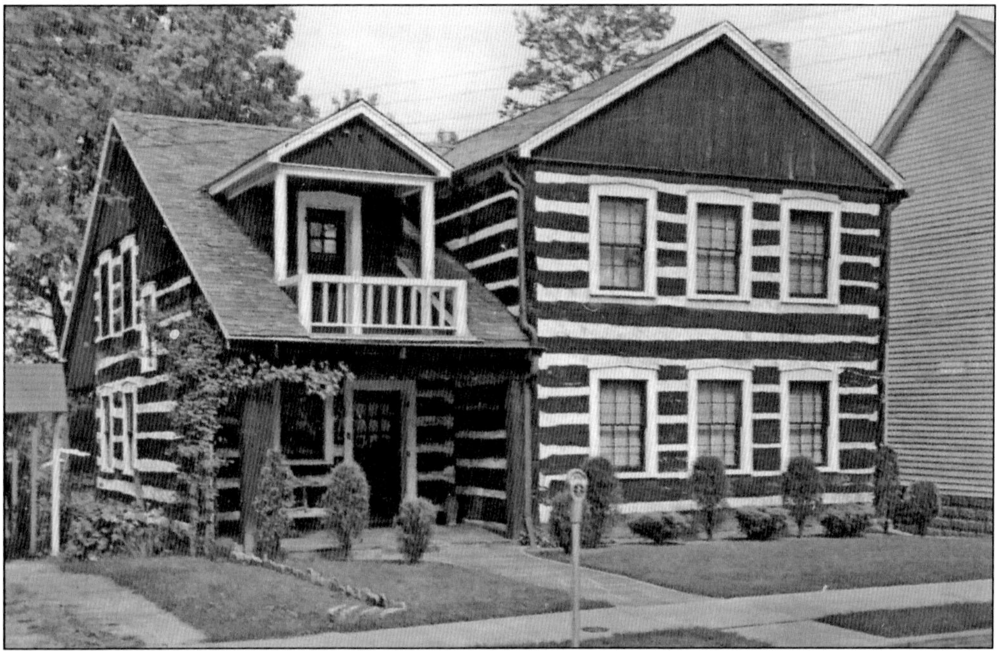

One of the city's most endearing and enduring sites is the Old Log Cabin on Court Street, the oldest house in Cynthiana. Built in 1790, its many occupants over the years included a young Henry Clay, who practiced law in the building in 1806. Cynthiana's first newspaper, the *Guardian of Liberty*, was printed here, as was the widely used textbook Guthrie's Arithmetic. Later the log cabin was the home of radio station WCYN. (Courtesy of the Cynthiana–Harrison County Museum.)

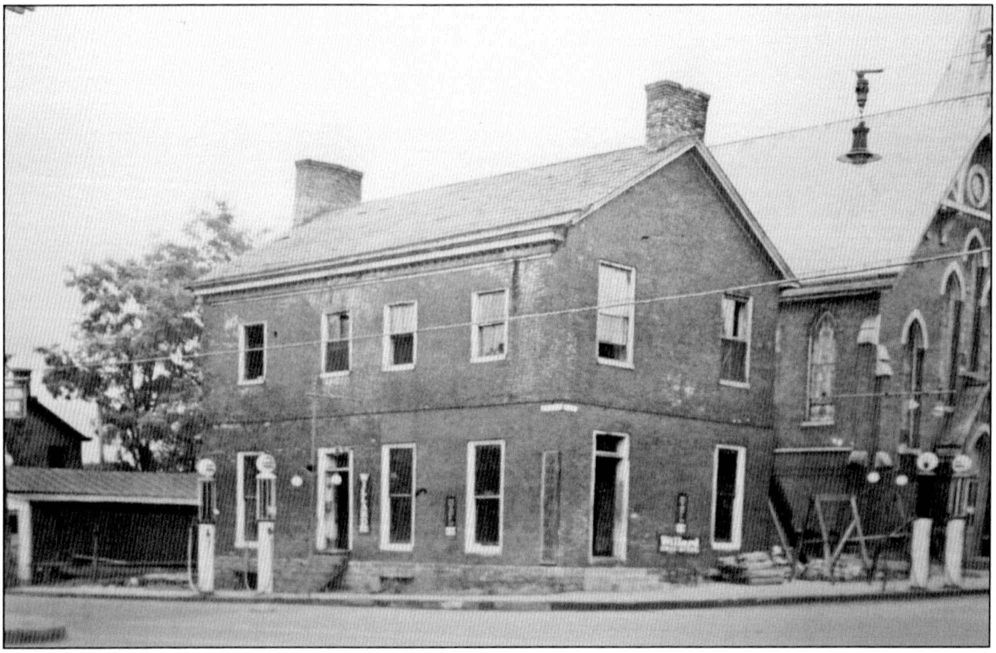

The oldest brick house in Cynthiana stood from 1805 to 1936 at the corner of Main and Pleasant Streets, next to Cynthiana Presbyterian Church. (Courtesy of the Cynthiana–Harrison County Museum.)

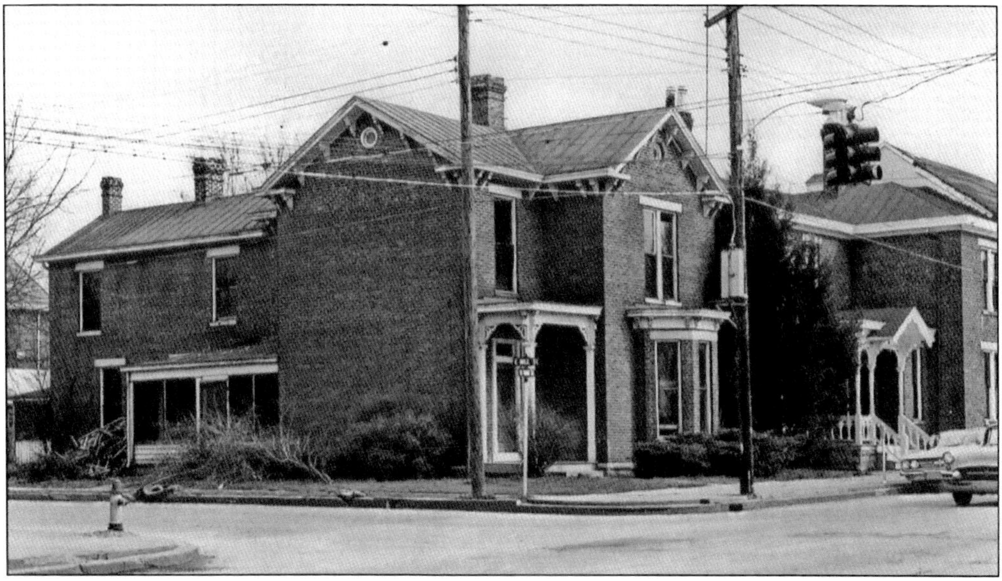

For years, this home stood out for visitors coming from the north on U.S. Route 27. It was situated at the southeast corner of Mill and Main Streets. (Courtesy of the Cynthiana–Harrison County Public Library's James Saunders Whaley Collection.)

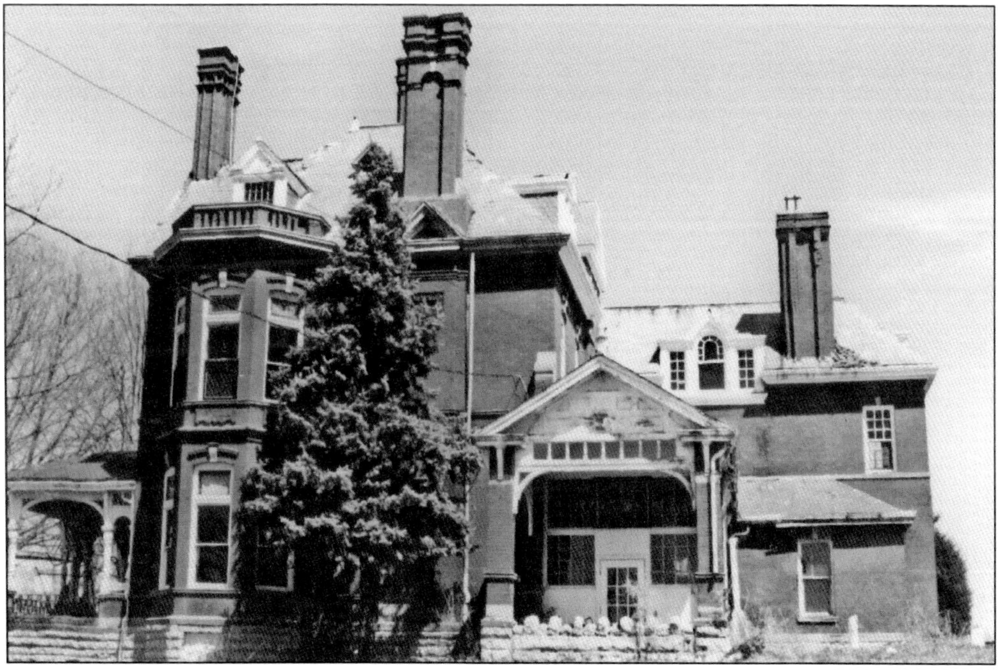

A former Kentucky legislator, distiller, and horse breeder, Thomas Jefferson Megibben built the 27-room Victorian mansion known as Monticello in 1883. This side view shows part of the ornate detail work on the Cynthiana landmark. Later Dr. Henry and Caroline Bromley owned the home. A fire destroyed the iconic structure, named for Pres. Thomas Jefferson's Monticello in Virginia, on July 8, 1985. (Courtesy of the Cynthiana–Harrison County Museum.)

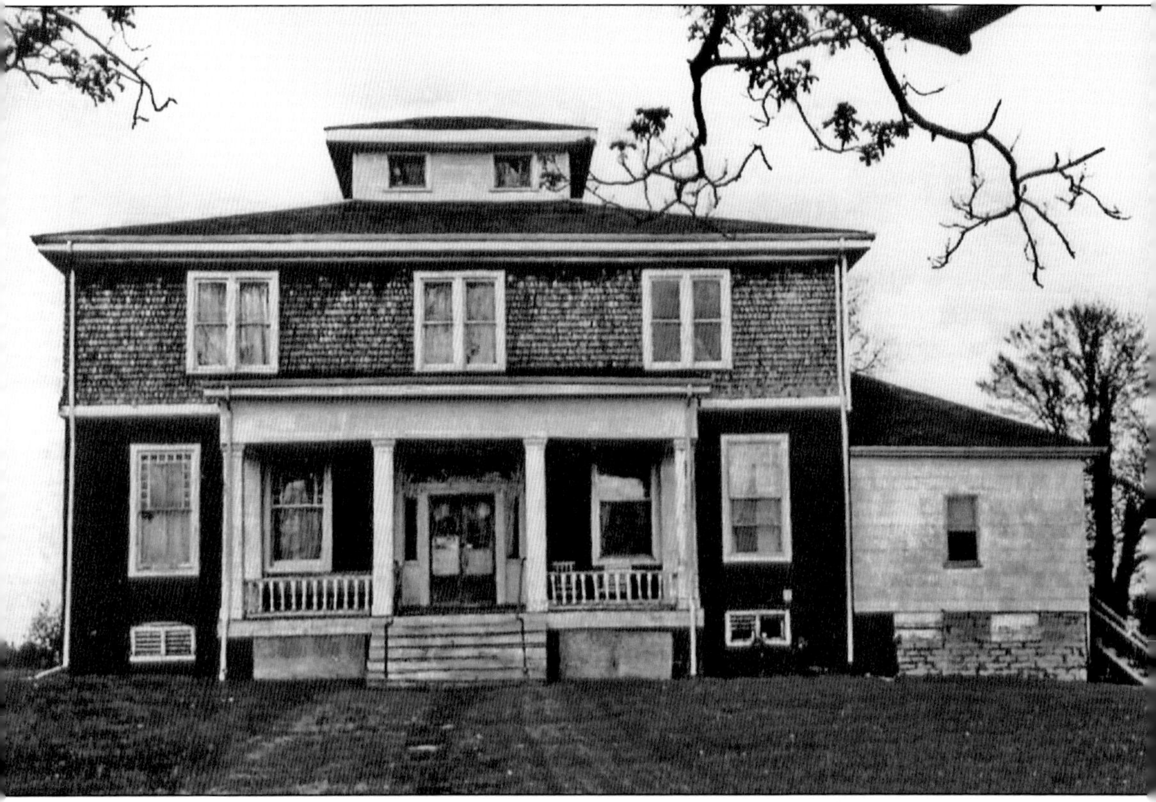

The Handy House, off U.S. Route 62, was built around 1816 for Col. William Brown, a prosperous farm owner. In her 1894 book *Chronicles of Cynthiana*, writer Lucinda Rogers Boyd said of Brown: "During the first third of the present century, the most eminent member of the Cynthiana bar after William K. Wall was, no doubt William Brown. . . . He became very wealthy, owning 1,000 acres of land and many slaves." Other Handy Farm owners over the years included Dr. Joel C. Frazer, a physician, and William T. Handy, who purchased the 165-acre farm from Frazer in 1883 for $18,000. In 2002, the city and county governments bought the house and surrounding acreage. (Courtesy of the Cynthiana–Harrison County Museum.)

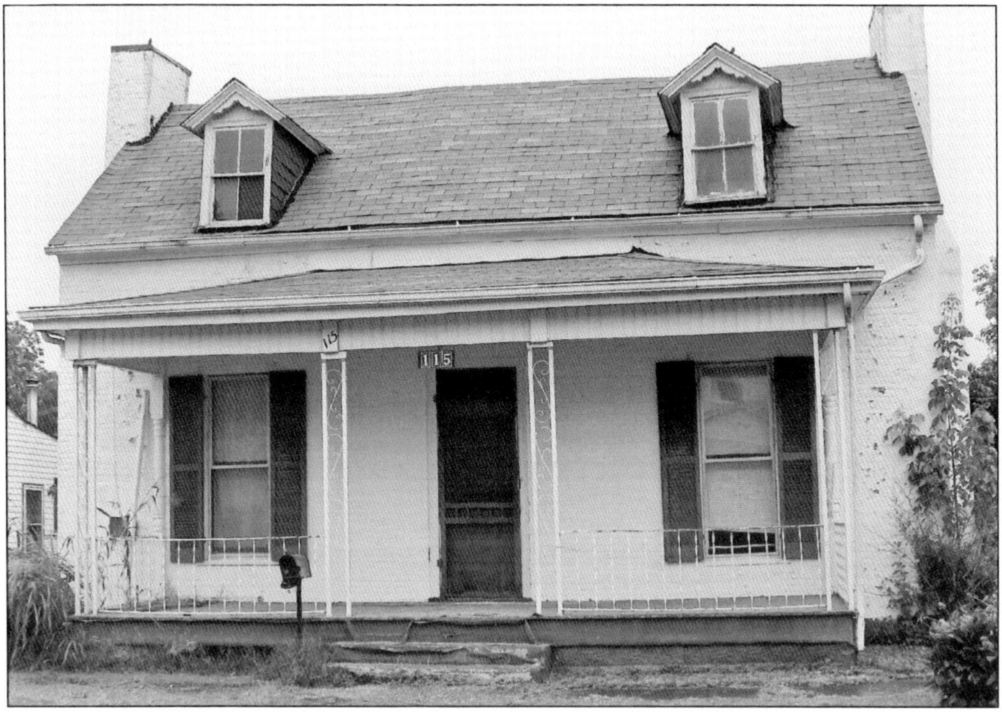

Walter Edward Scott, better known as "Death Valley Scotty," was born in 1872 at 115 North Locust Street. The son of George and Anna Scott, who gained a reputation as a performer and con man who became involved in gold-mining scams, is the name behind a mansion in Death Valley called Scotty's Castle. The castle is now a property of the National Park Service, whose description of Scott says: "Walter Scott, Death Valley Scotty, convinced everyone that he had built the castle with money from his rich secret mines in the area. Albert Mussey Johnson actually built the house as a vacation getaway for himself and his wife, Bessie. Scotty was the mystery, the cowboy, and the entertainer, but he was also a friend." The Cynthiana man behind the mystery died in 1954 in Death Valley, but the fascination with him lives. (Photograph by M. Britt Kennerly.)

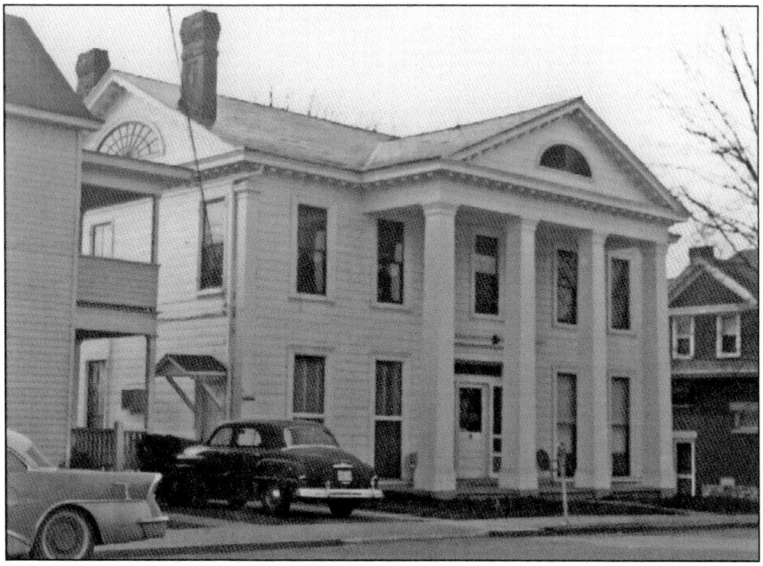

The Withers House, pictured here in 1961, stood for years on Court Street near the Old Log Cabin. The site where it stood became home to the Goodyear Tire and Rubber Company business a few years later. (Courtesy of William A. Penn.)

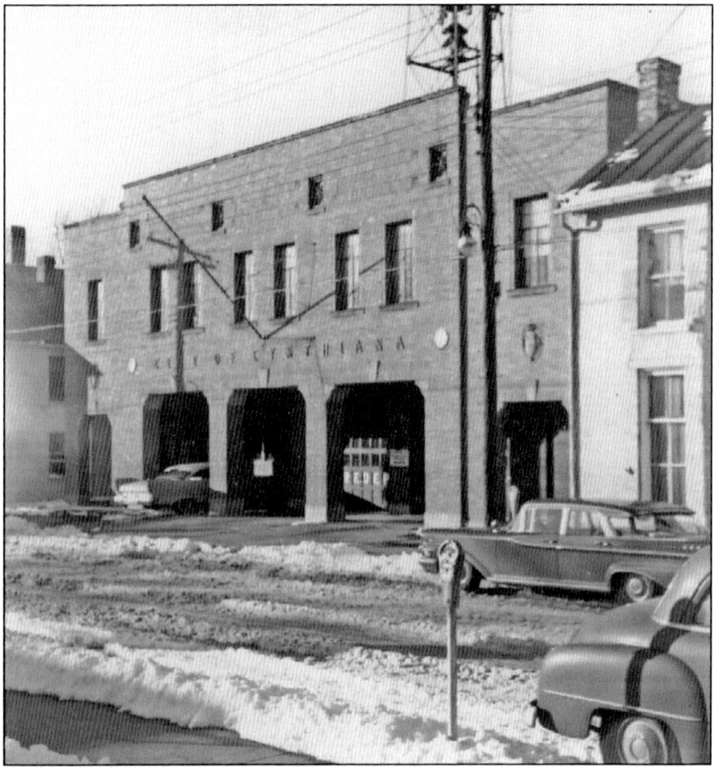

Across several decades, Cynthiana City Hall has played home to everything from the fire department to the commissioners' meeting room to turkey bingo games at Thanksgiving. The public library was housed on the building's second floor from 1930 until a new facility opened on South Church Street in the early 1960s. (Courtesy of William A. Penn.)

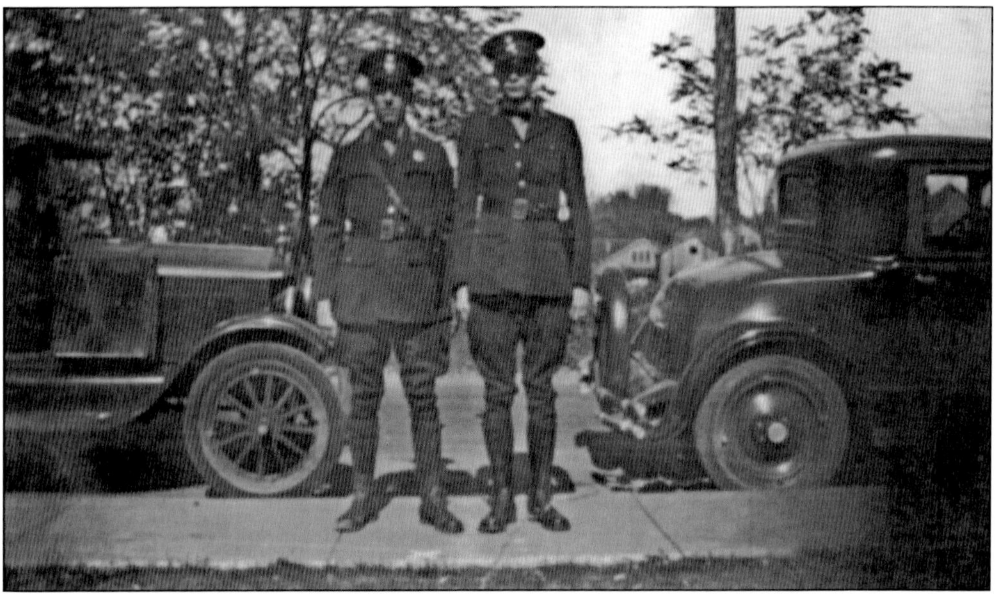

Harrison County deputy sheriffs Virgil Florence (left) and Odus Kitchen look ready for action in 1931. (Courtesy of the Cynthiana–Harrison County Museum.)

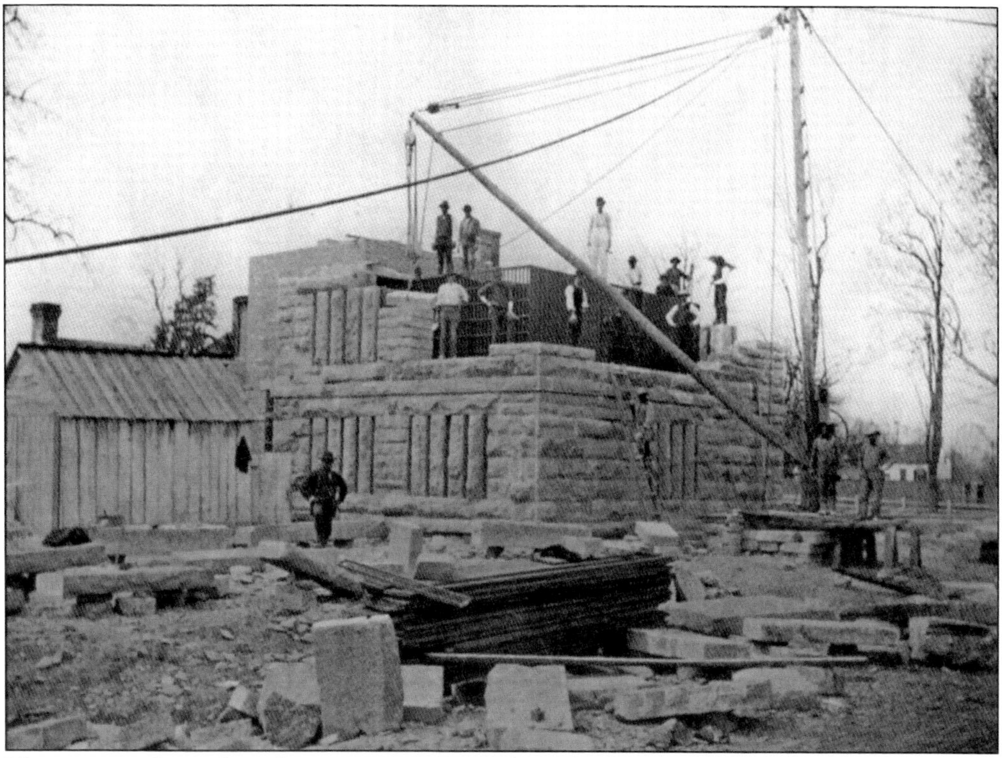

The county jail, seen here during construction and in a shot from the early 1960s, was built in 1886 on West Pike Street. Builders were John Robert "J. R." Poindexter and Thomas Lowry. The total bill for construction was $10,538.65—$8,850 for the contract price, with $1,520.25 added to the bill for extras and another $168.40 for repairs to the jail residence. (Above courtesy of the Cynthiana–Harrison County Museum; below courtesy of William A. Penn.)

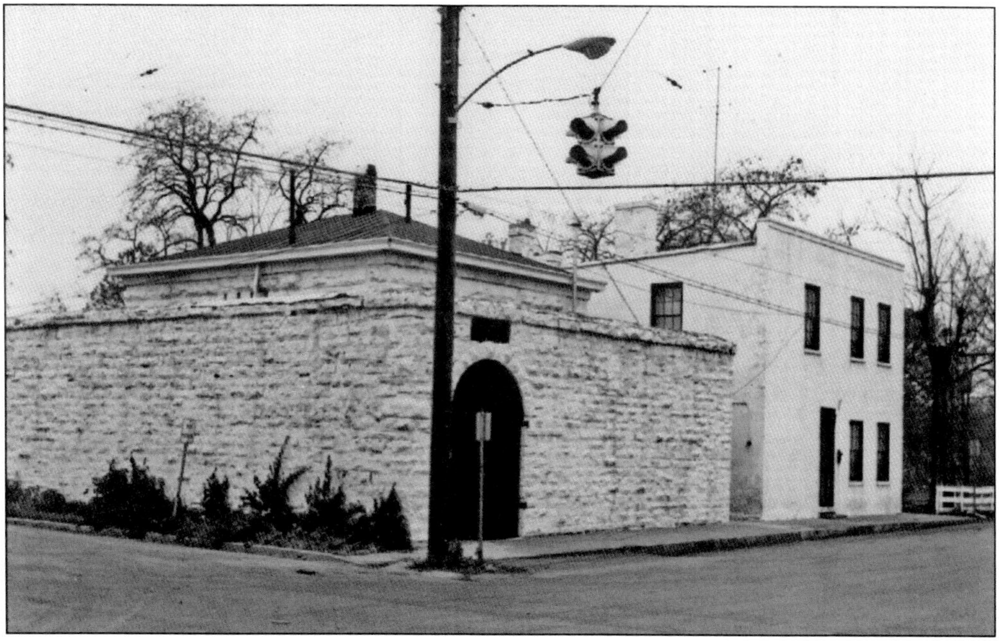

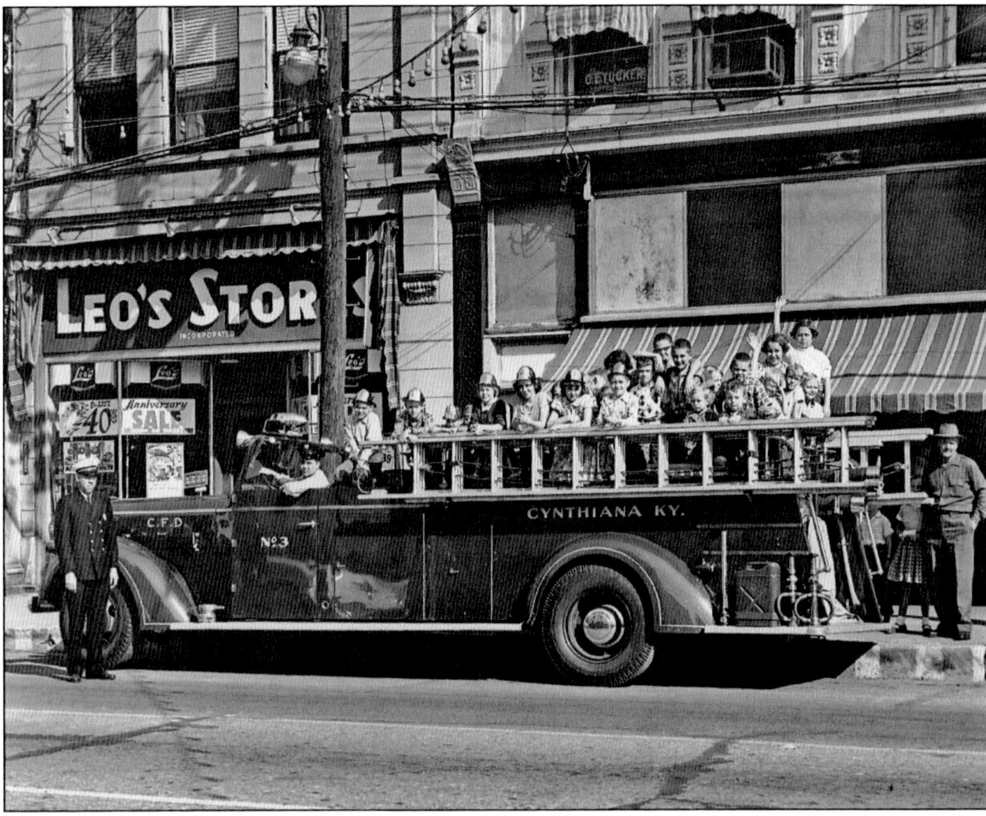

In the early 1960s, children sit on a fire truck in front of Leo's Store on Main Street. (Courtesy of the Cynthiana Fire Department.)

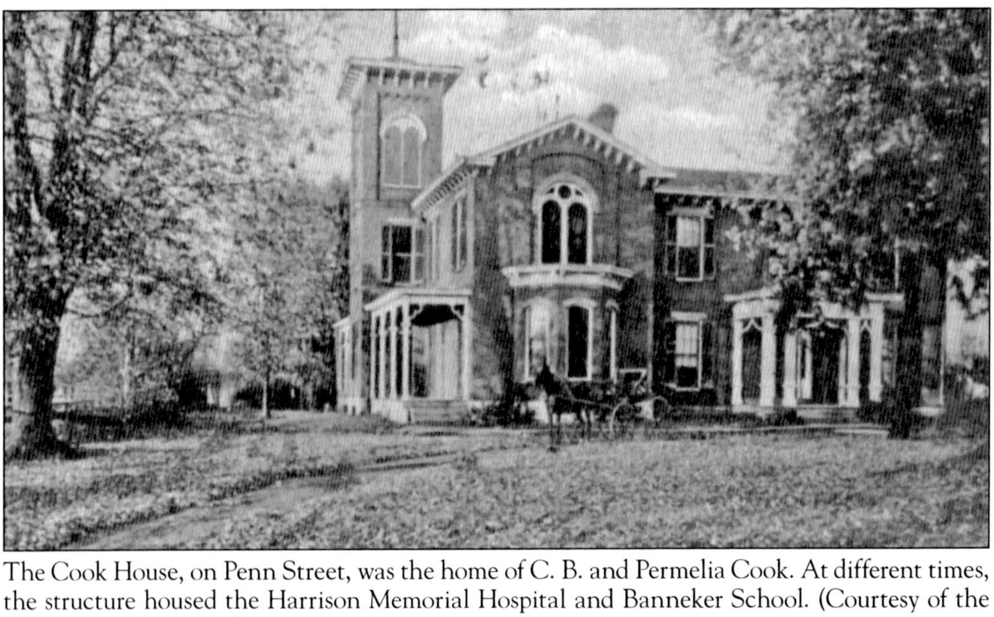

The Cook House, on Penn Street, was the home of C. B. and Permelia Cook. At different times, the structure housed the Harrison Memorial Hospital and Banneker School. (Courtesy of the Cynthiana–Harrison County Museum.)

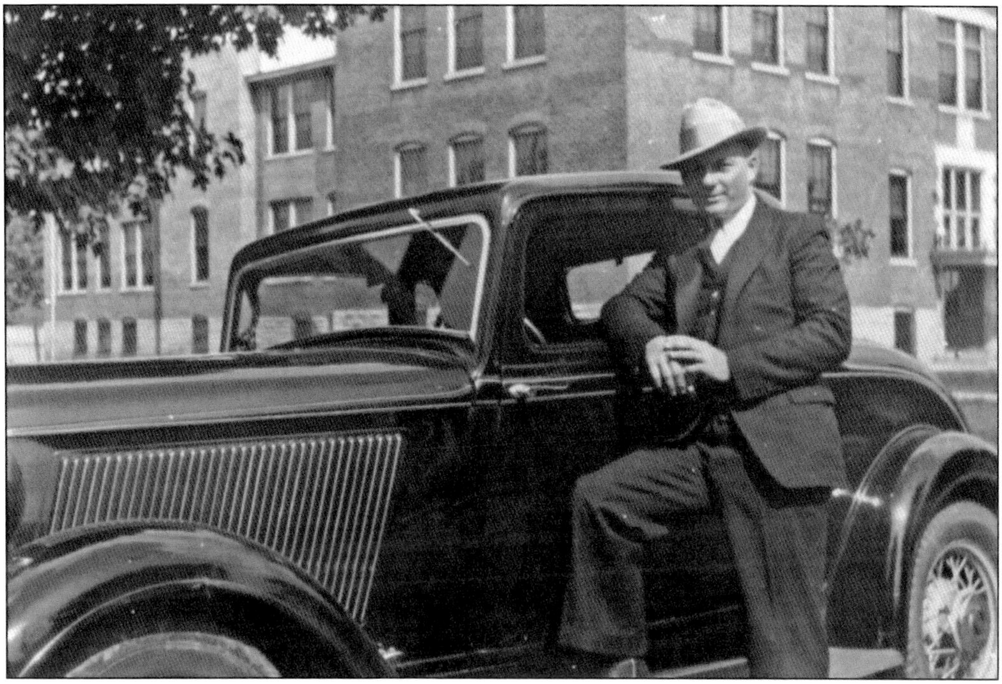

William Kaufman is dressed to impress as he stands beside his Plymouth near Marshall School in the 1930s. (Courtesy of the Cynthiana–Harrison County Museum.)

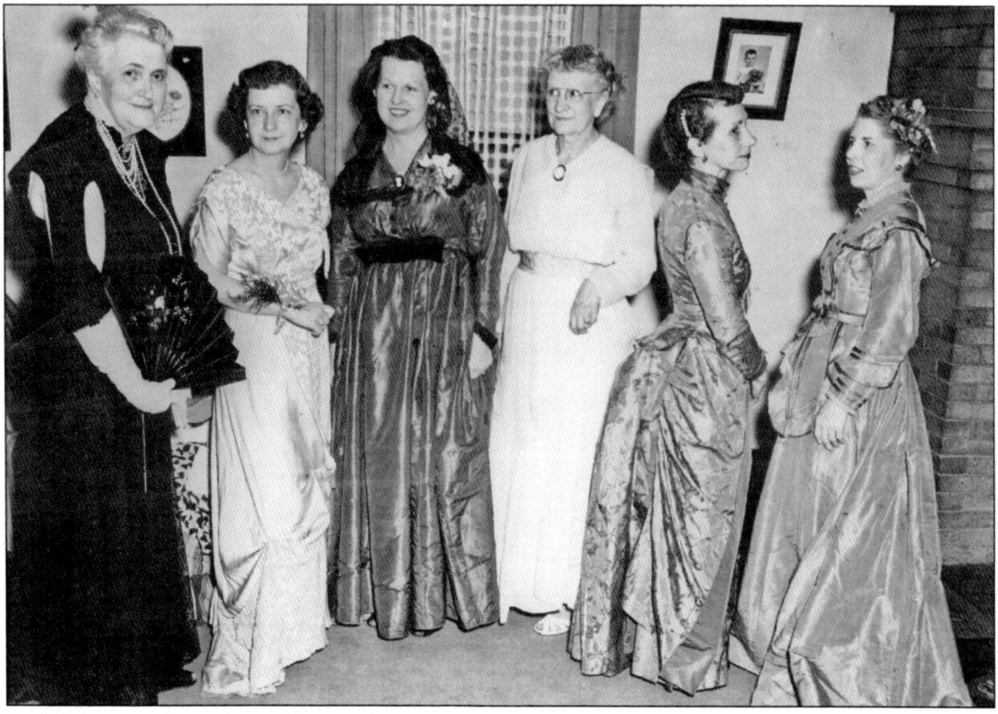

Stylishly attired members of a Cynthiana woman's club in the 1950s are, from left to right, Gladys Rankin, Eloise Wiglesworth, Marcella Franks, Prudence Whitaker, Jessie Moore McDaniel, and Fay Jewett. (Courtesy of Dean Peak.)

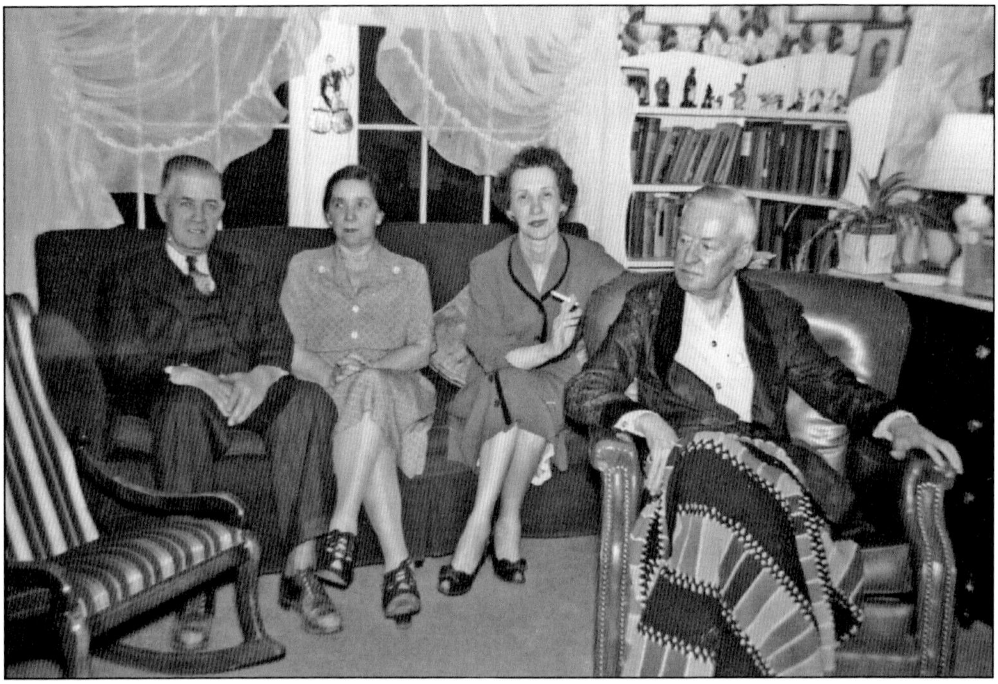

Local tobacco warehouse owner John Roy Peak Sr. and his wife, Frances Moore Peak (left), spent an evening with Jessie and John McDaniel (right). (Courtesy of Dean Peak.)

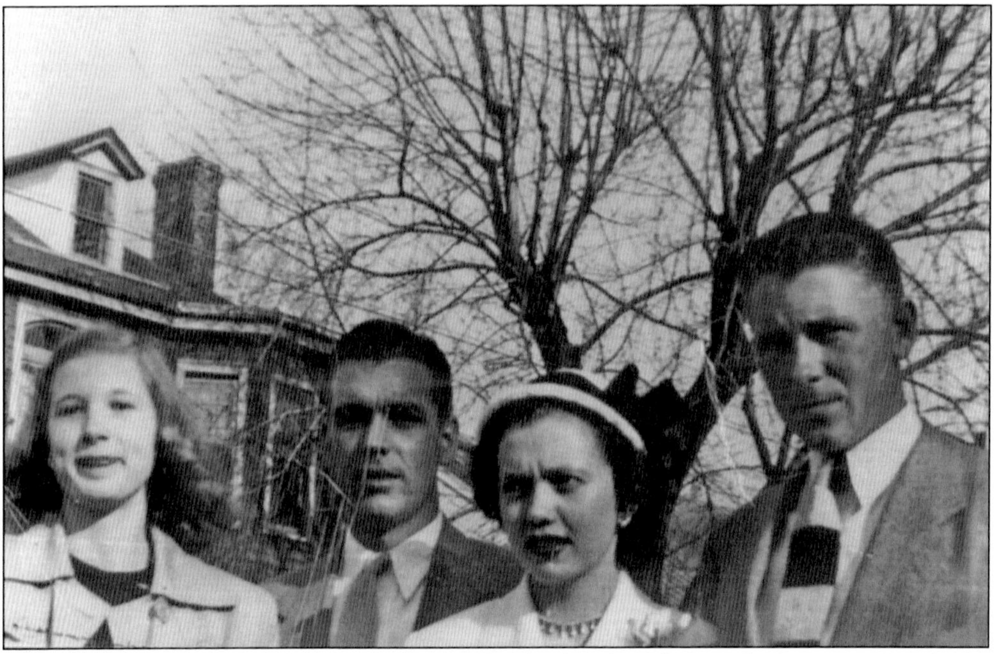

Seen here in the 1950s, Ruth Midden Box and her husband, Lark Box, the longtime Cynthiana postmaster (left), were good friends with Norma and Bonny Dailey (right). Lark Box and Bonny Dailey met as children, served in the same U.S. Marine Corps unit, and stayed friends as adults. (Courtesy of Thomas and Teresa Dailey.)

Four

HALLS OF LEARNING

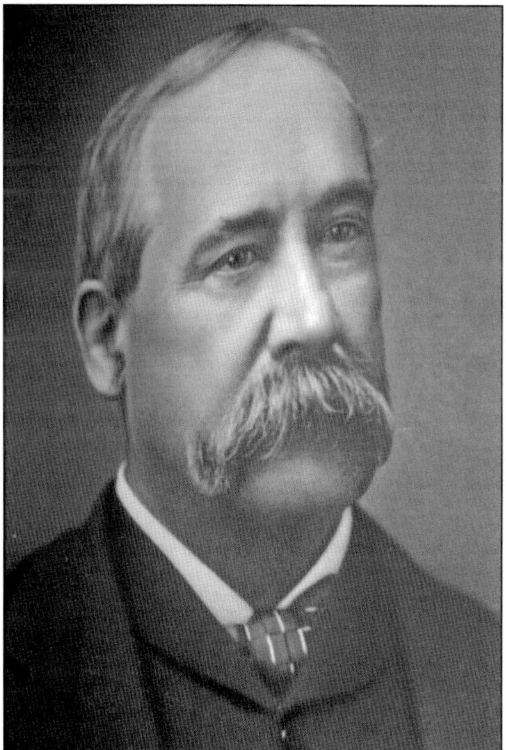

Lucius Gardner Marshall became the first principal the Cynthiana Public School in 1872, serving until his death on September 19, 1885. (Courtesy of Biancke's Restaurant.)

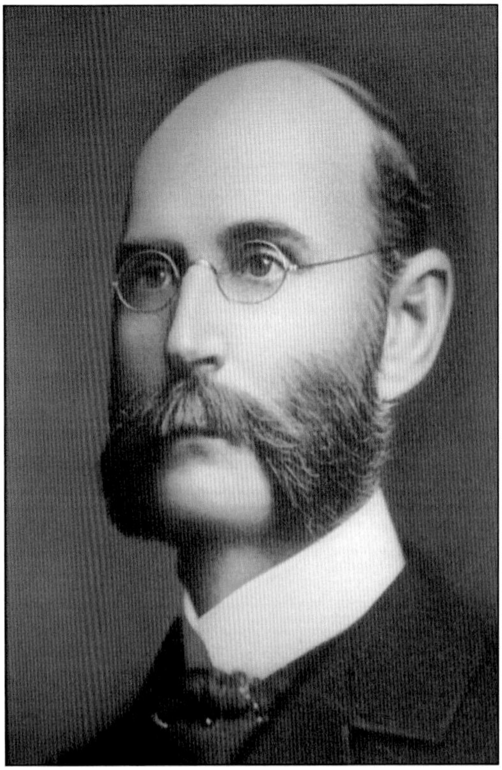

Charles Augustine Leonard was principal of Cynthiana Public School from 1886 until 1908. (Courtesy of Biancke's Restaurant.)

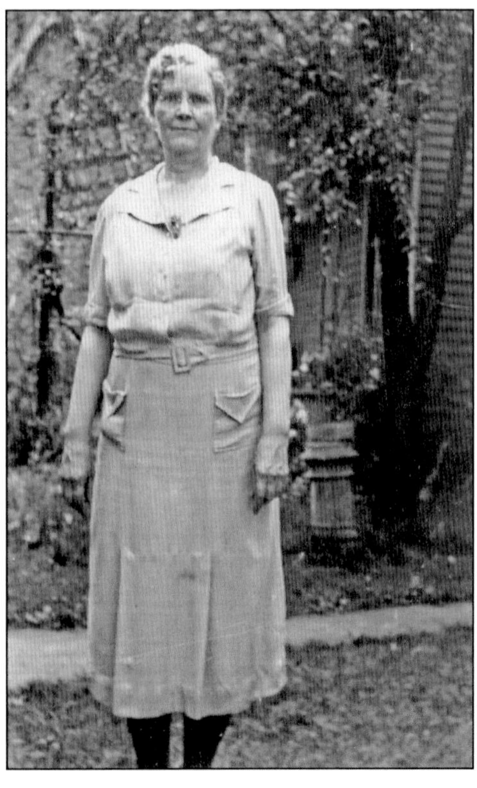

Teacher Fannie Zoller was a trusted and respected educator who ran her own school. Student chairs from Zoller's school and Sarah Lail's Little Red Schoolhouse are on display at the Cynthiana–Harrison County Museum along with items from Smith Classical School and Banneker School. Zoller died in 1956. (Courtesy of the Cynthiana–Harrison County Museum.)

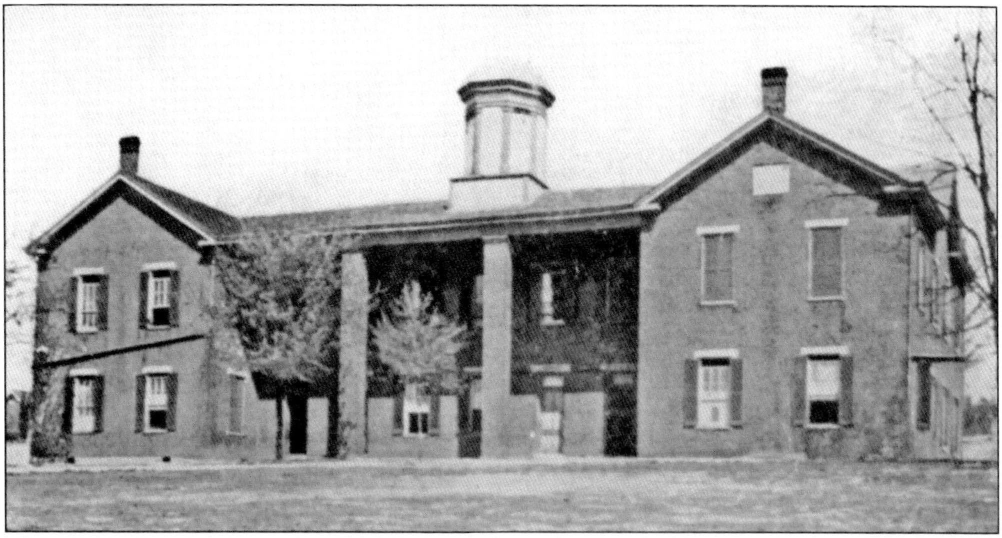

The *Log Cabin* newspaper reported in 1896 that "the Cynthiana Graded City School is the continuation of Harrison Academy, which was founded in 1804, under a legislative charter approved December 22, 1798. The trustees were granted six thousand acres of vacant land located on the south side of Green river. One stipulation was that the lands should revert to the State, if the trustees did not within ten years establish a school with at least twelve scholars. Harrison Academy was organized in the sixth year after the charter was granted." The Cynthiana Graded City School stood on the east side of Church Street between Pike and Pleasant Streets. In 1908, a new school was built on the south side of Bridge Street at Clifton Road. The school was lost to fire on January 21, 1918, leading to the erection of a new Cynthiana High School that was occupied by October 1919. (Courtesy of the Cynthiana–Harrison County Museum.)

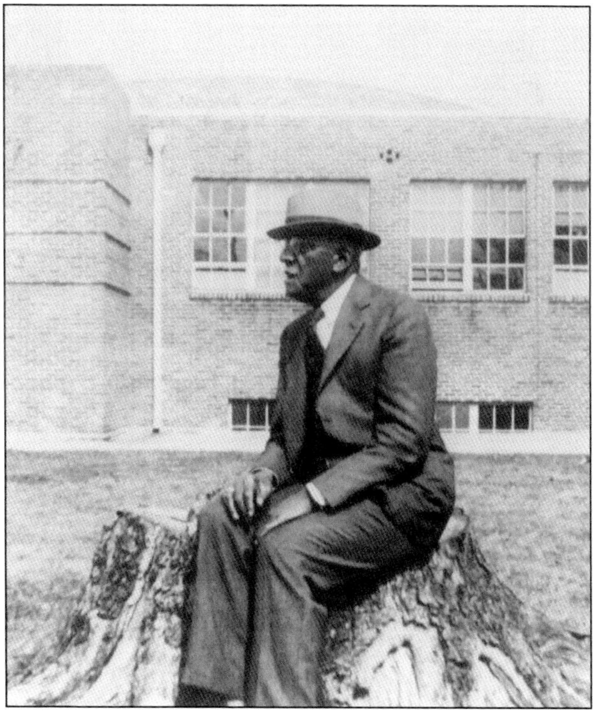

Prof. W. E. Newsom is seated in front of Banneker School, the educational home for the city's African American students for many years. Banneker was consolidated with Cynthiana High School in September 1956. Newsom, who became the school's first principal in 1913, retired as Banneker principal in 1941, followed in the role by E. O. David of Cynthiana. Banneker, built in 1937, was named for famed mathematician and astronomer Benjamin Banneker (1731–1806). Newsom was at the helm of the school when he penned a poem titled "Ode to Banneker," which opens with the lines, "Banneker circled by shrub and tree, Tis with delight we honor thee, Thy opened door provides us cheer, A safe retreat is given here." (Courtesy of the Cynthiana–Harrison County Museum.)

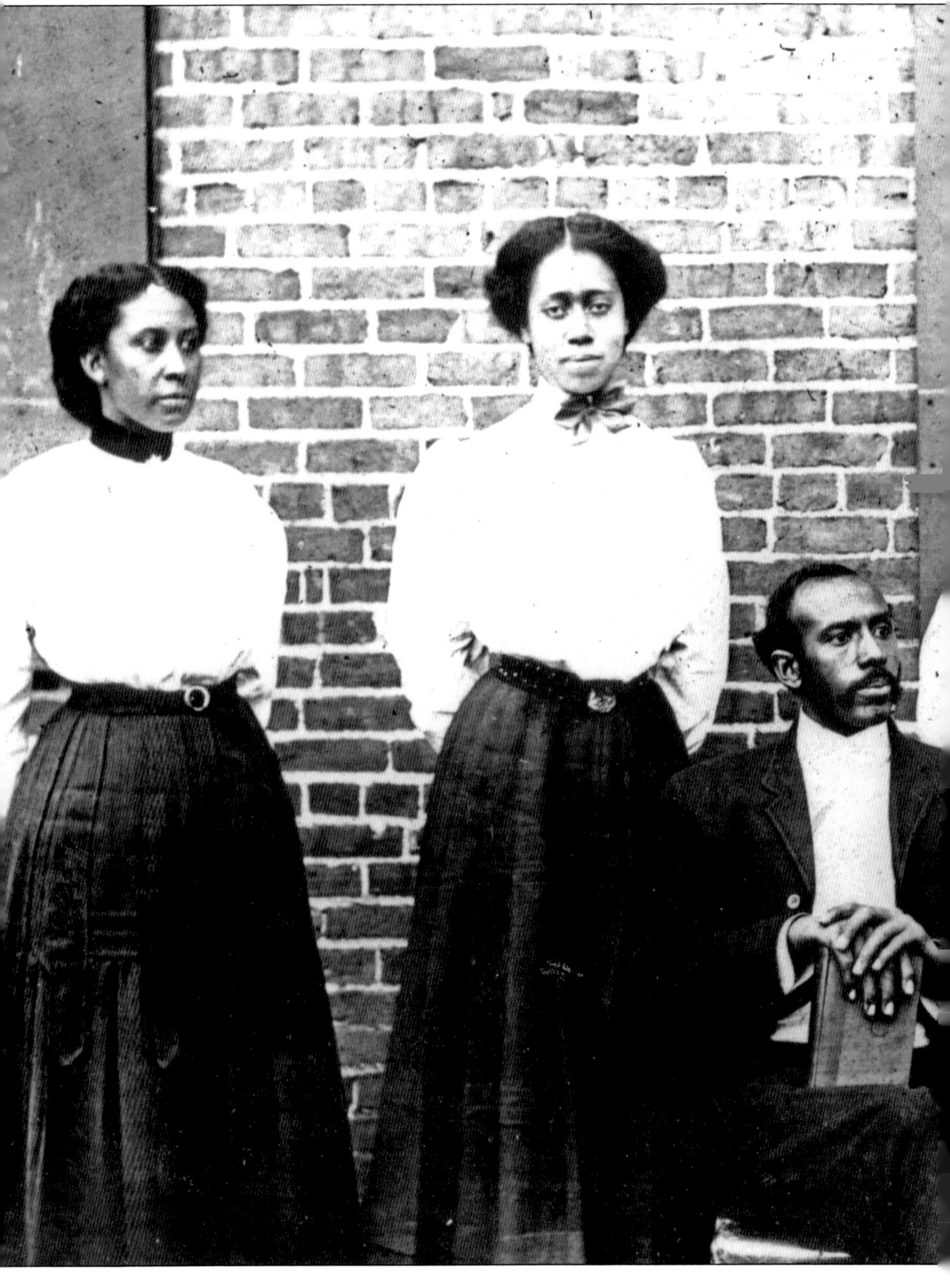

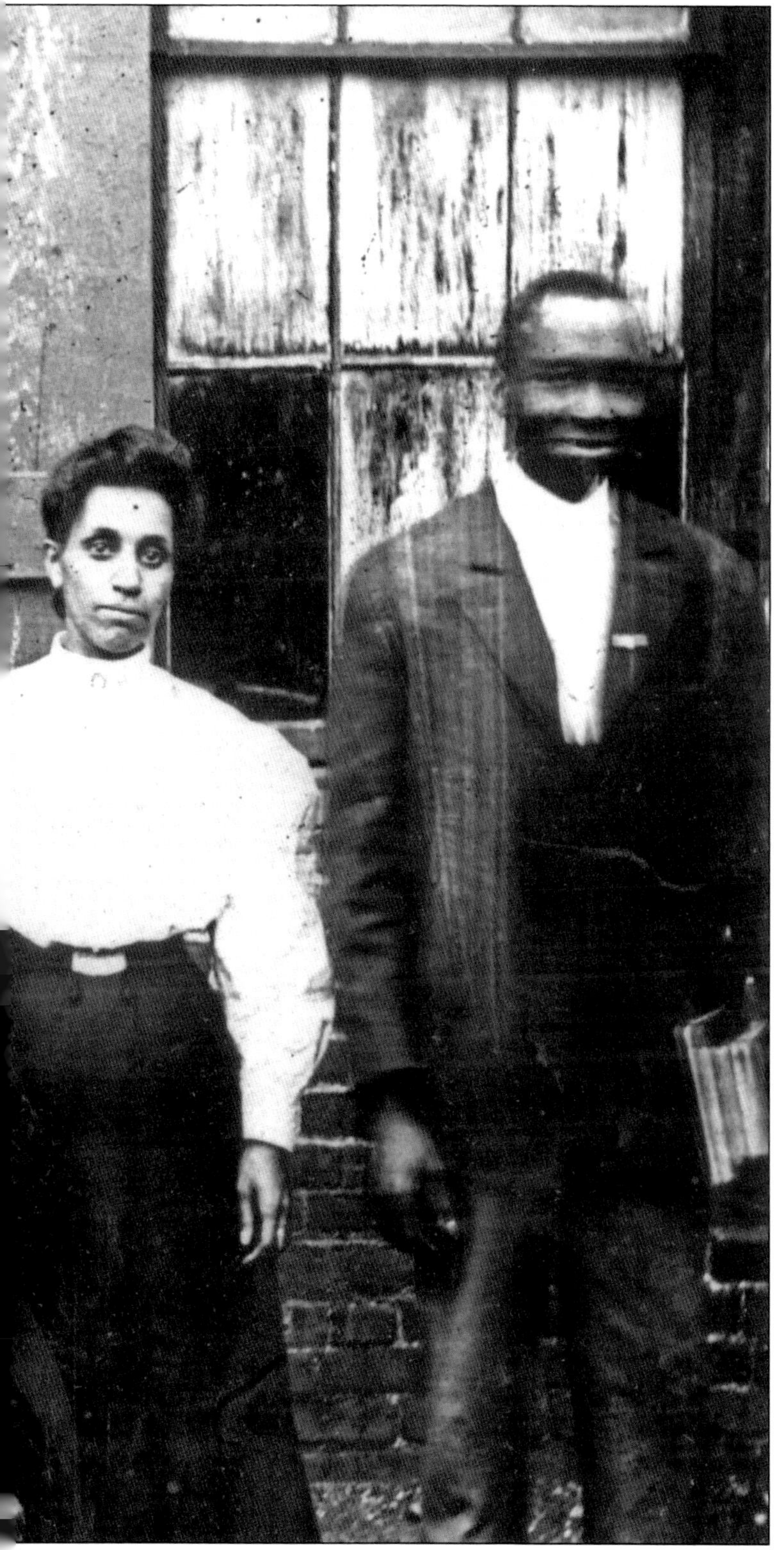

Faculty members at the Cynthiana Colored School in 1908 were, from left to right, Daisy Bober, Hattie Paton, Prof. W. C. Orton, Mrs. W. C. Orton, and Thomas J. Mason. (Courtesy of the Cynthiana–Harrison County Museum.)

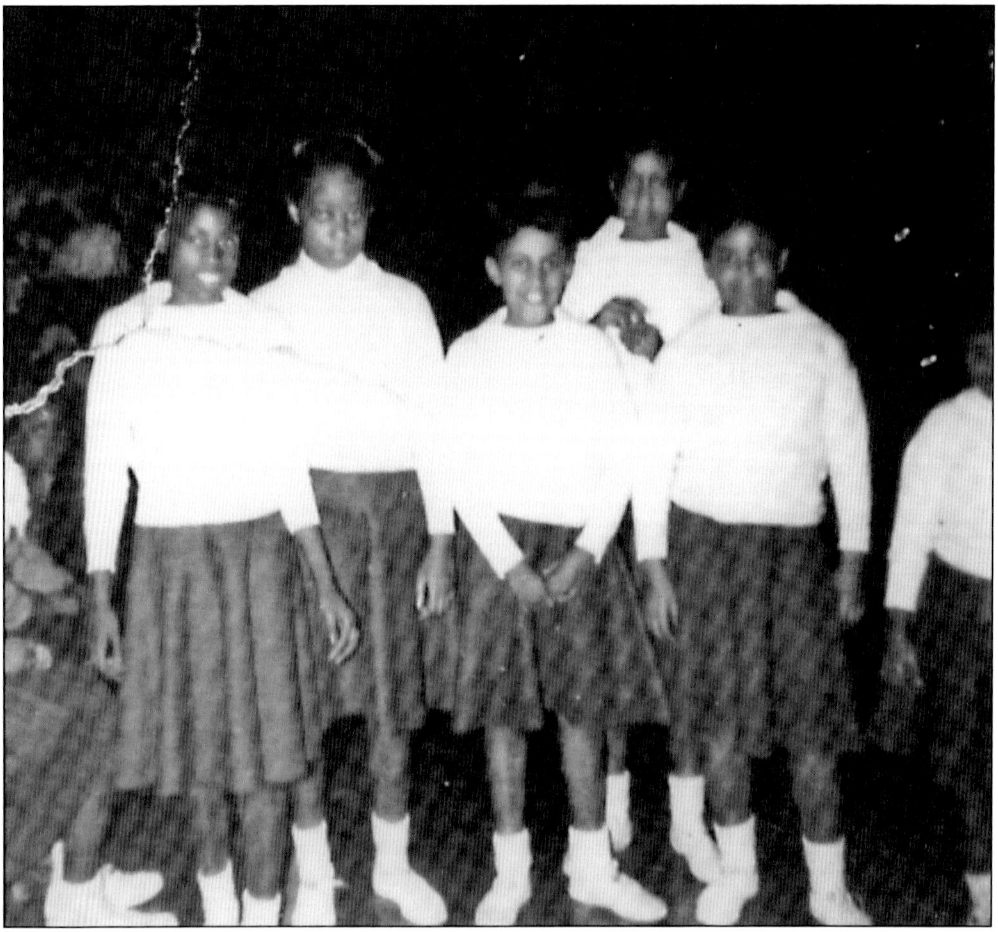

From left to right, Carlotta Conner, Janice Wilson, Linda Prather, Patricia L. Allen, Cheryl Adair, and Brenda Johnson were Banneker School cheerleaders during the school's last year of existence. (Courtesy of Alice Allen/*Cynthiana Democrat*.)

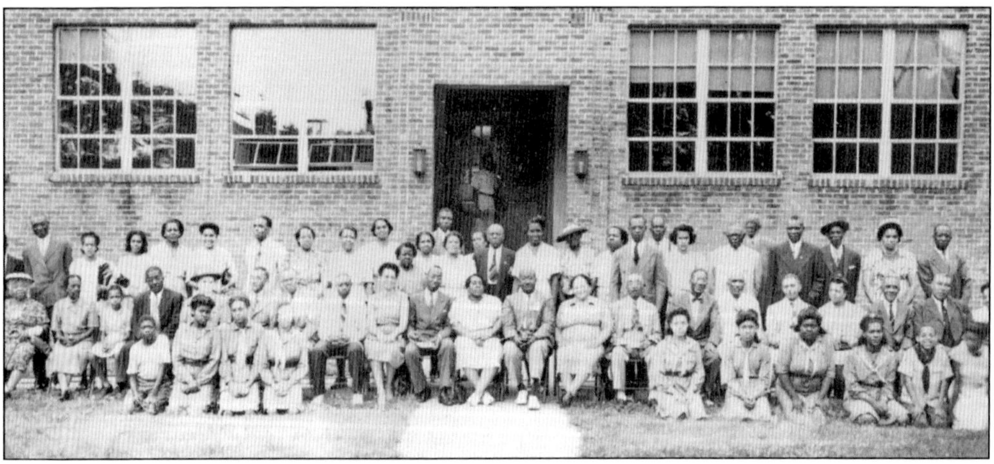

Parents and teachers gather in front of Banneker School in this undated photograph. (Courtesy of Alice Allen/*Cynthiana Democrat*.)

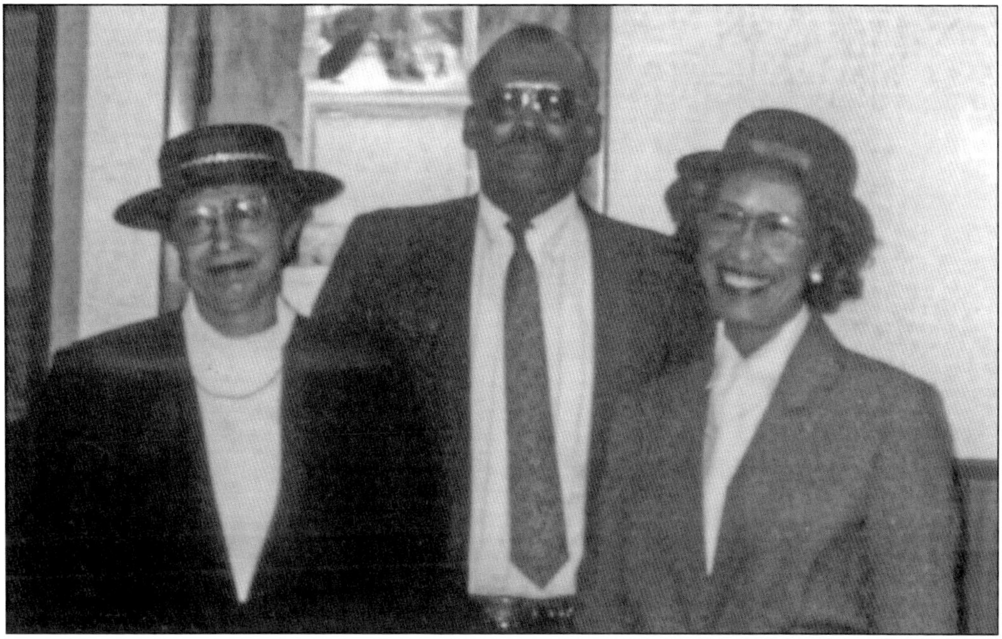

From left to right, siblings Teresa, Baldwin, and Marilyn David were students at Banneker School, where their father, E. O. David, was principal and their mother, Vivian, was a teacher. Teresa became a social worker, Baldwin became a Cynthiana volunteer firefighter and 911 operator, and Marilyn became a nurse. (Courtesy of Marilyn David Wash.)

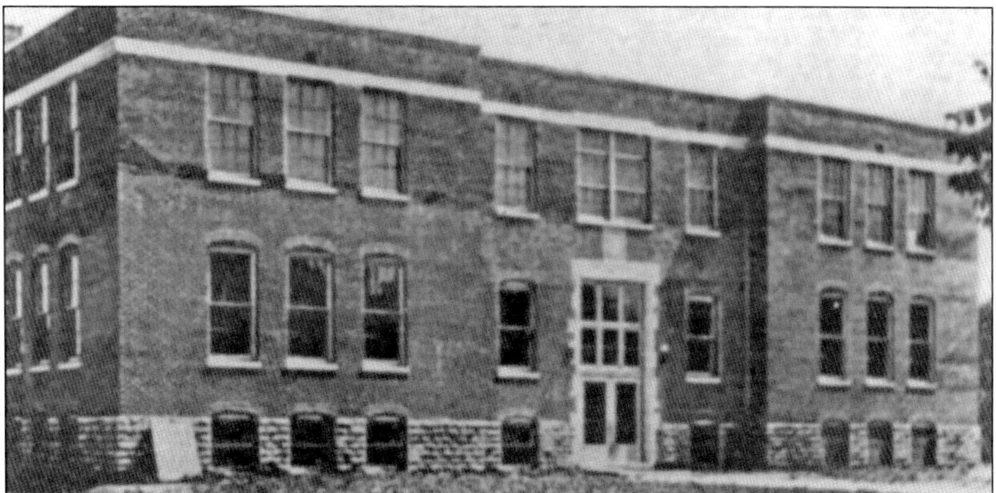

In January 1922, Marshall School opened in Cynthiana in the 200 block of West Pleasant Street, offering classes in first through sixth grade. It was located where the Family Dollar Store now stands and was named for local educator and principal I. G. Marshall. (Courtesy of the Cynthiana–Harrison County Museum.)

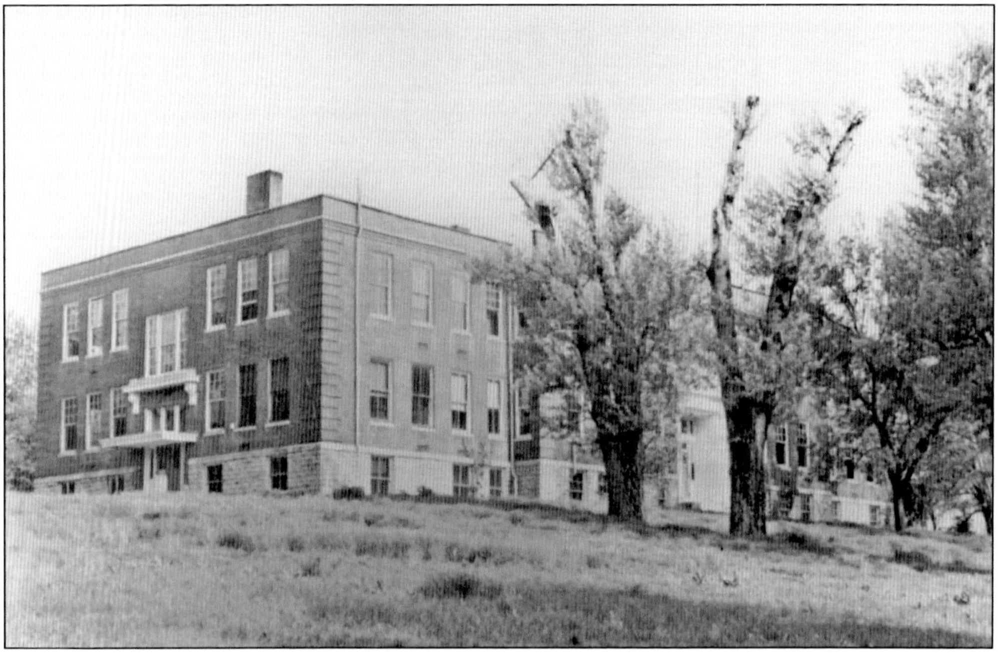

Cynthiana High School welcomed its first students in September 1872 and was the home of the Bulldogs until the school's closure in June 1962. The first official CHS newspaper was called *The Record* and was published on February 25, 1915, by the school's senior class. (Courtesy of the Cynthiana–Harrison County Museum.)

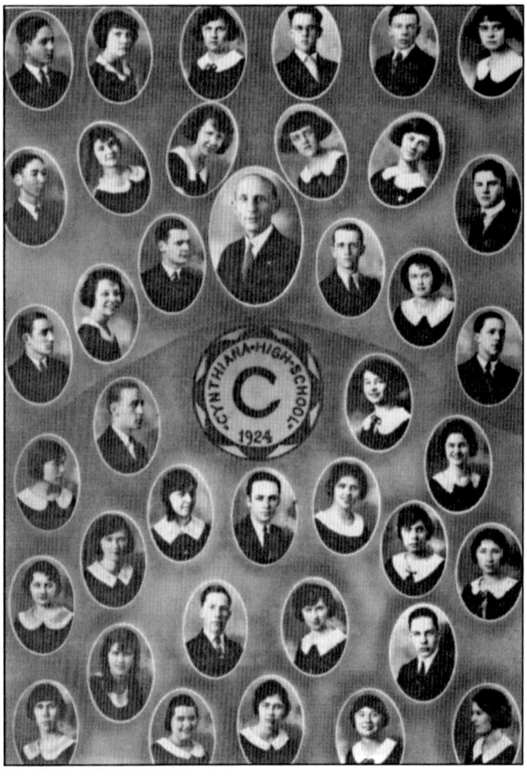

Members of the class of 1924 at Cynthiana High School were Richard Ammerman, Anna G. Arnold, Catherine Dee Bailey, Christine Bailey, Gladys Bell, Jessie Berry, Renaker Berry, Elizabeth Box, Sarah Garnett Carroll, Jack Cason, Minnie Caswell, Forrest Cleveland, Allen Clifford, Alice E. Cox, James Cromwell, Iva Rose Crosthwaite, Marjory Joyce Fields, Hugh Ella Humphrey, George Moore Jameson, Eddythe Elizabeth Jennings, John Prentiss Lair, Mary Lair, Amelia Ann Lang, Margaret Linehan, Claud Marsh, Gladys Marsh, Eugene May, Robert McCarthy, Elva McKenney, William Parrish, Mary Payne, Mary Margaret Richer, Roy Shingleton, H. Tod Smiser, Virginia Smith, Gray Tucker, Betsy Wyles, and Irene Wyles. (Courtesy of the Cynthiana High School Alumni Association.)

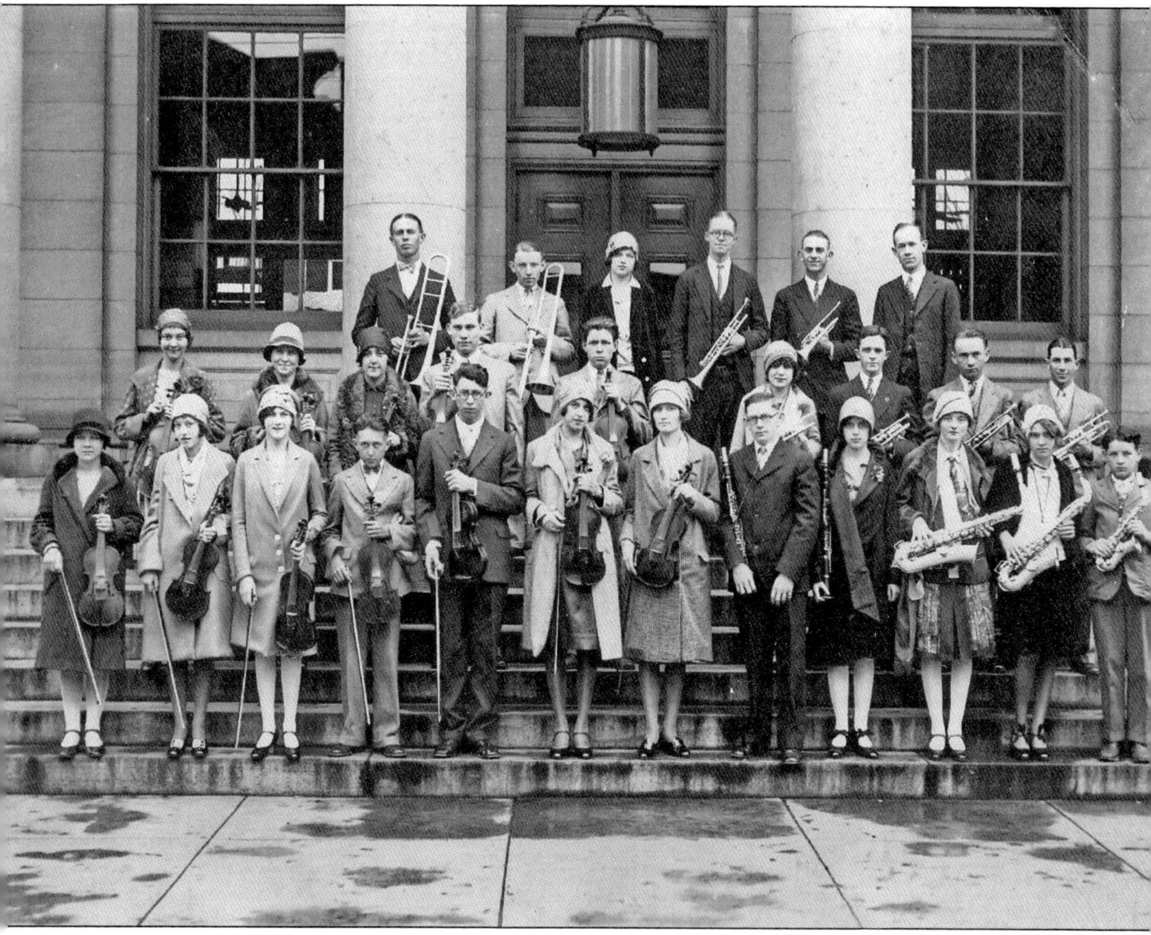

The Cynthiana High School orchestra, around 1928, stood at the ready in front of the city's old post office. (Courtesy of the Cynthiana–Harrison County Museum/Anna Myers McKee.)

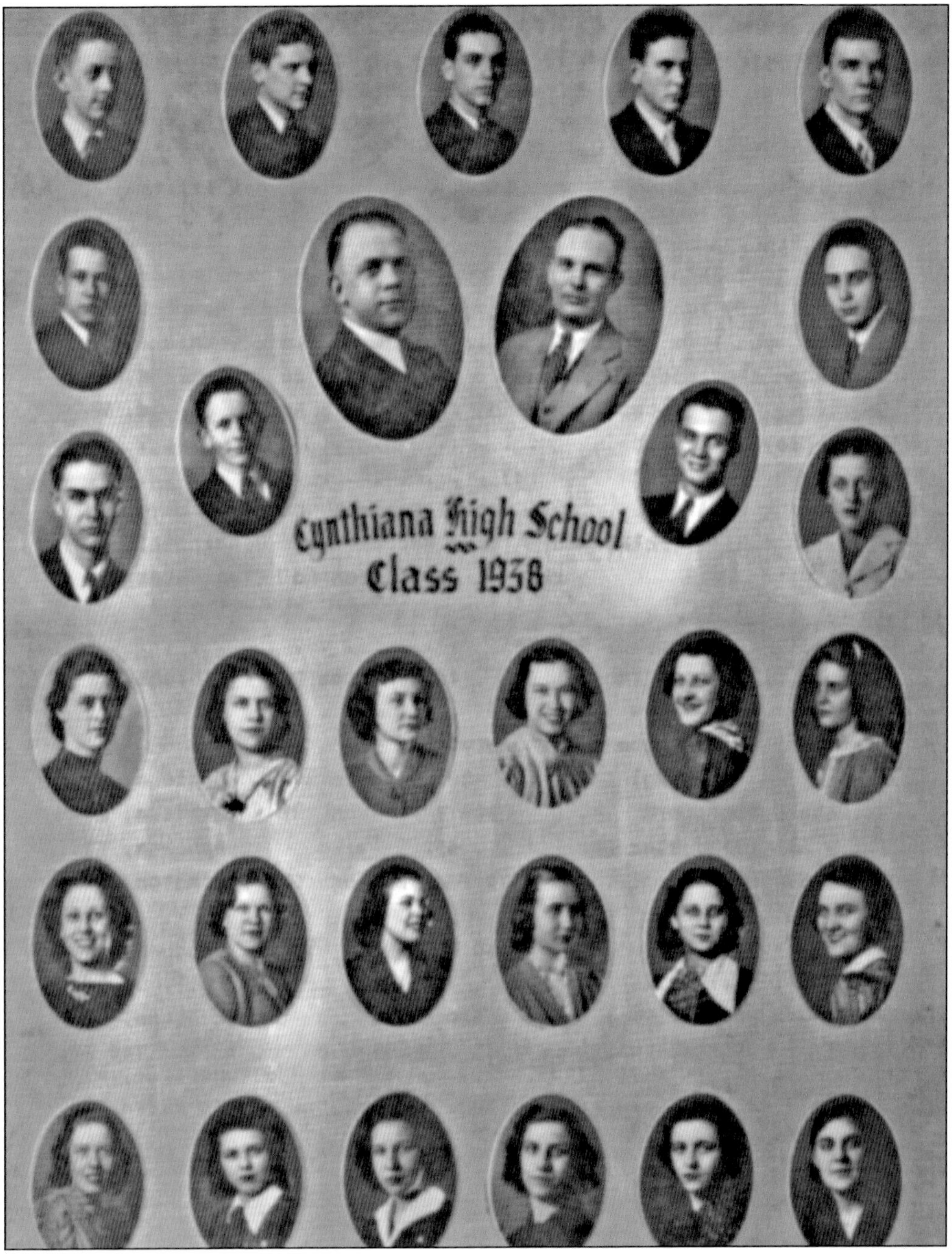

Cynthiana High School class of 1938 graduates were Marguerite Ruth Adams, Dorothy Alleen Argo, Georgie Lorene Arnold, Virginia Barnett, Evelyn Reese Cobb, Beaulah Christine Colvin, Mildred Louise Colvin, Alline Donovan, William Floyd Fightmaster, Margaret Fitzgerald, Helen Button Grater, William Henry Heck, Helen Kerr, James Gano Lail, William Bennett Morgan, Stella Loraine Platt, Margaret Pulliam, Christine Renaker, Vivian Ruth Rice, Henry Milton Robertson, Houston Rees Rose, Maude Paxton Ross, Ralph Slade, Mary Martha Thompson, Hershel Lee Turner, Sue Ruth VanDeren, Arthur Joseph Walsh, Mayme Lee Yarnell and Robert Kirkland Young. (Courtesy of the Cynthiana High School Alumni Association.)

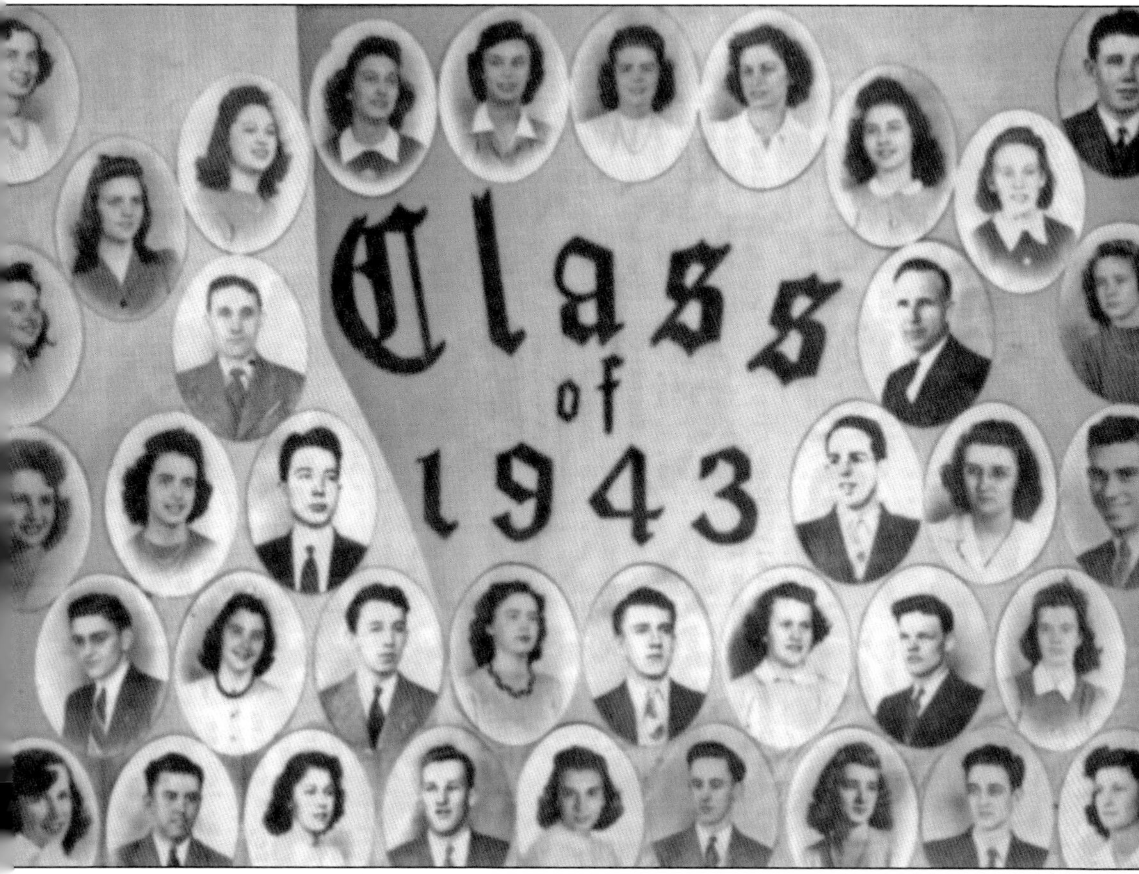

The Cynthiana High School class of 1943 claimed as its own Minerva Ruth Adams, William Hersil Carr, Ruby Joyce Cason, Taylor Cason Jr., Ollie Jewell Clifford, Charles Ray Cooper, Virginia Miriam Faulconer, Jeanne Fightmaster, Cornelius John Fitzgerald, Wayne Wheeler Fitzgerald, William Curtis Hall, Elaine Hamilton Humphrey, Louise Madison Jewett, Jimmie Kimbrough, Sara Jane Kimbrough, Geneva Mildred Lemons, George N. Levi, Eubie Mae Martin, Betty Midden, George Bernard Midden, Alice Bagby Owsley, Rufus B. Pulliam, George Newton Reynolds, Dorothy Marie Scott, Joseph Craig Smith, Carol McStaton, Marjorie Jameson Taylor, Doris Ann Turner, Ellen Garman Turner, Betty Louise Walsh, Phyllis Ann Watkins, William A. Webber II, Mabel Lee Wells, Maxine Williams, and Maysie McDowell Williams. (Courtesy of the Cynthiana High School Alumni Association.)

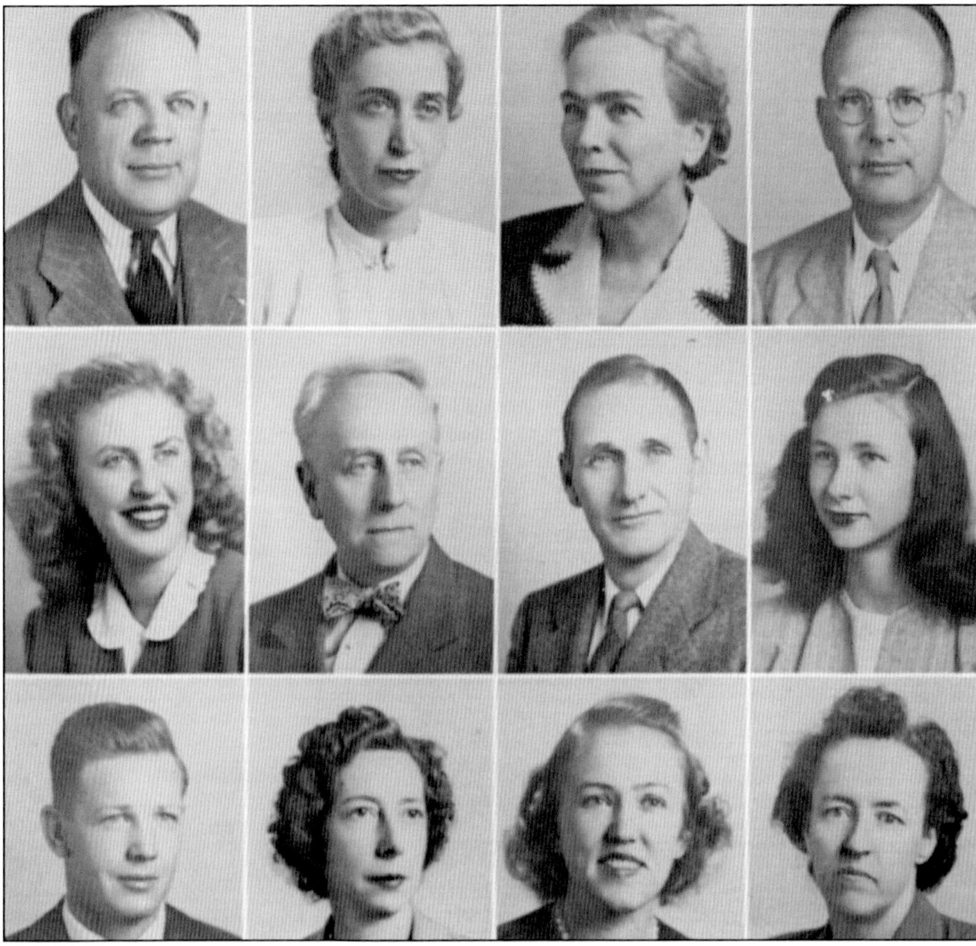

Faculty members at Cynthiana High School in 1948 were, from top to bottom and left to right, W. H. Cason, principal; Frances Conway; Cornelia Duffy; W. E. Lawson, superintendent; Sarah M. Leggett; H. D. Ingles; K. B. Stanfield; Jean Wright; J. Rocke; Marietta Sparks; Anna Meisel; and Sarah M. Van Deren. (Courtesy of the Cynthiana High School Alumni Association.)

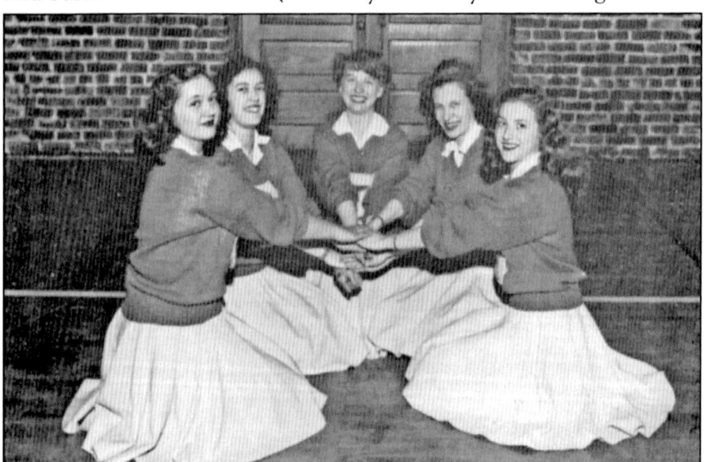

The "Green and White" at Cynthiana High School were cheered on in 1948 by, from left to right, Pat Hampton, Billee Bell Faulkner (captain), Bettie Lane Begley, Bonnie Lee McDonald, and Maxie McClain. (Courtesy of Helen McNees.)

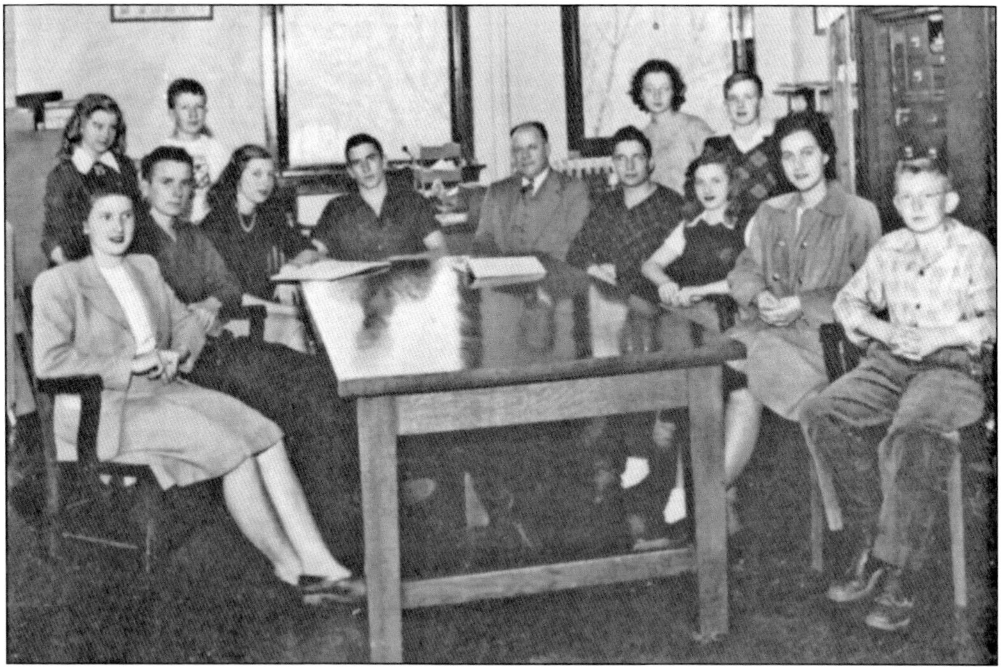

John Swinford, seated at the head of the table, was president of the 1948 activities council at Cynthiana High School. Swinford later became an attorney. Other council members were John Feeback, Ruth Midden, Jesse Adams, Marion Hardin, Henrietta Hasty, Janet Insko, Maxie McClain, Ann North, Elbert Smith, Joyce Taylor and Donald Withers. (Courtesy of the Cynthiana High School Alumni Association.)

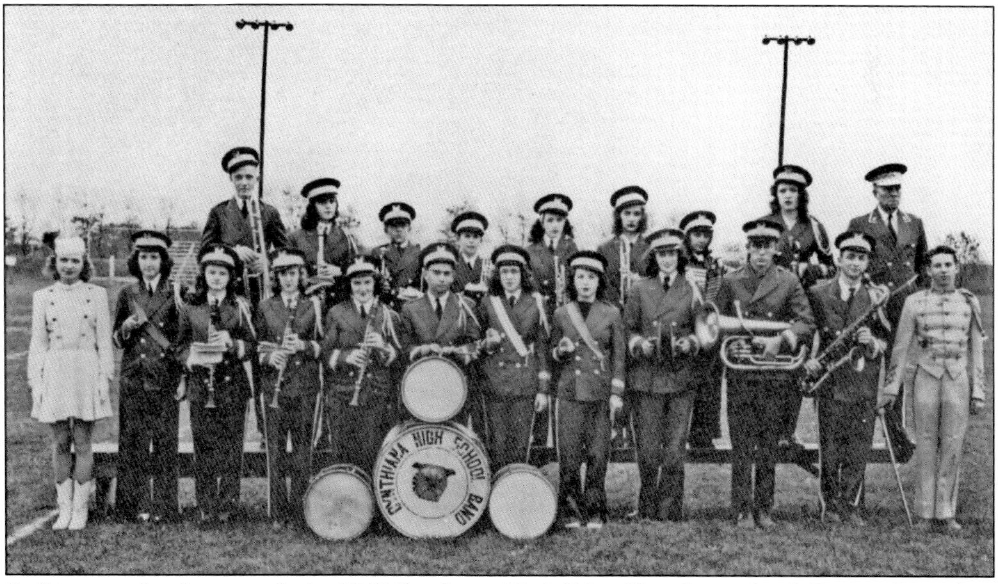

Striking up school spirit with the 1948 Cynthiana High School band were Sarah Barnes, Jacqueline Case, Elizabeth Crail, Paul Feix, Marjorie Gooden, Bonnie Insko, Margaret Keller, Harold Kendall, Linda Lowe, Henry Moody, Albert Nutgrass, Robert Pope, Katherine Reynolds, James Ritter, Christine Sosbe, Dorothy Stone, Carol Taylor, Joe Withers, and drum major Gerald Fitzgerald. (Courtesy of the Cynthiana High School Alumni Association.)

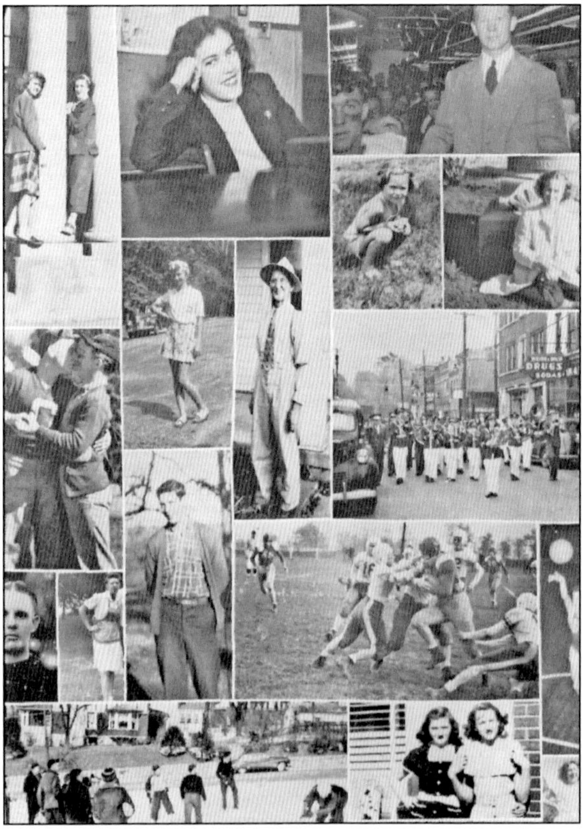

The 1948 Cynthiana yearbook featured a variety of snapshots of local life through the eyes of teenagers. (Courtesy of the Cynthiana High School Alumni Association.)

The 1950 activities council of Cynthiana High School posed for a yearbook photograph. They are, clockwise from left on the front row, Larry Shadd, Ruth Tolle, David McCauley, Patsy Lemons, Frazier Palmer, Janet Insko, Barkley Baird, Carol Conrad, Janice Withers and Dan Howk. On the back row, from left to right, Kelly "Pop" Stanfield, Sue Douglas, Lane Taylor, and Cornelia Duffy. (Courtesy of the Cynthiana High School Alumni Association.)

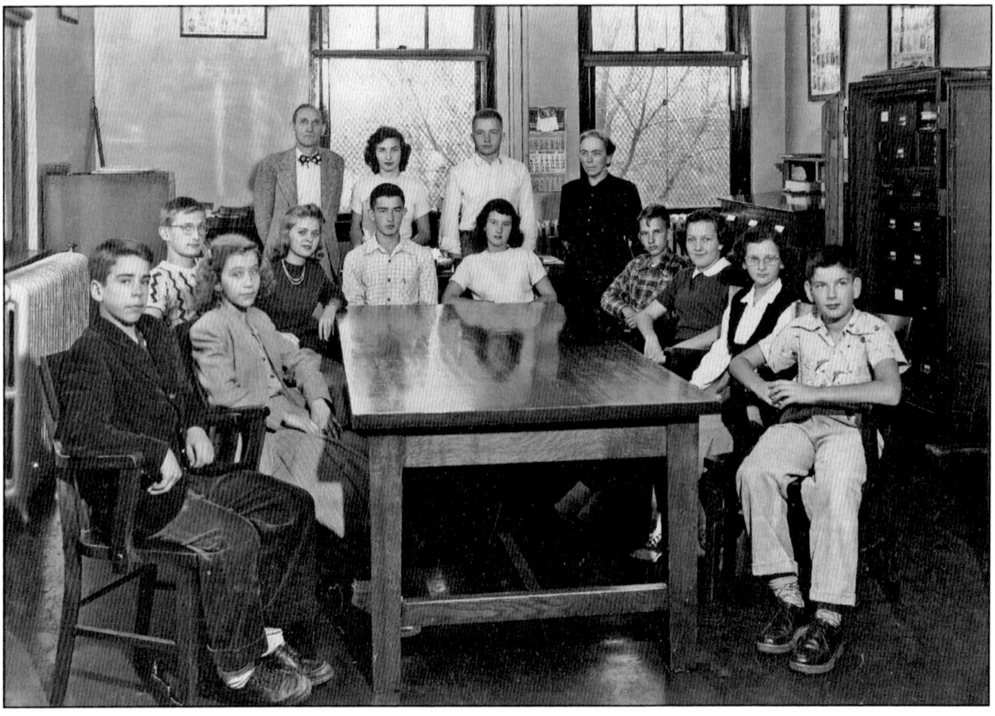

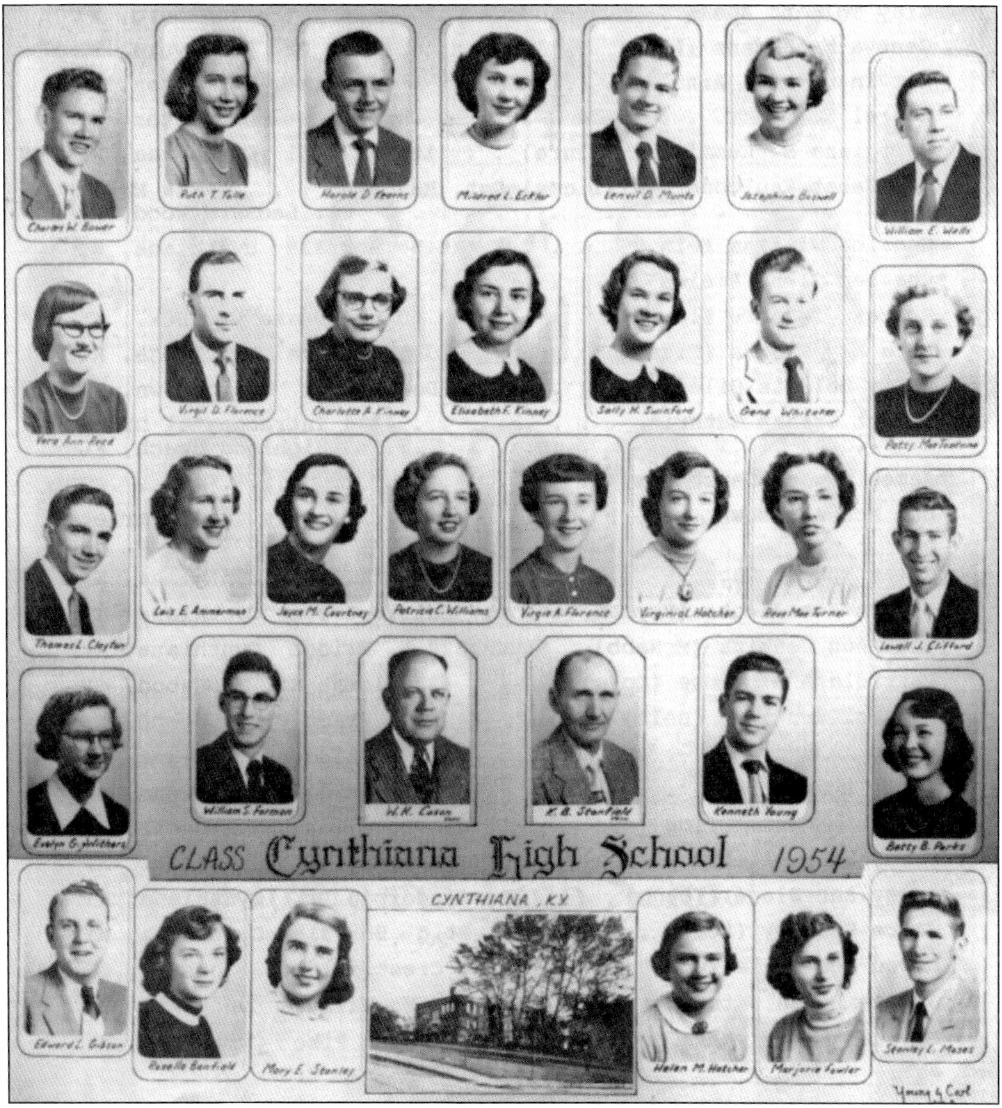

Members of the class of 1954 were Lois Ammerman, Rozella Banfield, Josephine Boswell, Charles W. Bower, Thomas Lee Clayton, Lowell Jackson Clifford, Joyce Marie Courtney, Mildred Louise Ecklar, Virgil David Florence, Virgie Ann Florence, William Simpson Foreman, Marjorie Fowler, Edward Louis Gibson, Helen Hatcher, Virginia Hatcher, Harold David Kearns, Charlotte Kinney, Elizabeth Faye Kinney, Stanley Lewis Moses, Lenvil D. Muntz, Betty Bruce Parks, Vera Reed, Mary Elizabeth Stanley, Sarah Hanson Swinford, Patricia Mae Toadvine, Ruth Taylor Tolle, Reva Mae Turner, William Edgar "Willie" Wells, Gene Whitaker, Patricia Carol Williams, Evelyn Gale Withers, and Kenneth Young. (Courtesy of the Cynthiana High School Alumni Association.)

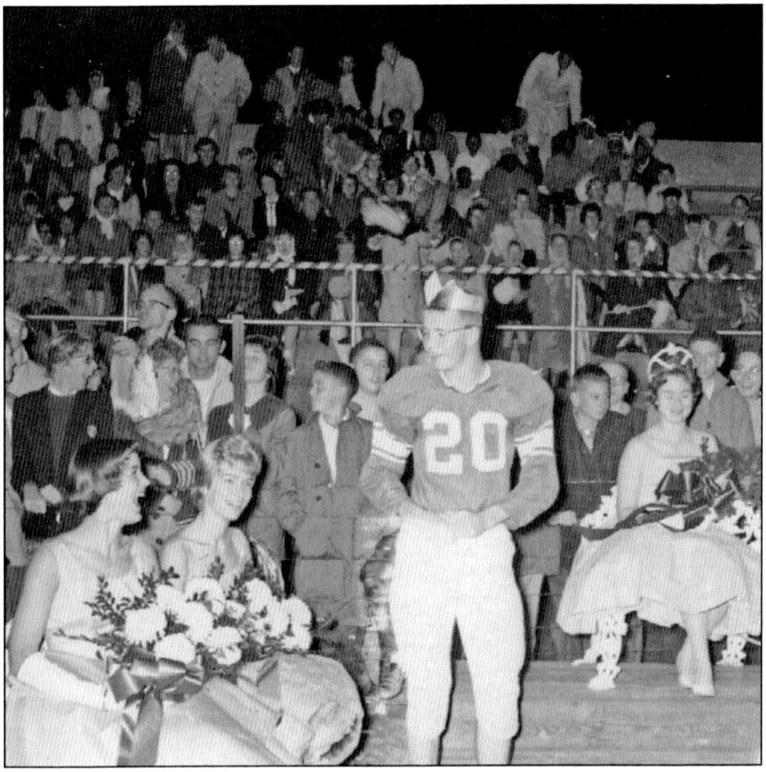

A grinning Bill Penn was named Cynthiana High School's homecoming king in 1961. His queen, seated to his left, was Terry Ann Sorrell. Attendants were senior Martha Bell, at Penn's right, and junior Alice Stewart, seated at Bell's right. (Courtesy of William A. Penn.)

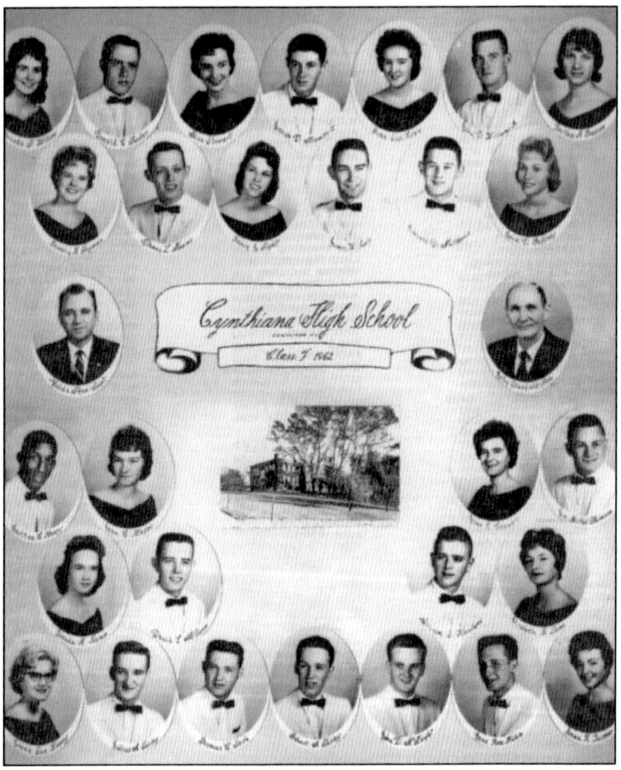

The last graduating seniors at Cynthiana High School marched in 1962. They were Joseph Dennis Biancke II, Joan Carol Criswell, Nancy Jo Fight, Beverly Kay Fryman, Carol Donia Gaffney, Bertha Alice Grayson, Brenda Mae Hamm, William Stewart Haviland, Carlton Eugene Henry, James William Juett, Danny Lee Kearns, Connie Sue Kinney, Elizabeth Bradford Lane, Jean Carolyn Magee, Everett Dale Matthews, David Lawrence McEwan, John David McKnight, Lavon Stanley Page, Lois S. Powell, Gene Ross Richie, Mona Sue Richie, Julius Allan Shirley, Robert Anson Shirley, Alice Stewart, Thomas Clay Stith, Joe McKee Thomson, Donald Carr Tucker, Anna Russell Turner, John Denny Williams Jr., and Brenda Frances Wilson. (Courtesy of the Cynthiana High School Alumni Association.)

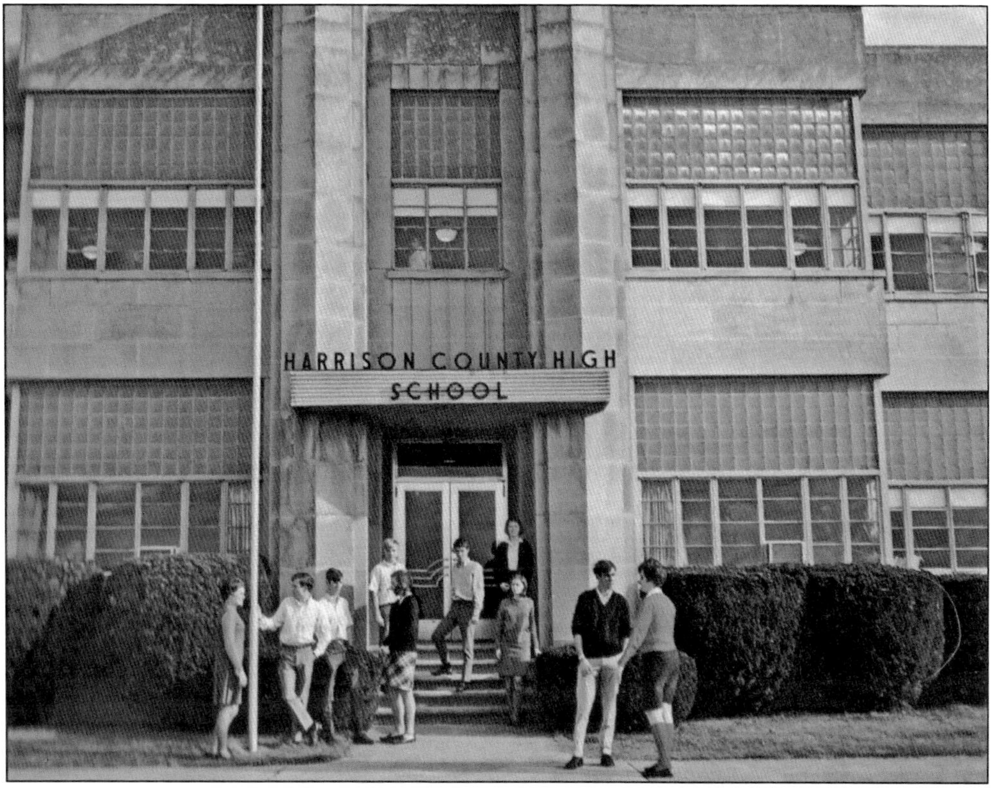

Students from the class of 1969 gather in front of Harrison County High School, home of the Thorobreds, on Webster Avenue. After county schools in communities neighboring Cynthiana closed in the spring of 1950, Harrison County High School graduated its first class in 1951. In 1962, Cynthiana High School also merged with Harrison County High School. (Courtesy of Harrison County High School)

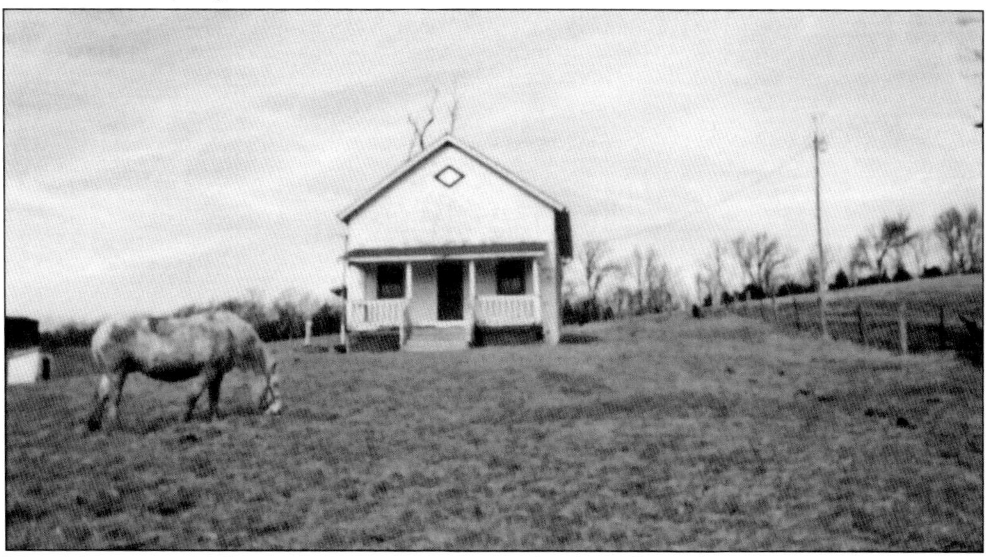

New Liberty, one of the county's many one-room schools in the early 20th century, is shown in an undated photograph. (Courtesy of the Cynthiana–Harrison County Museum.)

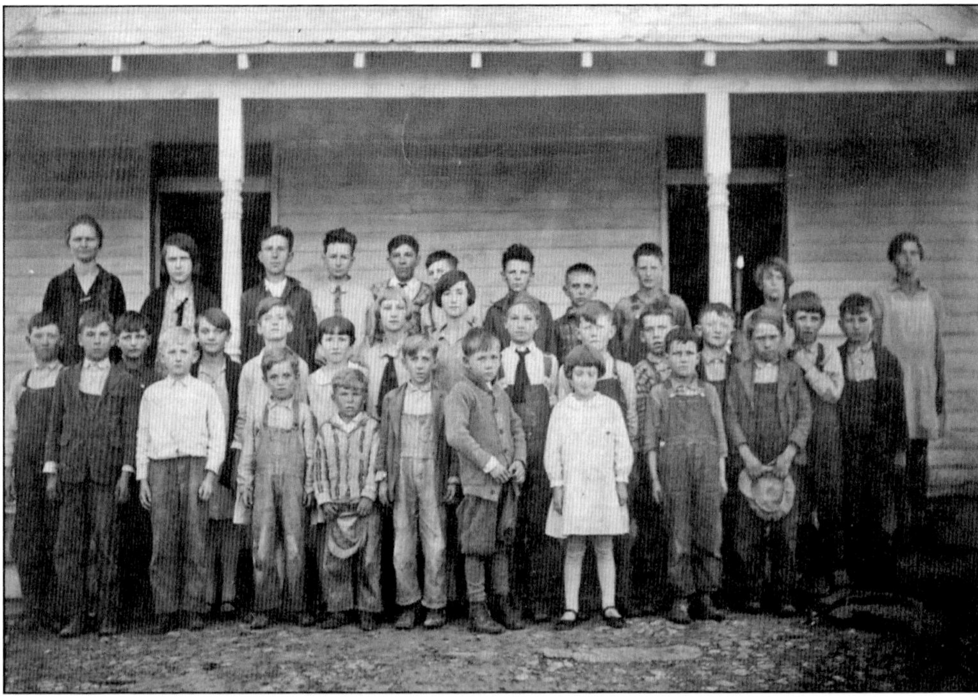

Bessie Perkins (back left), who taught at one-room schools in Harrison County between 1915 and 1925, stands with her class in front of the White Oak School around 1915. Her students included Renaker Casey, Felix Humphrey, and Lula Myrtle Perkins. (Courtesy of Helen Harney.)

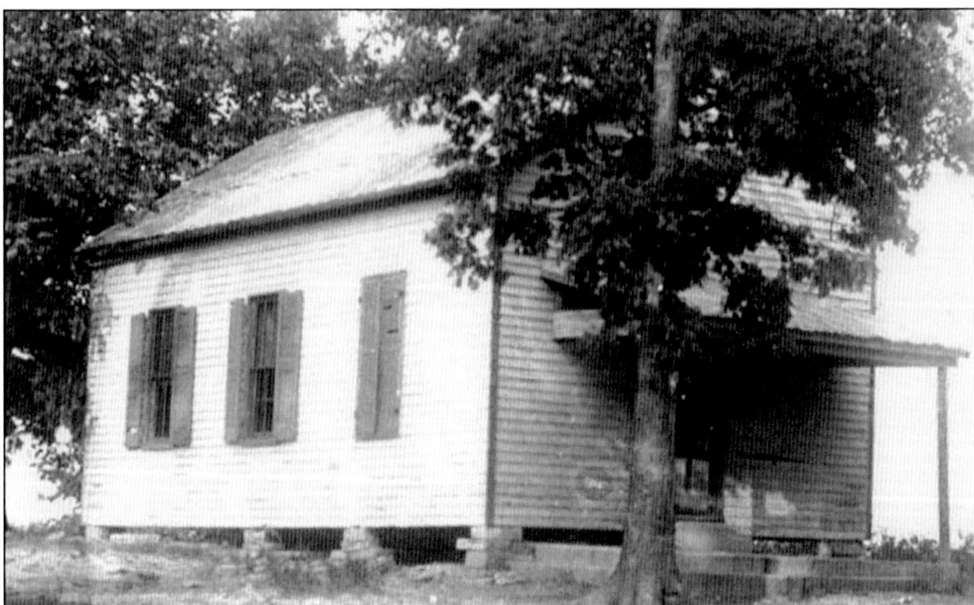

This country school was the educational home for students around Salem. (Courtesy of the Cynthiana–Harrison County Museum.)

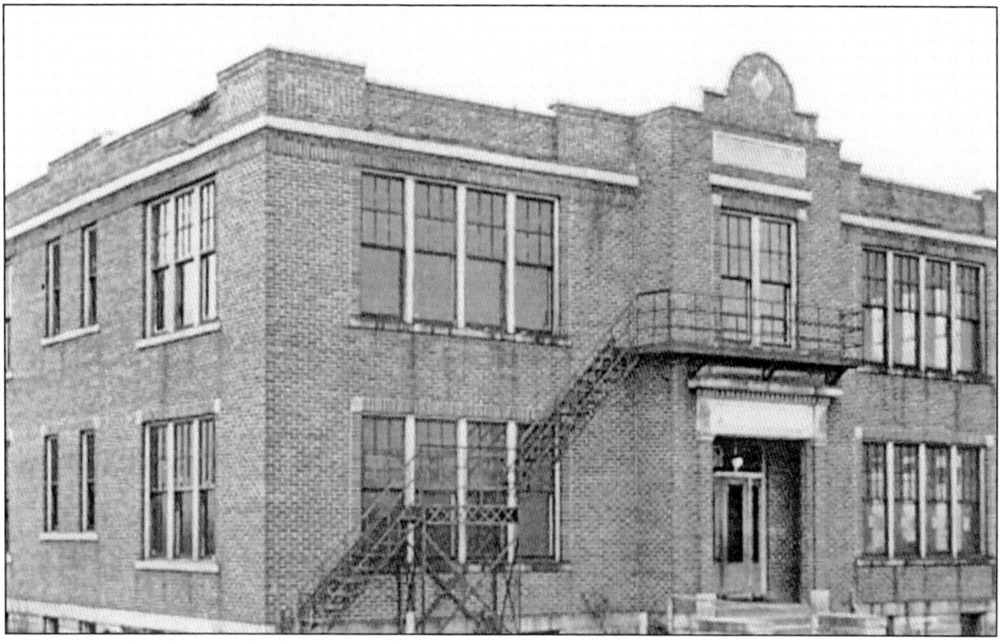

The class of 1950 was the last to graduate from Berry High School. That year, Berry and other county schools were consolidated with Harrison County High School. The old school was built in 1917, after a fire consumed the Berry Independent School. (Courtesy of Patty Adams.)

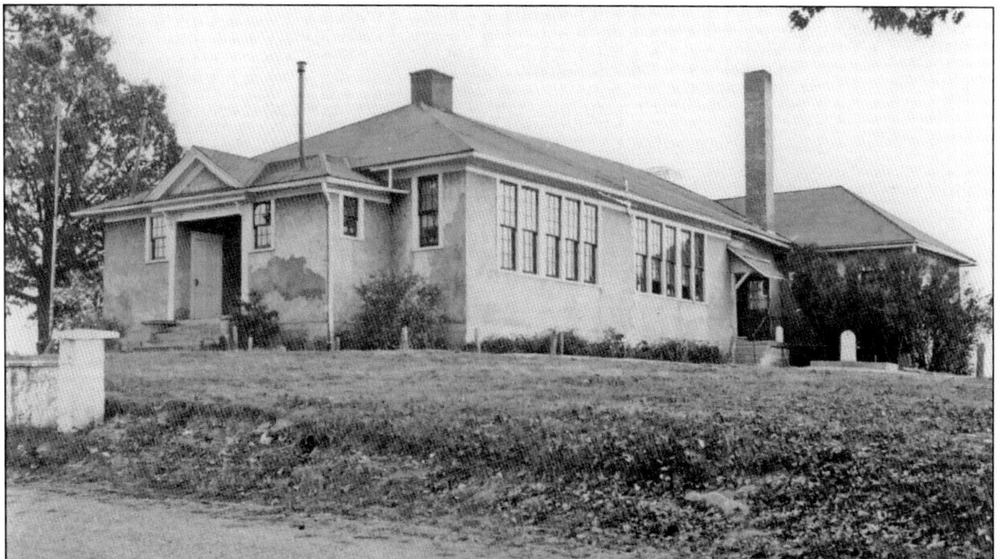

Built with just four rooms in 1923, Renaker School offered instruction until 1950. (Courtesy of the Cynthiana–Harrison County Museum.)

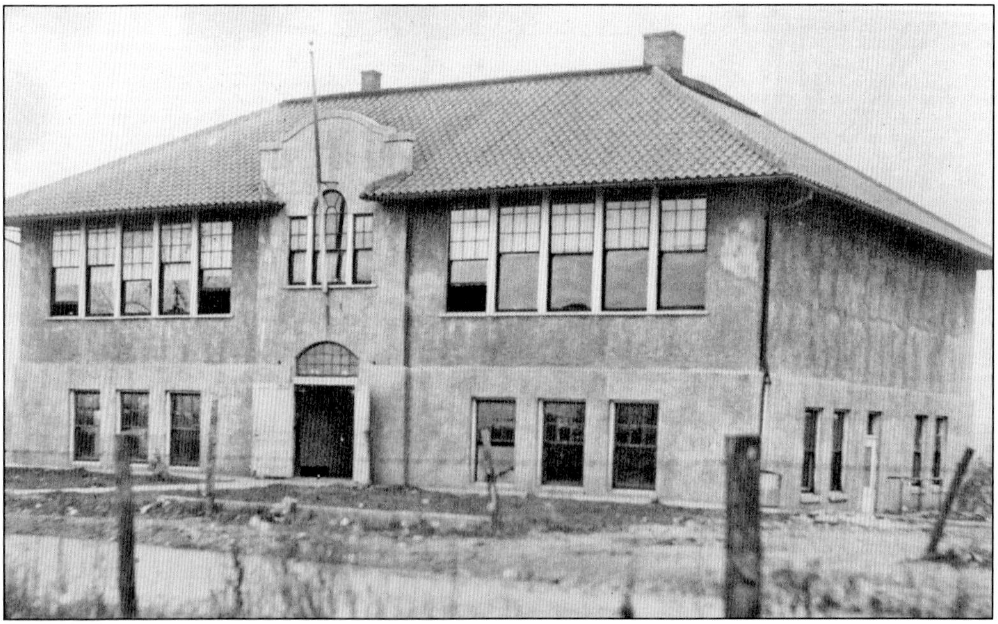

The first graduates of the Sunrise School received their diplomas in 1922, with the last class graduating in 1940. (Courtesy of the Cynthiana–Harrison County Museum.)

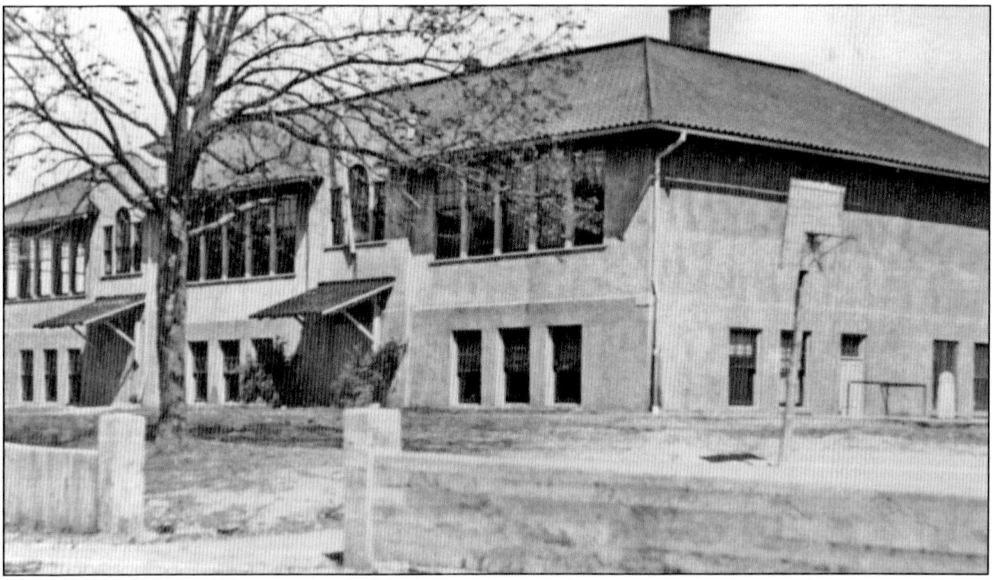

Buena Vista School opened in 1920. Educators during its last year of operation, 1964, included Verna Pickering Teasley, a second-grade instructor who died in 2009 at age 96, and principal Raymond Ward. (Courtesy of the Cynthiana–Harrison County Museum.)

Five

Faith of Our Families

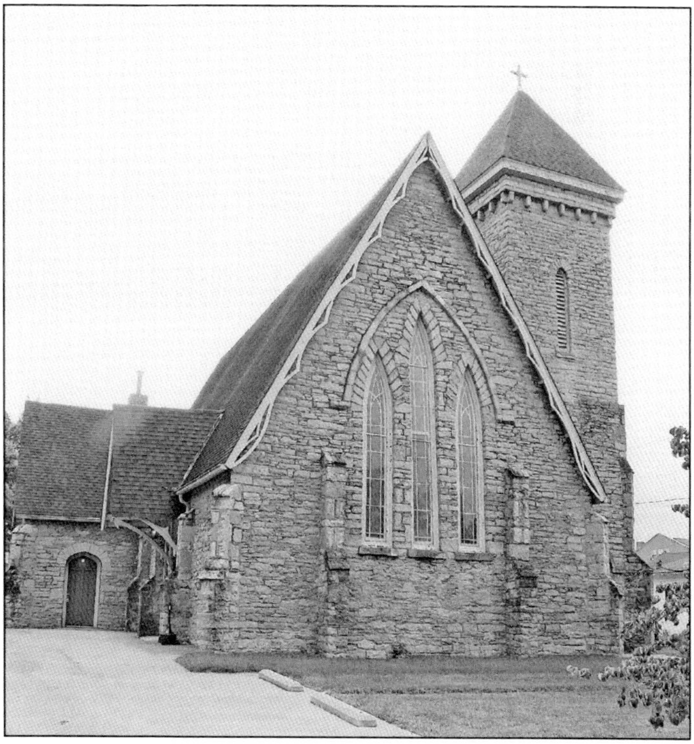

The oldest church building in Cynthiana is the Church of the Advent, home to the city's Episcopal congregation at 118 North Walnut Street. The building's cornerstone was laid in May 1855. Members relate that the beautiful oak altar was carved by women of the church in the 19th century and that during the Civil War, wounded soldiers were treated inside the church. (Photograph by Kate Darnell.)

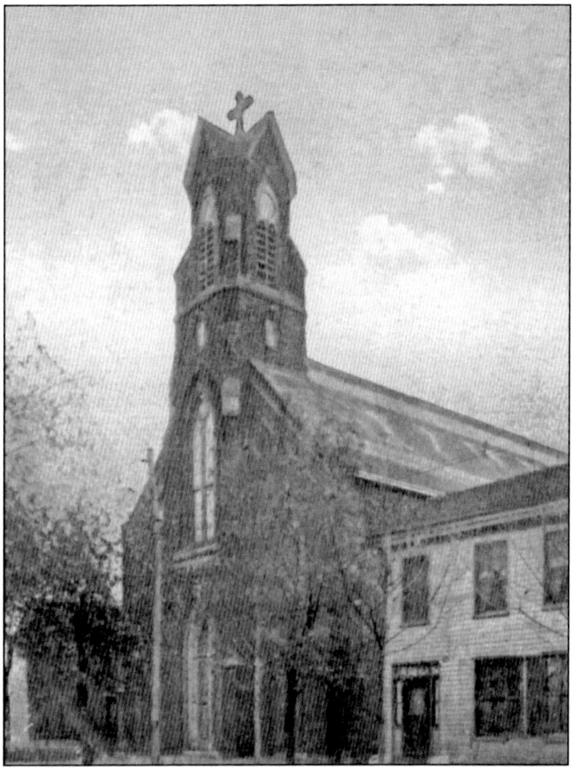

According to the St. Edward Catholic Church, Catholics were present in Harrison County as early as 1825. In 1852, the Right Reverend George Carroll, first bishop of Covington, decided a mission should be established in Cynthiana, as many Irish workers were moving in to lay track for the Kentucky Central Railroad. The first Catholic church in Cynthiana was dedicated on Ascension Day in 1864. A new church was started in 1871, and on October 29, 1876, the second church building at 123 North Walnut Street was dedicated. Sadly a blaze destroyed the building and rectory on December 30, 1965. Surviving the fire was a statue of the Blessed Virgin Mary, which became known as the Miracle Statue. The present-day church was dedicated on November 3, 1968, built on the same site as the beloved second building. (Courtesy of Flossie Gasser.)

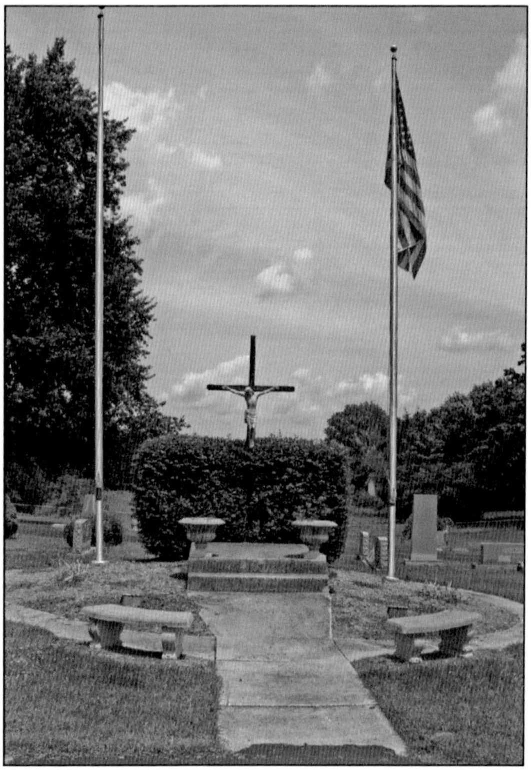

The serene St. Edward Cemetery is just north of downtown Cynthiana off U.S. Route 27. In 1869, according to church records, 30 acres at the intersection of A. Keller and Falmouth Pikes were purchased from Harrison Magee for $3,000. Some of that ground became the church cemetery. (Photograph by Linda H. Moore.)

Cynthiana's first Methodist church was completed in 1820, destroyed by fire in 1845, and rebuilt that same year. The First United Methodist Church's third building, at Pike and Church Streets, was erected in 1870. (Courtesy of the Cynthiana–Harrison County Museum.)

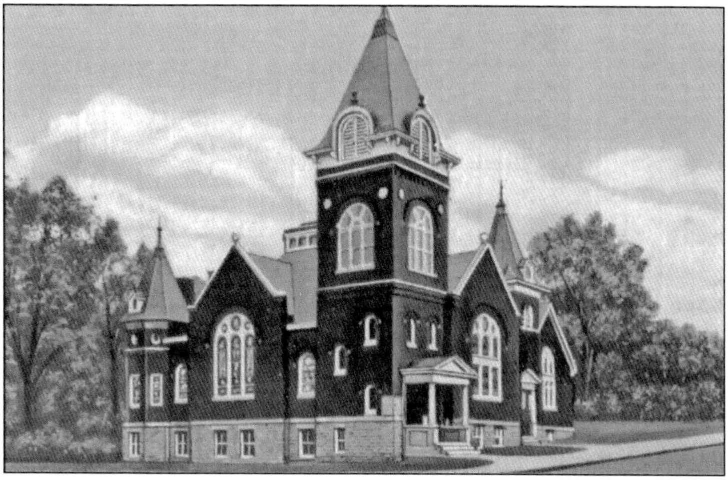

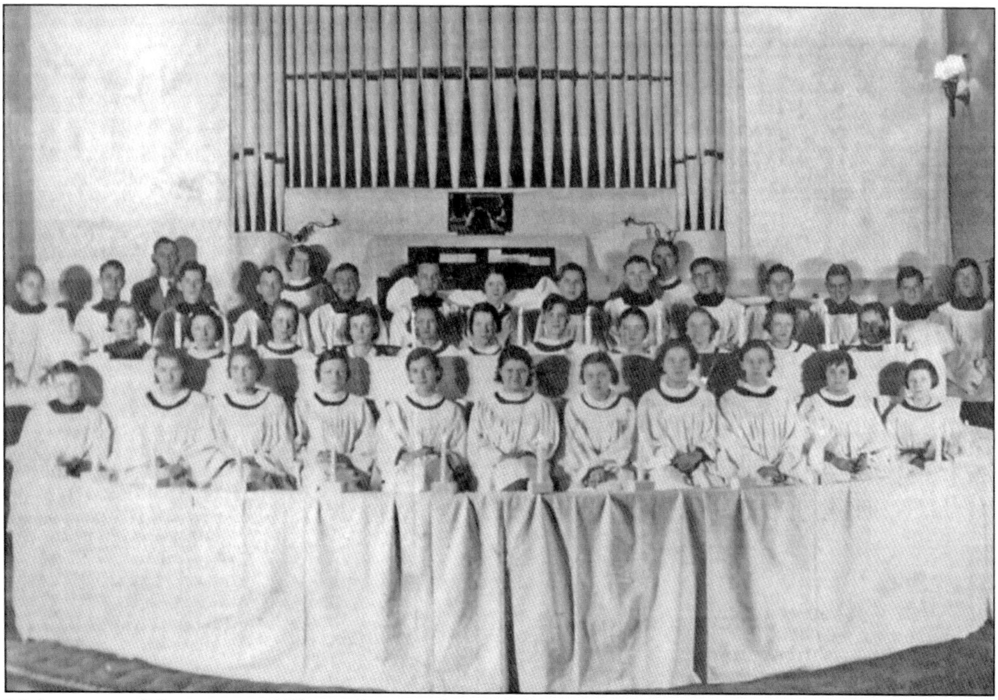

Making a joyful noise in 1935 are the members of the First United Methodist Church choir. From left to right are (first row) unidentified, Louise Williams, Alice Garnett Kendall, Cecil Martin, Helen Ecklar, Jane Osborne, Virginia Ruddler, Elsie Wood, Louise Spurrior, Jackie Ecklar, and Ester McKnight; (second row) Anna Sue Toadvine, Marian Martin, Zella Kitchen, Ruth McKnight, Elizabeth Crawford, Helen Cooper, Nancy McKnight, Christine Kearns, Anna Sue VanDeren, Ester Williams, and Loraine McCauley; (third row) Gus Palas Jr., Kirkland Young, George Phillips, Wade Hill, Roy Harney, Stanley Houston, Beatrice Kitchen Keith, Tommy Williams, Billy Giles, Roy Kitchen, Theodore Selin, John Morgan, Bennett Morgan, and Harold Dunn. Ruth Fryman directed the choir. (Courtesy of the Cynthiana–Harrison County Museum.)

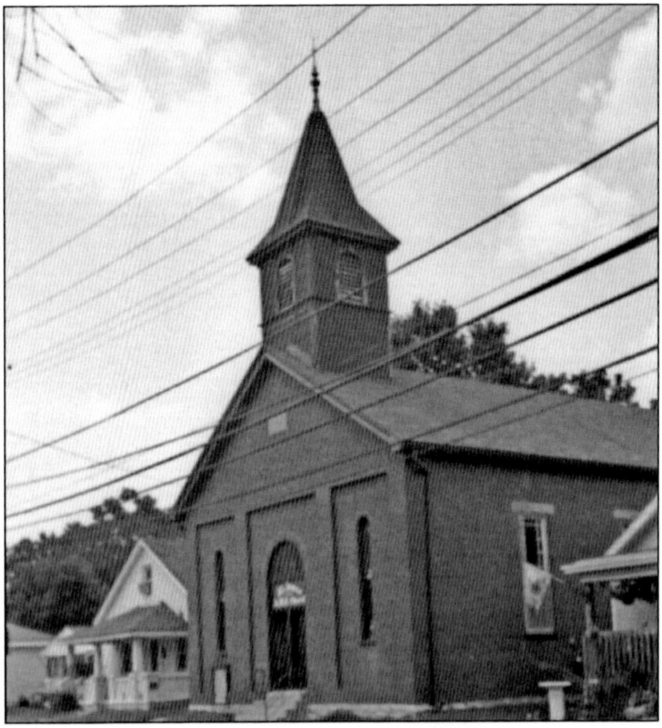

The Harrison County Historical Society records from 1905 show that three African American churches welcomed worshippers at that time: the Ebenezer Methodist Episcopal Church, the St. James A.M.E. Church (pictured here at its home on West Pleasant Street) and the Macedonian Baptist Church. Records also show that the St. James A.M.E. congregation built its first church in 1853. (Courtesy of Helen Harney.)

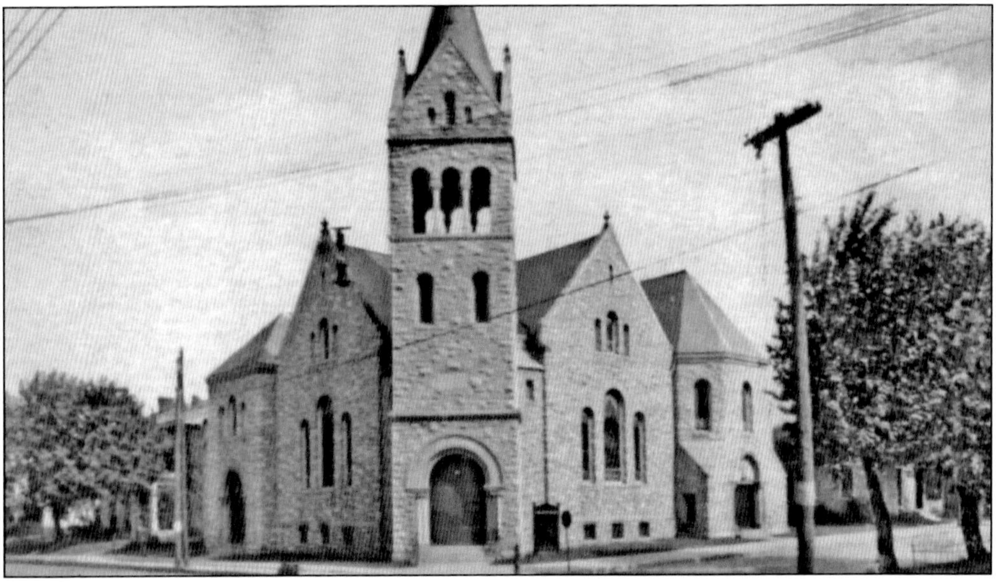

The Cynthiana Christian Church, at 202 North Main Street, traces its roots to a gathering of 11 people on July 24, 1827. For the first few years, the church says, "these founders gathered for worship at the courthouse and in homes of the members." In January 1829, worshippers paid $100 for a lot at Main and Mill Streets, completing the first church building for $3,500 in 1840. As at the Church of the Advent, the Cynthiana Christian Church opened its doors as a hospital for wounded Confederate soldiers after the Battle of Cynthiana. A second building was erected in 1899, with a June 16, 1901, dedication. The limestone building received a large addition in the 1990s. (Courtesy of the Cynthiana–Harrison County Museum.)

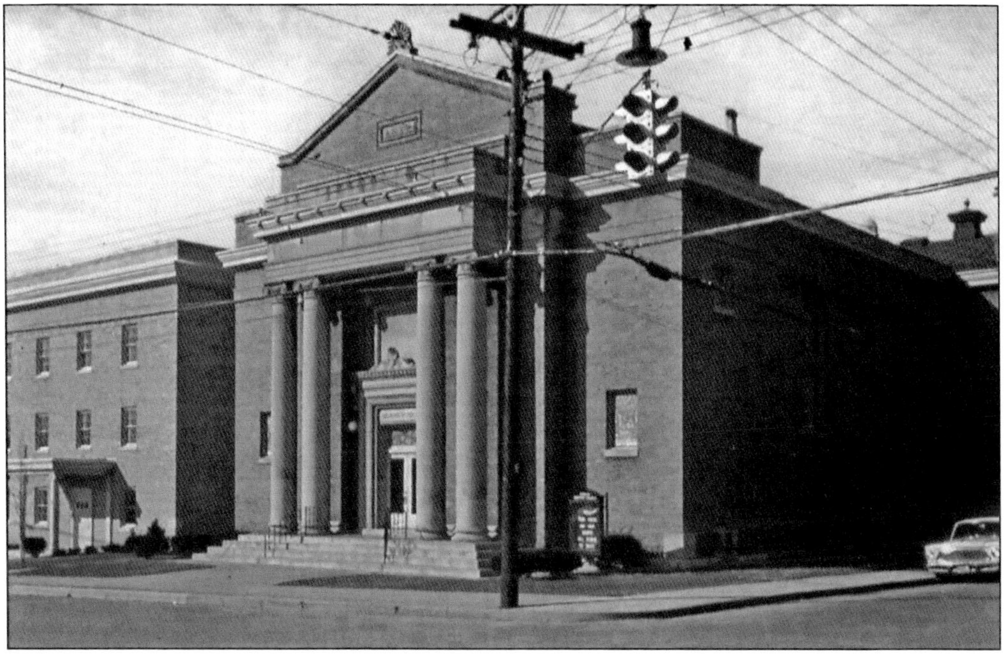

The Cynthiana Baptist Church's lineage dates to July 13, 1867, when several locals gathered to discuss building a Baptist church in the community. The first church home, with a price tag of $5,309, was dedicated on January 24, 1875, on a lot that cost $800. Between 1903 and 1908, membership grew from 200 to 350. The present sanctuary, at 212 East Pleasant Street, was built on the strength of such growth and was dedicated on December 26, 1915. The church's education building, adjacent to the church, was dedicated in 1963. (Courtesy of the Cynthiana–Harrison County Public Library's James Saunders Whaley Collection.)

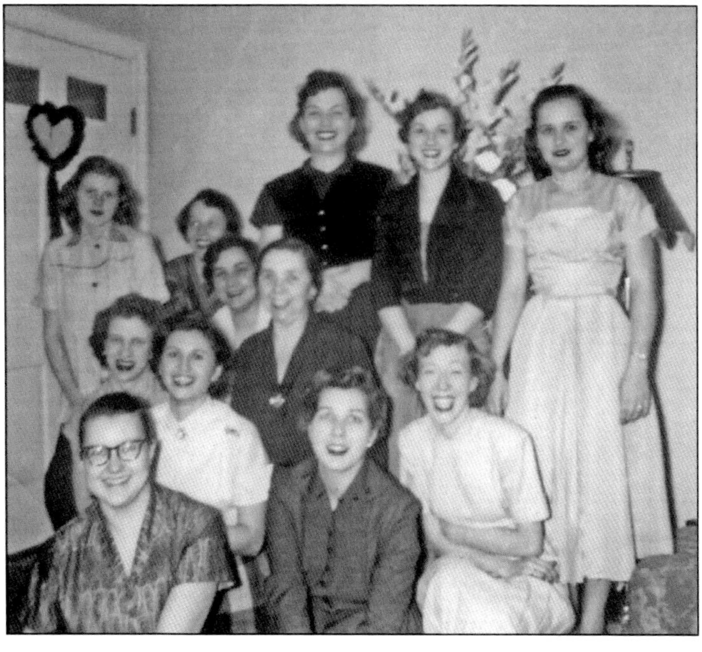

A group of Sunday school friends from the Cynthiana Baptist Church gather at the home of Betty Harney in the early 1950s. (Courtesy of Helen Harney.)

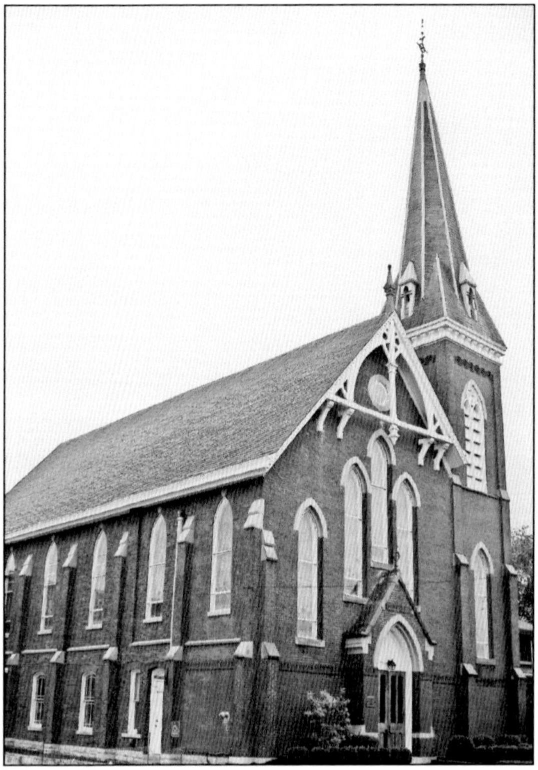

This Gothic redbrick structure at 103 North Main Street has been the home of the Cynthiana Presbyterian Church since 1880. It is the church's second structure at this site and is the second-oldest church building in the city. The Reverends W. H. Forsythe and Samuel Taylor formally organized the church in 1829. The total bill for the carpenters and brick masons building the church's first Main Street home came to $124.95, with the ladies of the congregation raising the money to pay for the turned work around the pulpit and a fund-raising drive so successful that the church was dedicated debt free. Forsythe convinced a local carpenter—Greenup Remington, who built the city's covered bridge in 1837—to make and paint the church doors, promising to pay for them when he got a "good fee for marrying a couple." In 1882, writer William Perrin called it "the most beautiful house of worship ever built in Harrison County." (Photograph by M. Britt Kennerly.)

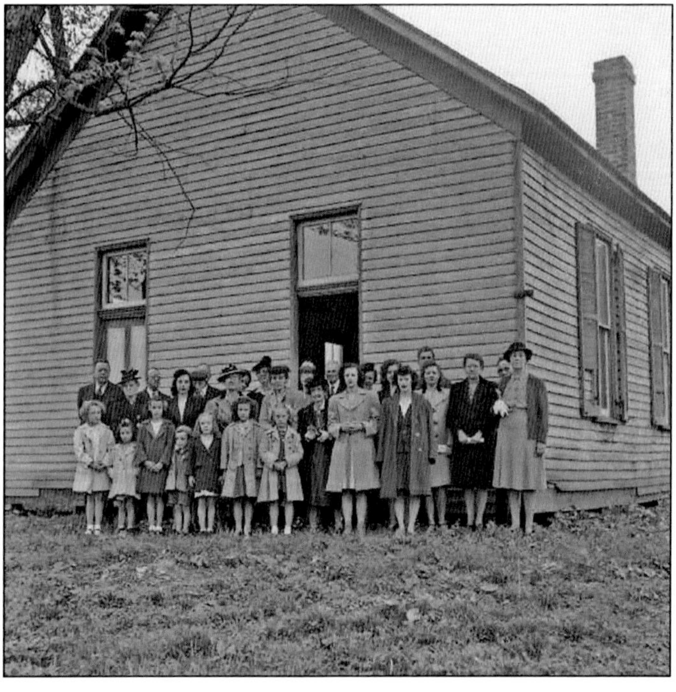

The countryside surrounding Cynthiana has long been home to small churches, many of which have been in existence for 100 years or longer. (Courtesy of the Cynthiana–Harrison County Museum.)

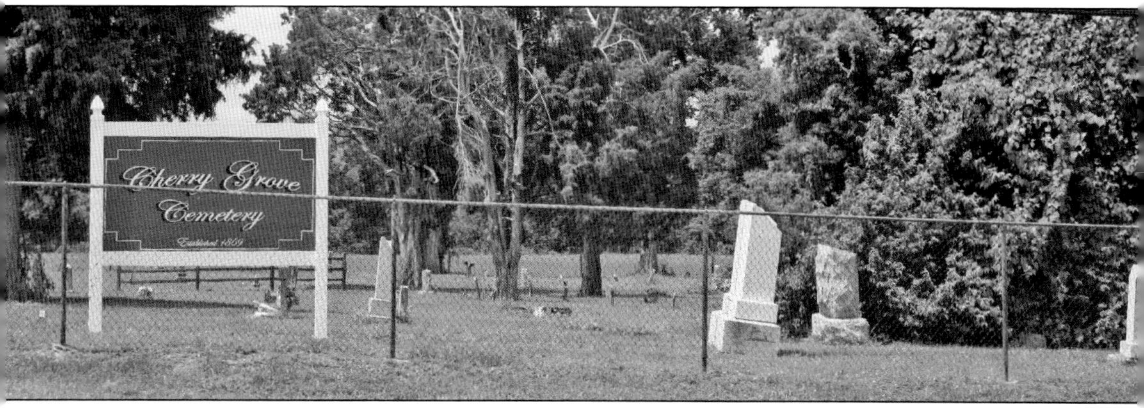

Cherry Grove Cemetery, off U.S. Route 27 across from McDonald's, is the final resting place for many of Cynthiana's African American pioneers. (Photograph by Linda H. Moore.)

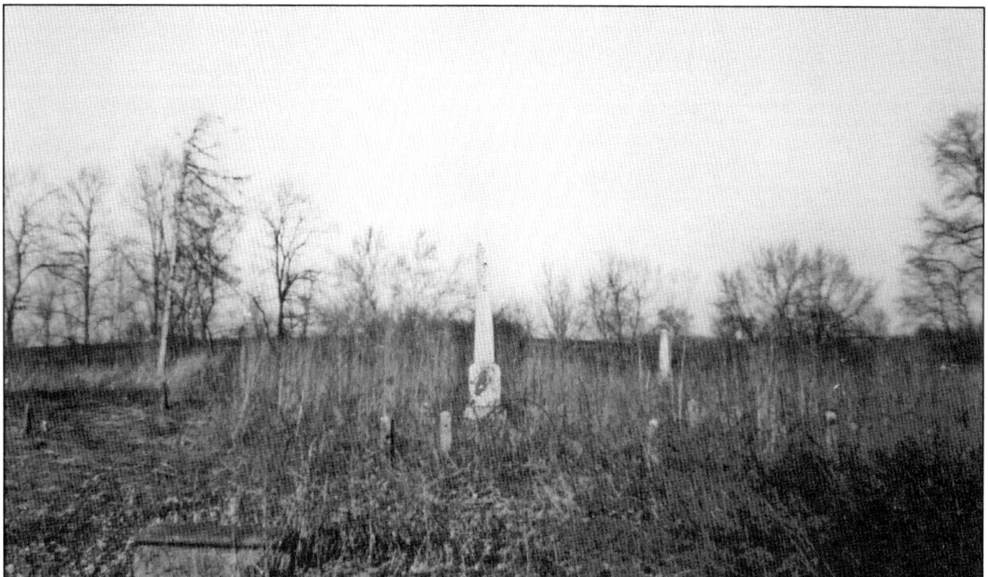

Robert Harrison, the man who named Cynthiana, deeded four acres to the city for the City Cemetery off Main Street on U.S. Route 27. It was the only burial ground in Cynthiana from 1793 to 1868, when Battle Grove Cemetery was built. The first mayor of Cynthiana, Samuel January, and many other notable people from the city's past are buried there. (Courtesy of William A. Penn.)

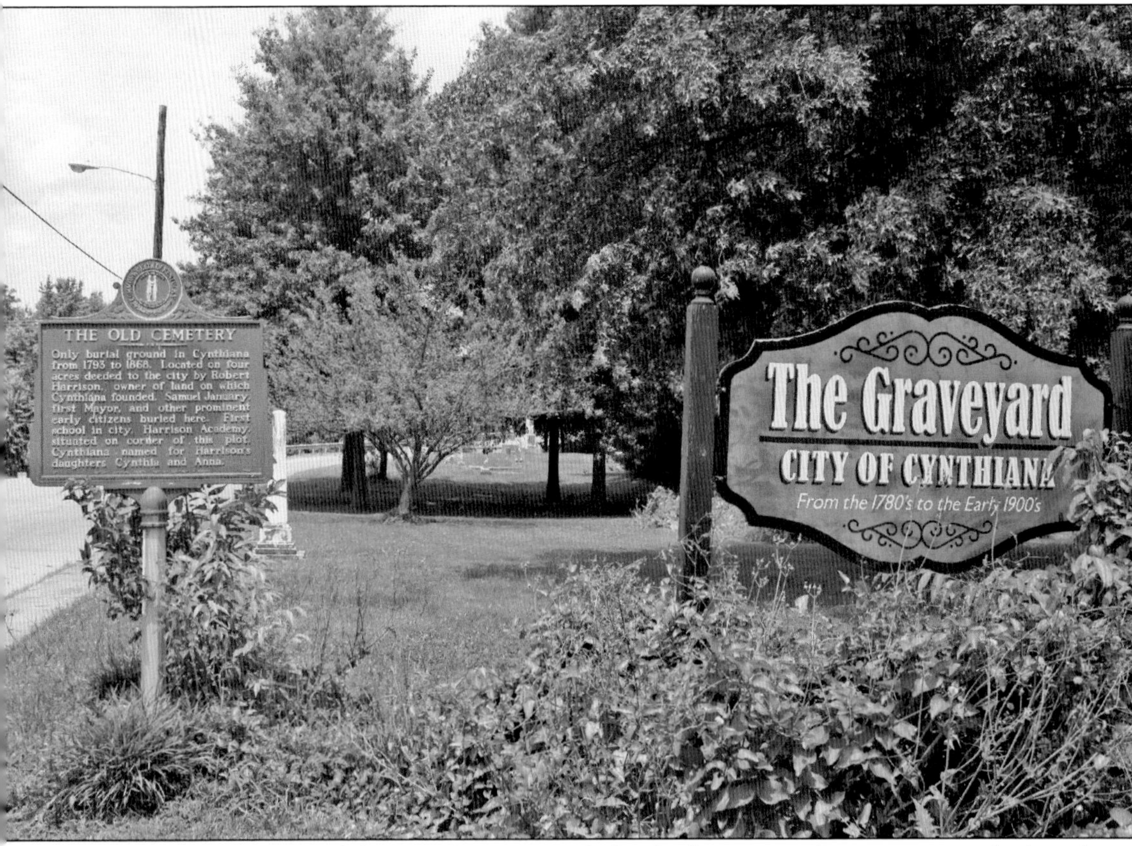

A modern-day view of the City Cemetery includes the historic marker recognizing the burial ground. (Photograph by Linda H. Moore.)

Six

DOWN TO BUSINESS

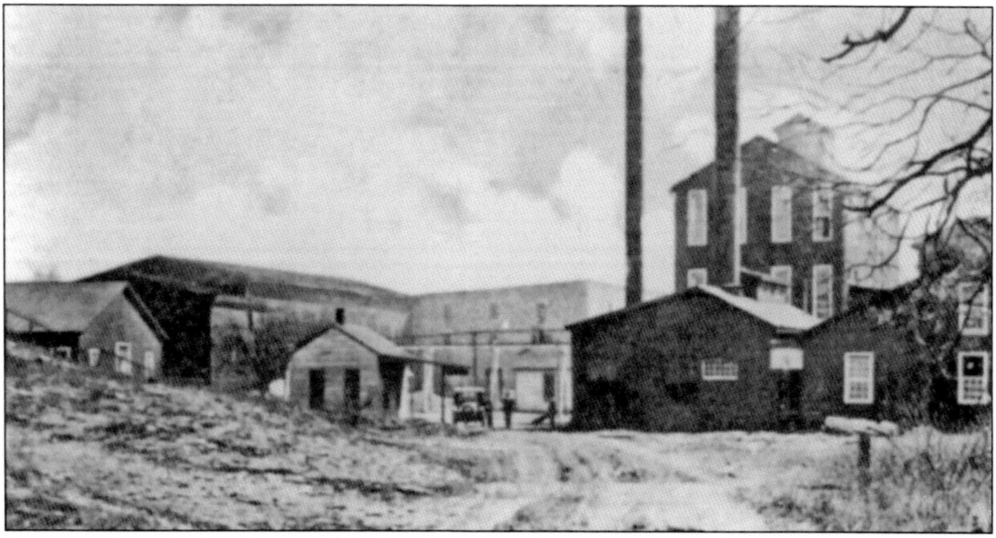

At one point in the 1900s, around 30 distilleries—including the A. Keller Distillery, pictured—were located in Harrison County. The A. Keller Dam spans the South Licking River about a mile and a half north of Cynthiana. According to the Harrison County Historical Society, it was originally built as a dam to store water for turning a water wheel, which would in turn furnish power for a flour mill. In 1840, the original owner sold the property and dam to Abram Keller, who converted it to a distillery. The distillery later became known as Ashbrook Brothers. Whiskey continued to be made there under the brand name of "Old A. Keller." (Courtesy of the Harrison County Historical Society.)

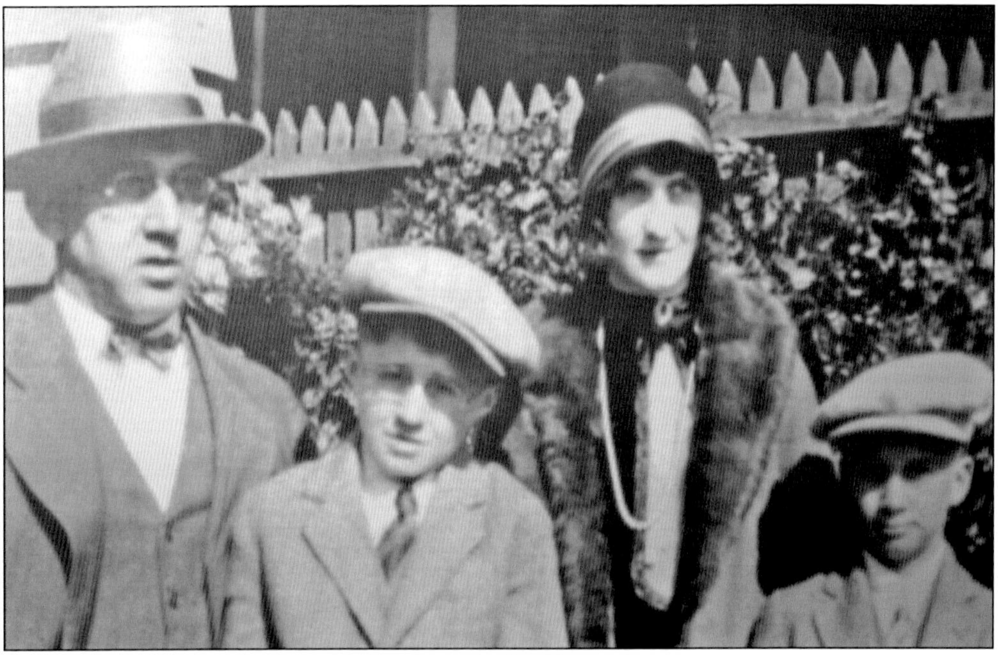

In 1894, Guido Biancke, a native of Lucca, Italy, and his wife, Clementina, opened a restaurant and fruit stand on Pike Street. They had two children, Joe D. and Amelia, who followed their parents in running Biancke's Restaurant on Main Street. The restaurant has survived and thrived for more than 100 years, feeding locals and out-of-towners. Pictured in an undated photograph are Joe D. Biancke, his wife, Stella, and sons Joe E. (left) and Harry (right). (Courtesy of Biancke's Restaurant.)

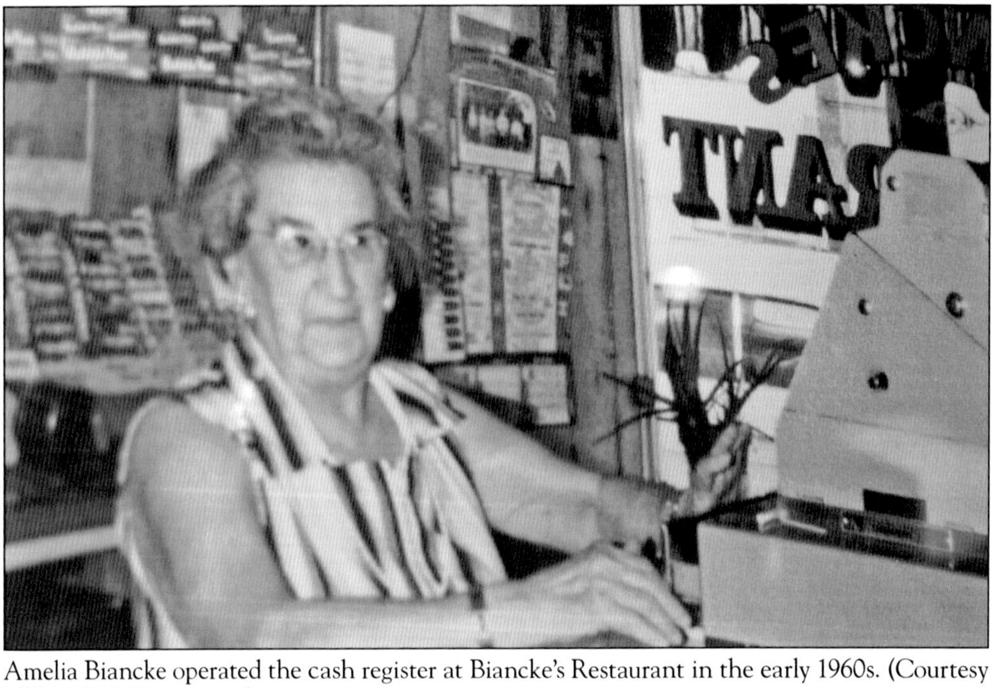

Amelia Biancke operated the cash register at Biancke's Restaurant in the early 1960s. (Courtesy of Biancke's Restaurant.)

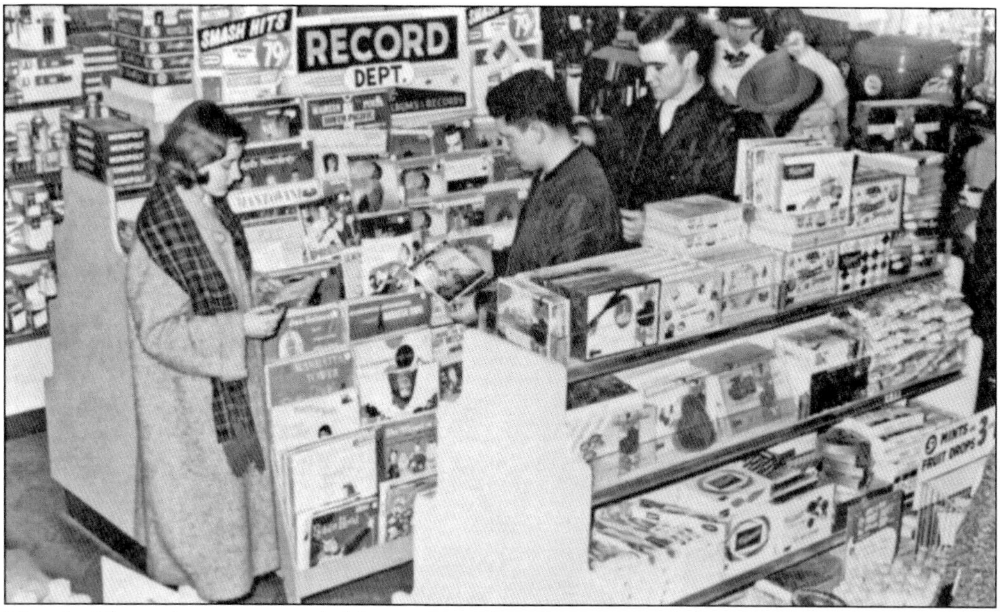

The dark-haired young man holding a record in the center of the photograph, John "Muff" Adams, hung out with other teenagers at Begley's drugstore on Pike Street in 1957. The store's soda fountain and lunch counter were a hit with people of all ages. (Courtesy of the Cynthiana High School Alumni Association.)

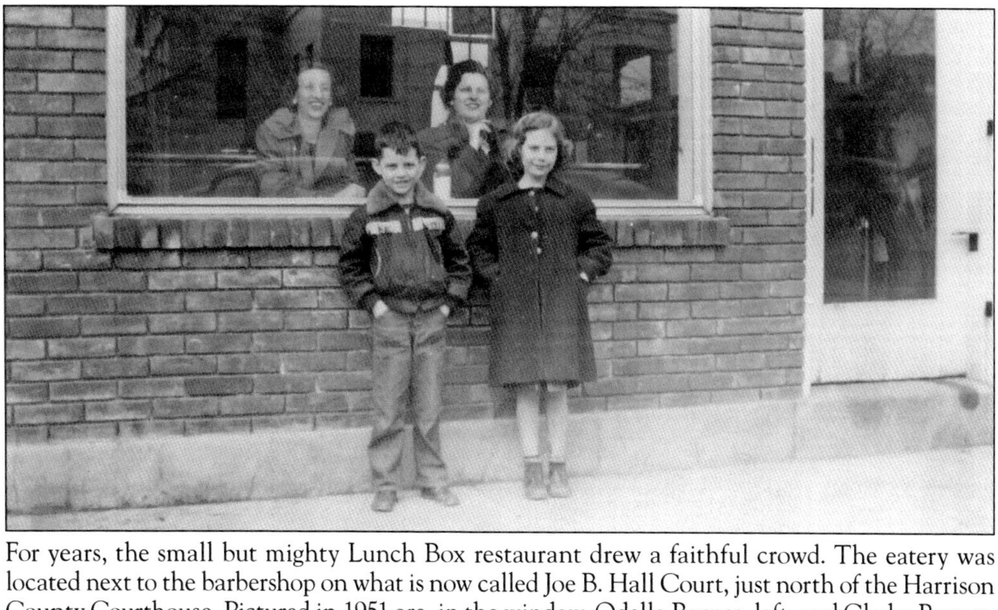

For years, the small but mighty Lunch Box restaurant drew a faithful crowd. The eatery was located next to the barbershop on what is now called Joe B. Hall Court, just north of the Harrison County Courthouse. Pictured in 1951 are, in the window, Odella Barnes, left, and Gladys Barnes. The children outside are David and Charlene Baldwin, whose parents, D. C. and Mary Nancy Baldwin, owned the restaurant at that time. (Courtesy of Helen Harney.)

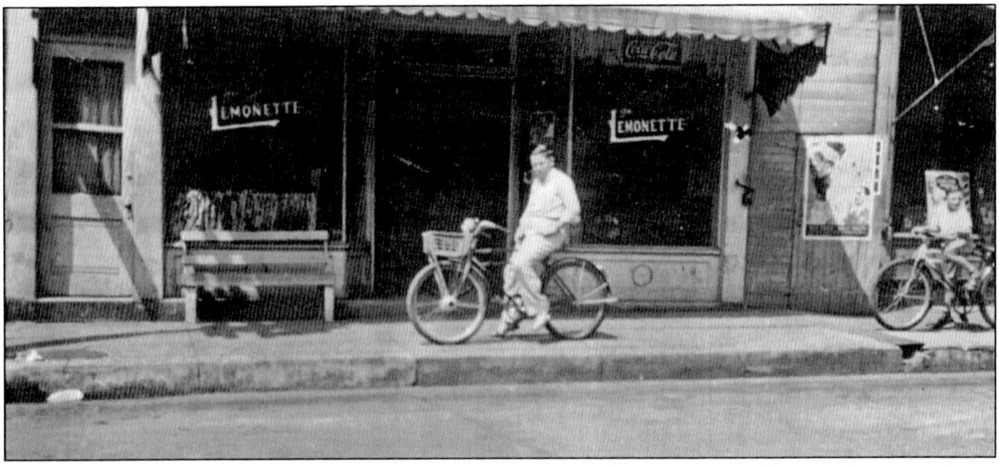

The Lemonette restaurant stood on Walnut Street, south of the Harrison Deposit Bank, and was a popular spot for hamburgers and hot dogs. Pictured here around 1940 is B. W. Martin, son of Lemonette owner Sam Martin. (Courtesy of the Cynthiana–Harrison County Museum.)

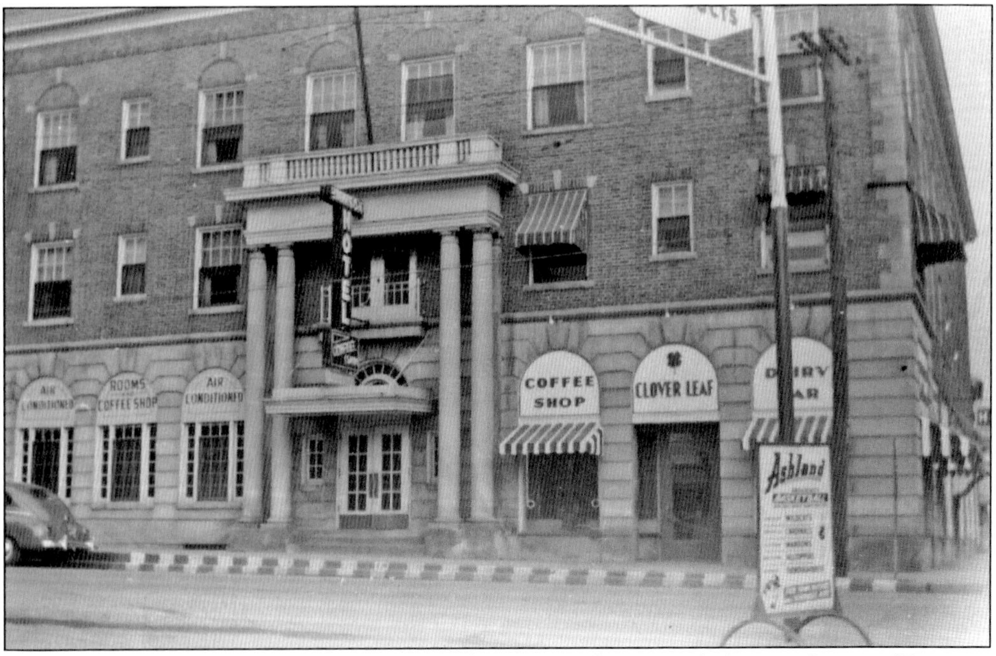

The Harrison Hotel opened in June 1925 at the corner of Main and Pleasant Streets. (Courtesy of the Cynthiana–Harrison County Museum.)

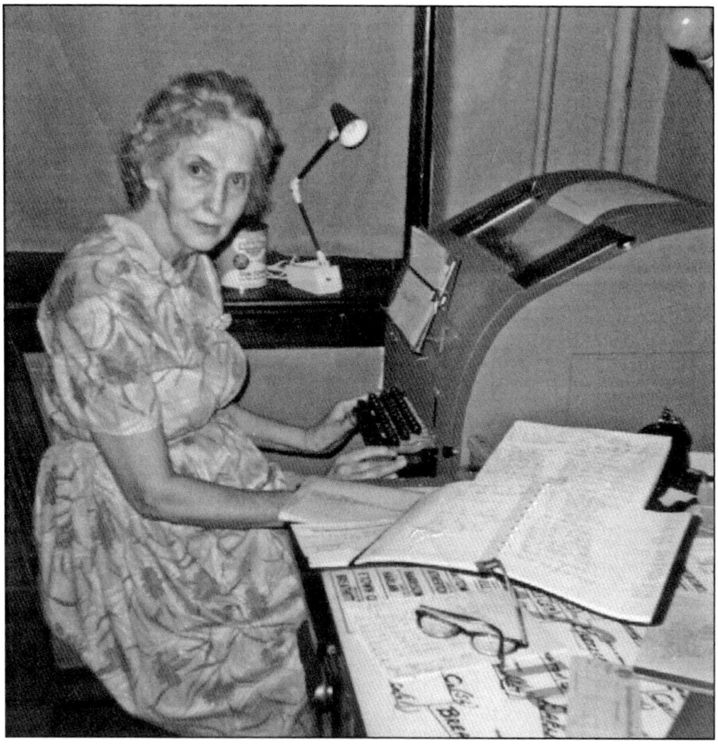

Katherine Rogers worked for many years at McKnight's Restaurant and also at the Harrison Hotel. (Courtesy of Helen Harney.)

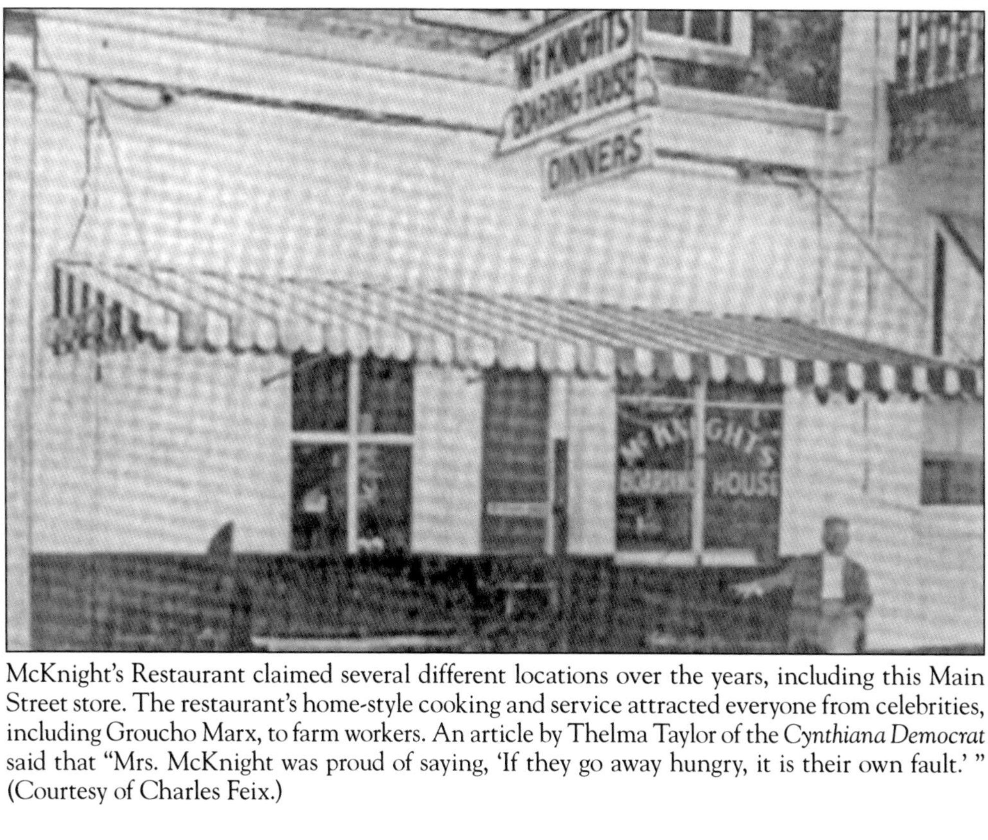

McKnight's Restaurant claimed several different locations over the years, including this Main Street store. The restaurant's home-style cooking and service attracted everyone from celebrities, including Groucho Marx, to farm workers. An article by Thelma Taylor of the *Cynthiana Democrat* said that "Mrs. McKnight was proud of saying, 'If they go away hungry, it is their own fault.' " (Courtesy of Charles Feix.)

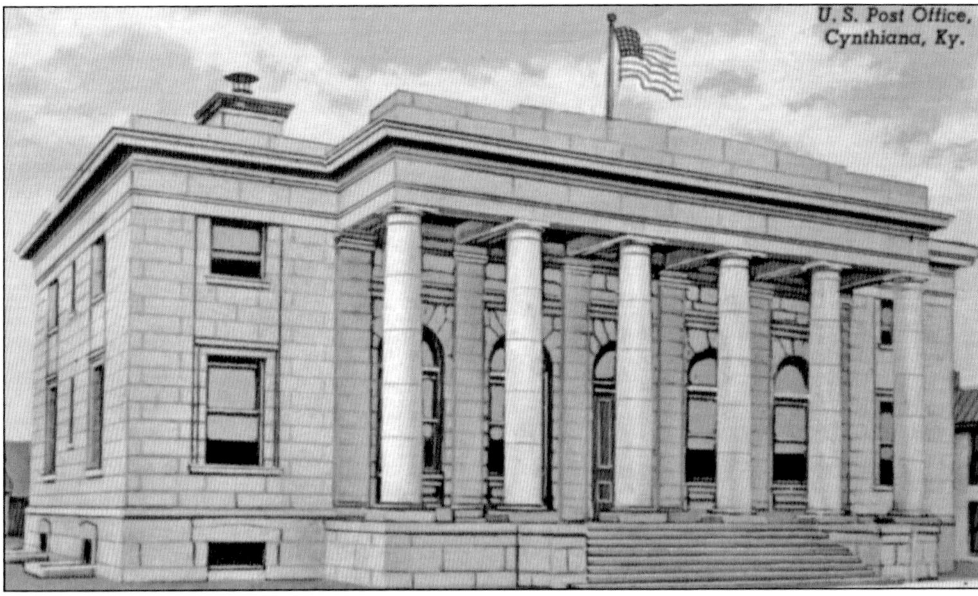

This postcard features a shot of the Cynthiana Post Office at its Walnut Street location, where mail service was based from 1914 until a new facility opened on Ladish Road in 1991. The first post office in Cynthiana opened in 1801. The city's postmasters have included three women. According to a 1928 John Cromwell column in the *Log Cabin*, Mattie Dee Todd, a niece of First Lady Mary Todd Lincoln, was postmaster from 1878 until 1895. Todd oversaw the building of a post office on the south side of Pike Street, two doors west of the Rohs Opera House. Bettie S. Moore, who took over for Todd, was the last female postmaster until Jackie Hill was appointed in 2001. (Courtesy of Helen Harney.)

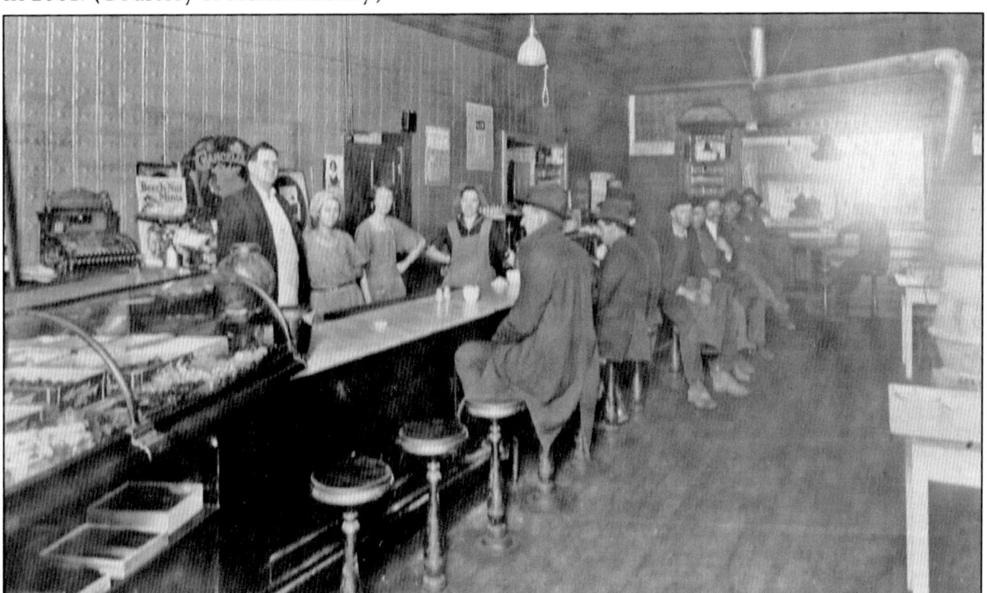

Around 1921, Beckett's store was located on the north side of Bridge Street, on the west side of the railroad tracks. Behind the counter are, from left to right, Robert Beckett, Ann Peddicord, Elsie Lowe, and Verna Beckett. (Courtesy of the Cynthiana–Harrison County Museum.)

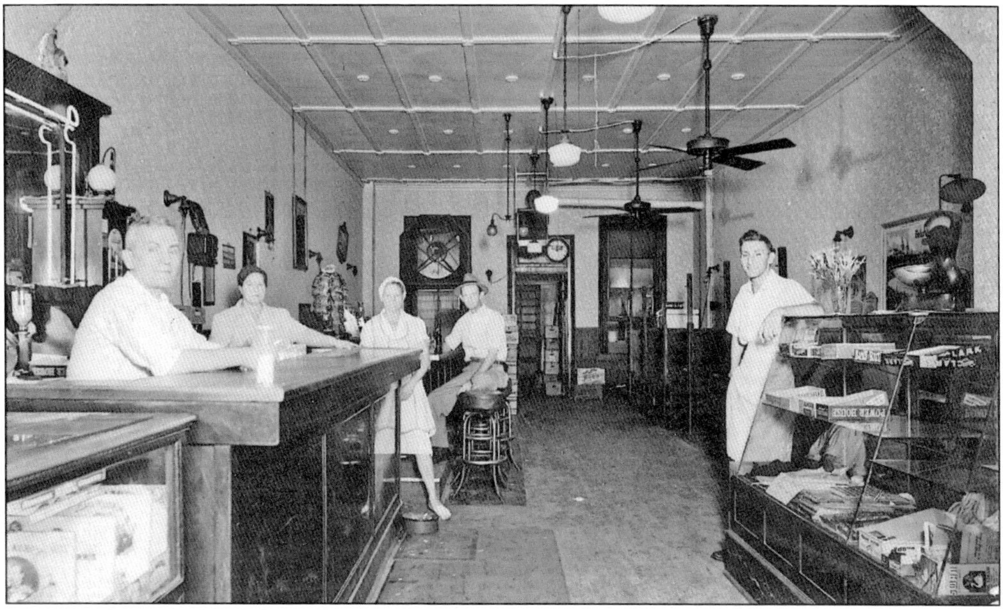

A 1948 photograph of the Palas Restaurant finds Gus Palas and his wife, Francis, behind the counter. (Courtesy of the Cynthiana–Harrison County Museum.)

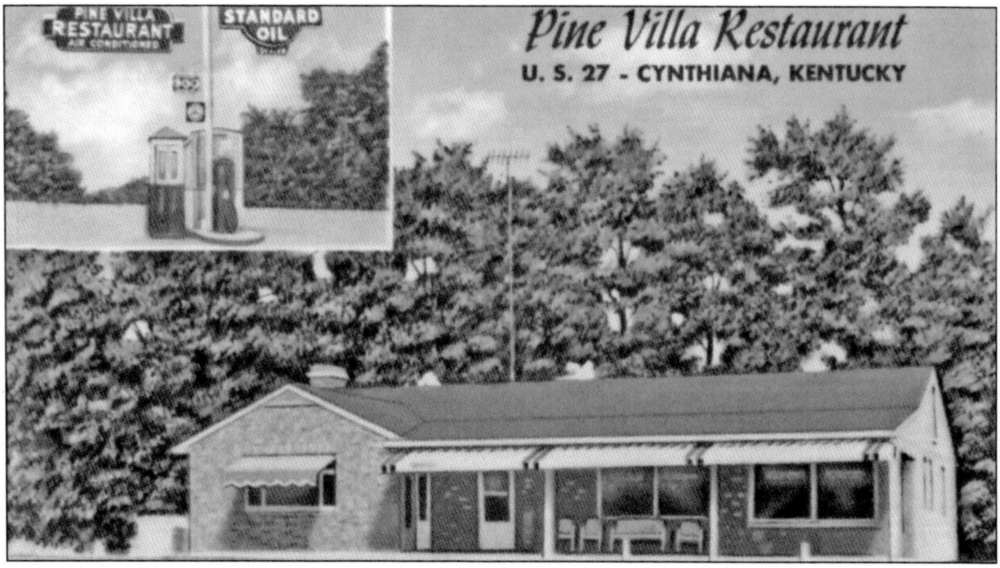

Just north of the city off U.S. Route 27, the Pine Villa Restaurant was a hit with travelers and residents alike and was celebrated on this vintage postcard. (Courtesy of the Cynthiana–Harrison County Museum.)

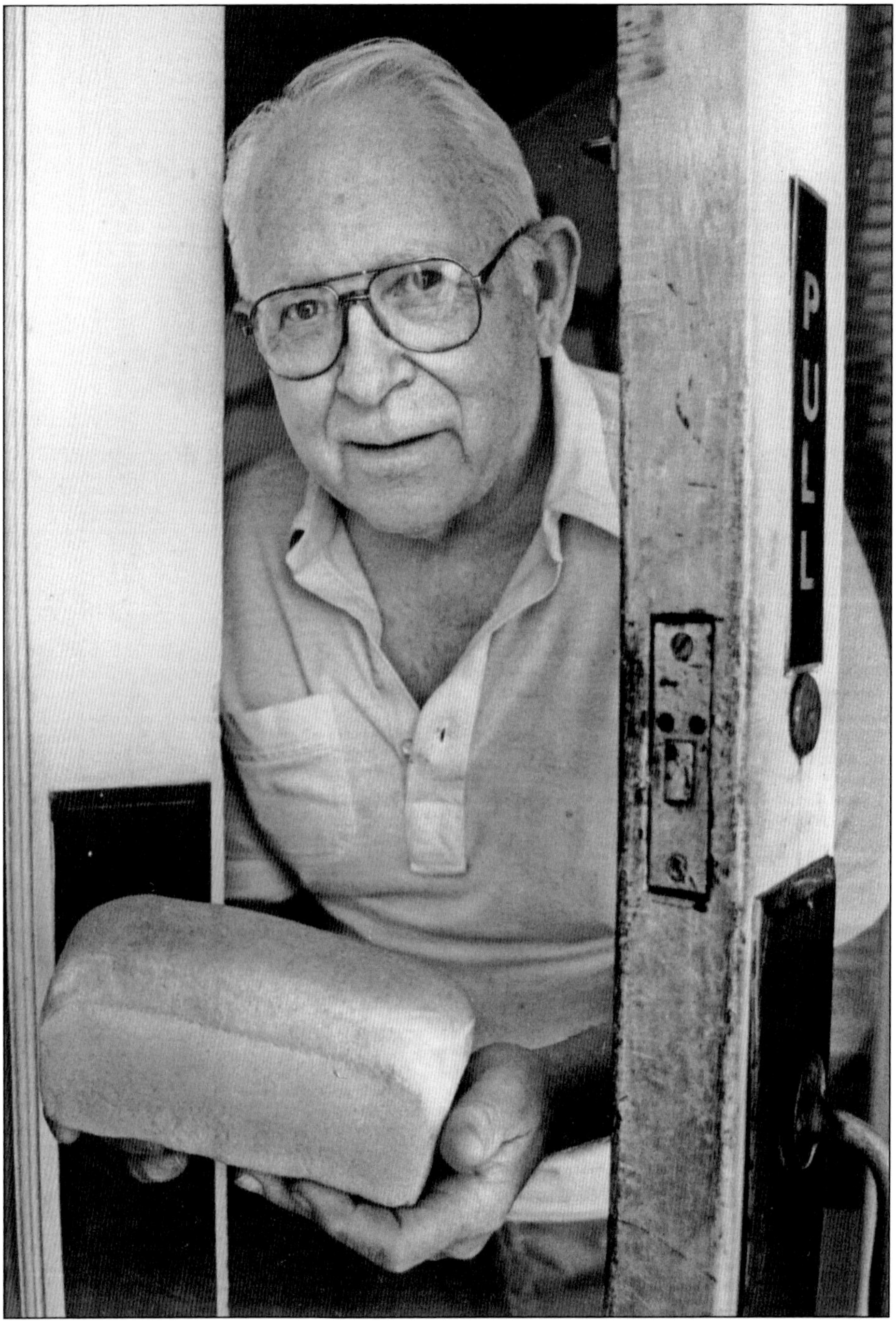

Baker Bonny Dailey is pictured with a loaf of his famous salt-rising bread. Dailey started his career in the Cynthia-Ann Bakery, and he became a head cook in the U.S. Marine Corps. He started his own bakery in Cynthiana and also ran several country club dining rooms. At one point, the Bonny Bakery made up to 2,500 loaves of salt-rising bread each week, luring customers from several states. Dailey and his wife later opened Village Inn Restaurant. (Courtesy of Thomas and Teresa Dailey.)

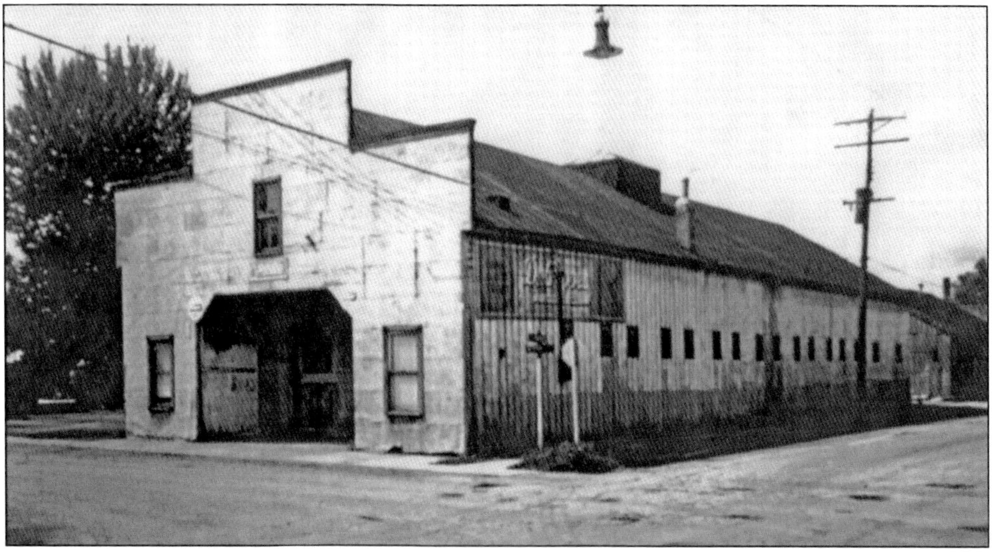

This site, at the northwest corner of Pike and Poplar Streets, housed diverse businesses over the years. In its early days, the location was the home of Cummins' Livery Stables. Pictured here in the 1940s, the former livery became a Dr Pepper bottling plant. The building was torn down in 1958, and a Kroger grocery store took its place on the landscape. (Courtesy of the Cynthiana–Harrison County Museum.)

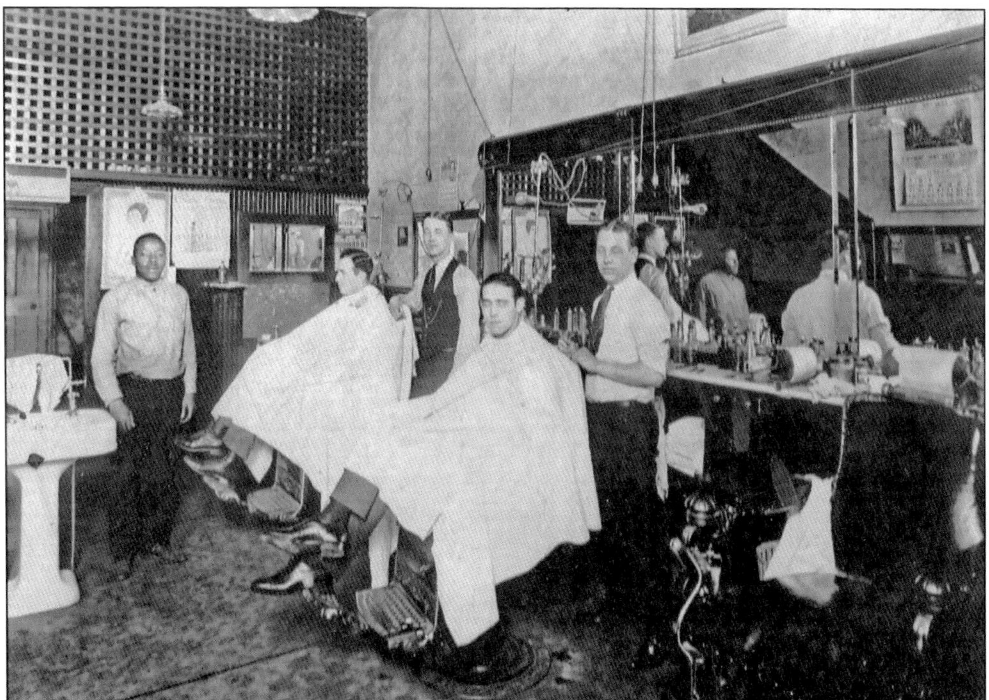

Barber Frank Pope is at the first chair in this 1923 photograph from a downtown shop, with Hussey Heck seated in the chair. Malcolm Reno is at the second chair; the shoeshine man was identified as Josh. (Courtesy of the Cynthiana–Harrison County Museum.)

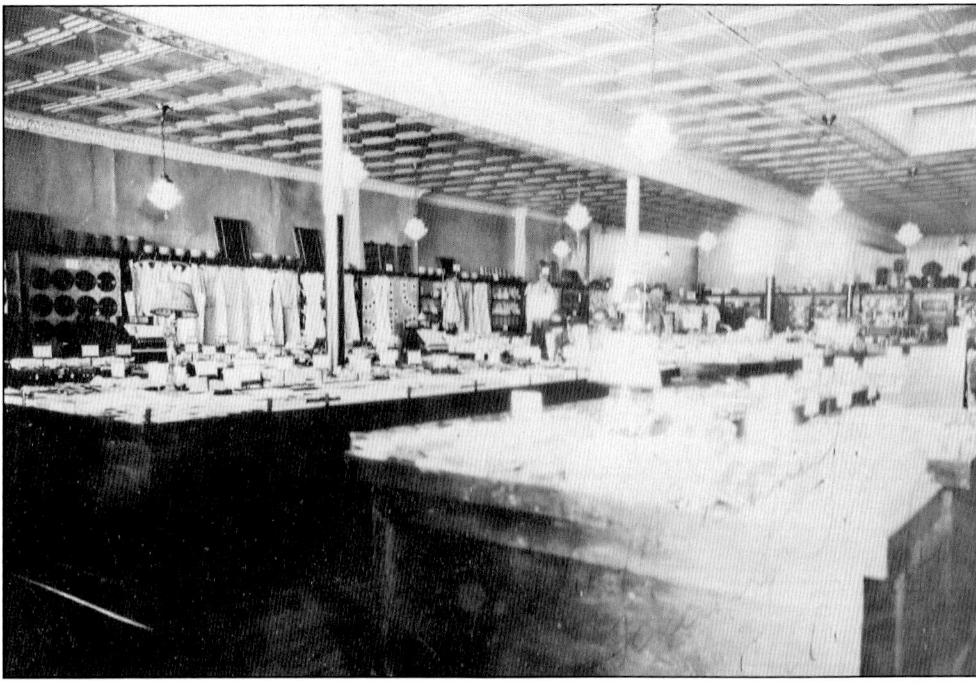

Marshall's Dime Store was located on Pike Street next to Veach Redd's. (Courtesy of the Cynthiana–Harrison County Museum.)

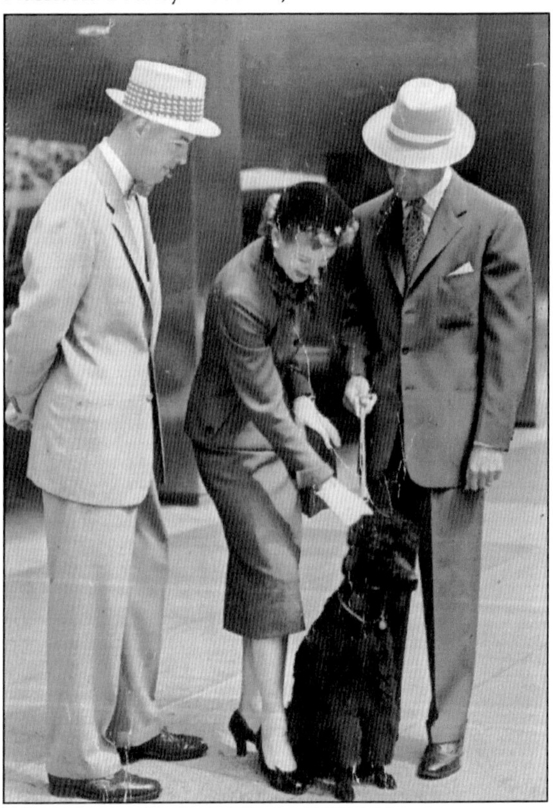

The M. Goldberg store on Main Street across from the Harrison County Courthouse was in business for more than 100 years before conducting its final sale and closing in early 2009. This 1953 postcard back trumpeted $29.95 suits: "You won't believe your eyes . . . when you see our NEW Palm Beach suits! Plaids, checks, stripes, nubby effects in smartest colors . . . wonderful fit . . . now smooth-feeling and wrinkle-resistant too!" Other clothing stores that did business in the city for decades included Pressman's—owned by a family whose kin include Cynthiana-born actor Lawrence Pressman of *Doogie Howser, M.D.* fame—Patton's, Lerman Brothers, the Clara Shoppe, and the Style Shop. (Courtesy of the Cynthiana–Harrison County Museum.)

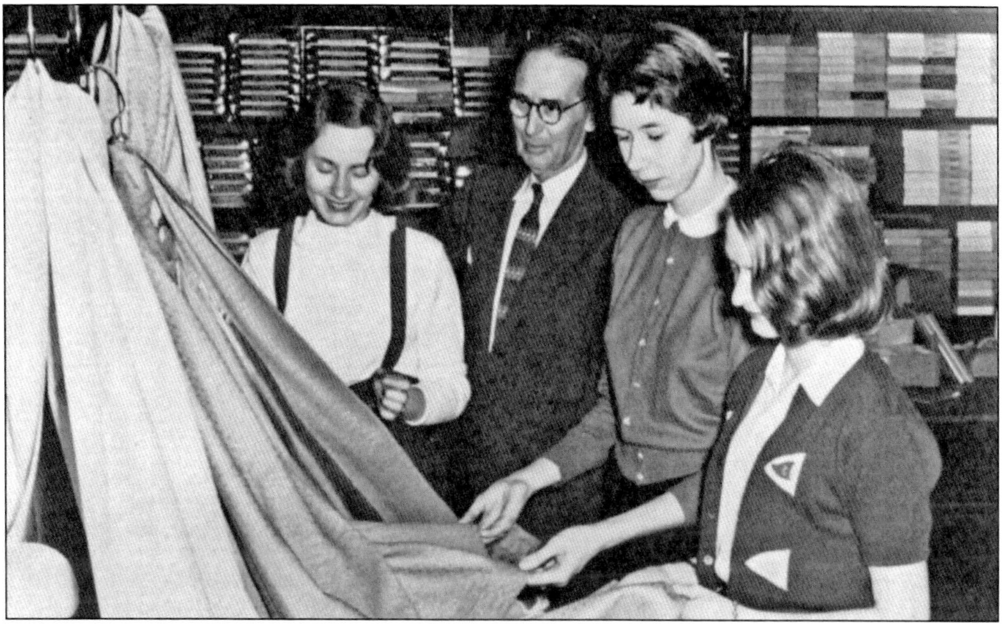

Patton's Dry Goods Store, a much-loved fixture on Main Street for many years, was a featured advertiser in the 1957 *Cynthian* yearbook. (Courtesy of the Cynthiana High School Alumni Association.)

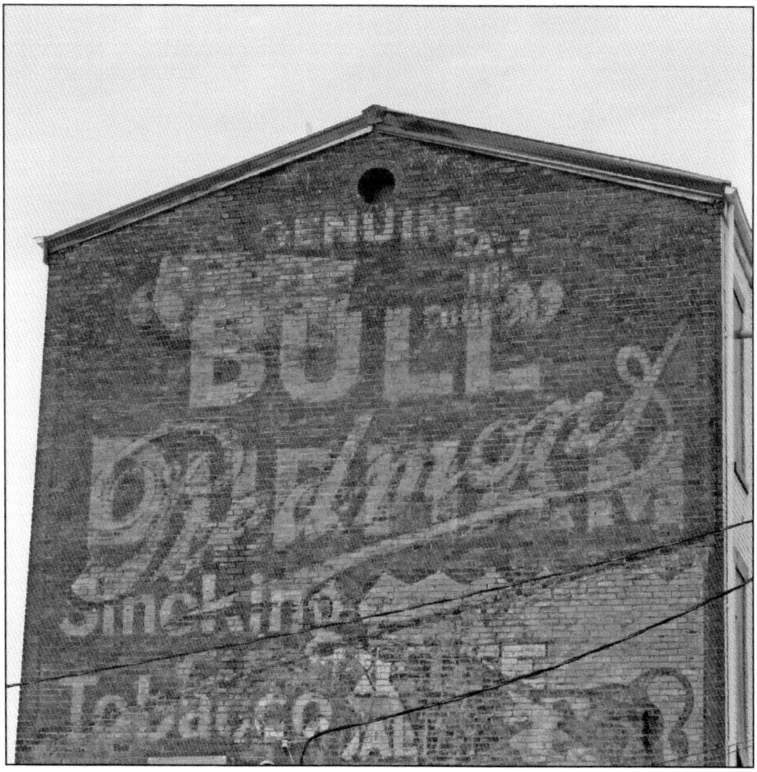

The Bull Durham sign painted on the building at 109 East Bridge Street has drawn the eye of drivers for decades. The structure has housed, among other businesses, an automotive supply store and most recently the China House Restaurant. (Photograph by Linda H. Moore.)

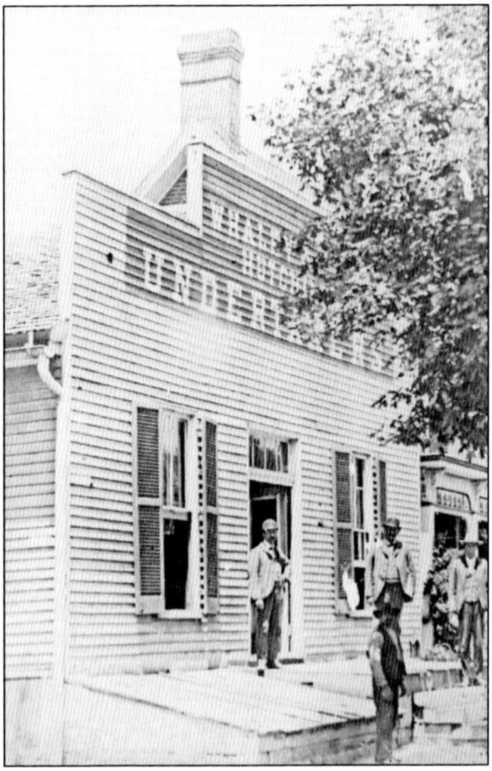

Whaley's Funeral Home is pictured in the 1800s on the west side of South Main Street near the old covered bridge and in the latter part of the 1900s. During the Civil War, the building was known as the Rankin House. Other historic funeral homes in Cynthiana were the J. L. Davis Funeral Home on the northeast corner of Poplar and Pleasant Streets and the Smith-Rees Funeral Home (1914–1976). (Both courtesy of the Cynthiana–Harrison County Museum.)

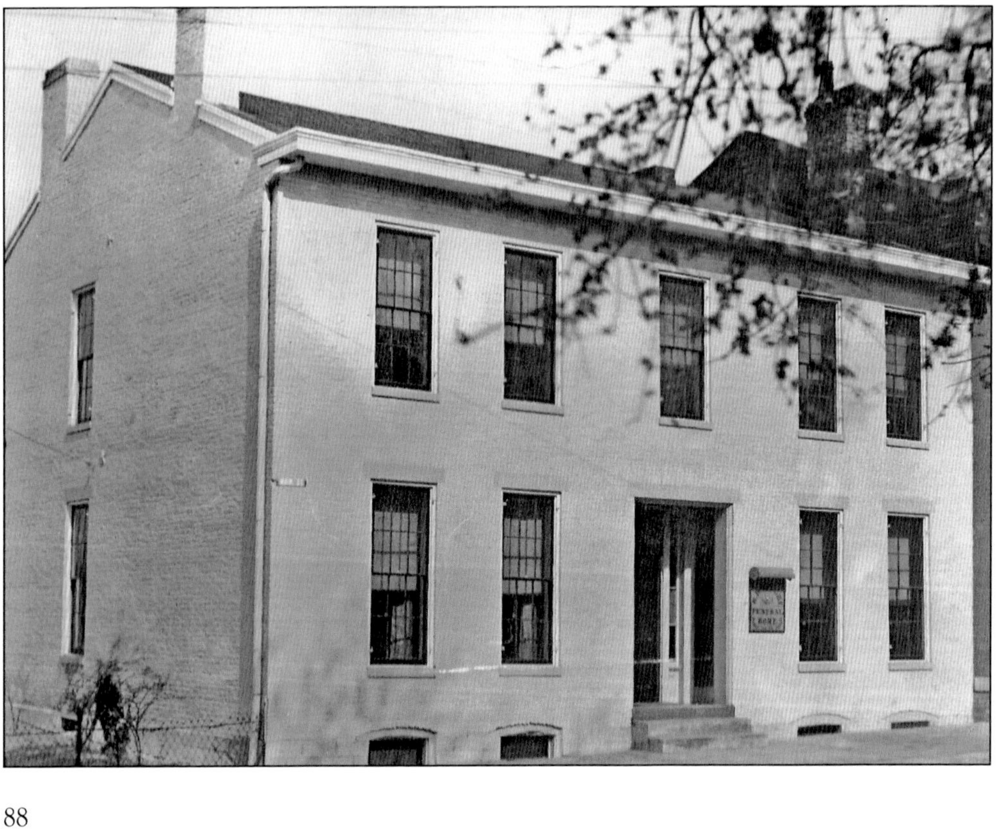

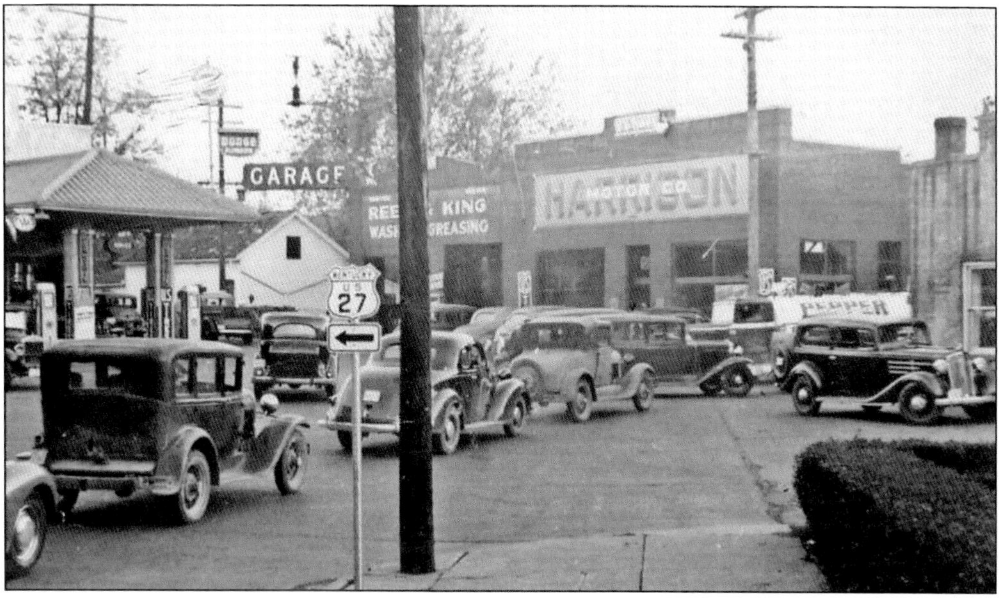

The original part of the Harrison Motor Building dated to 1880 and was used as livery stables. By 1920, it was converted to an automobile dealership with front and rear additions. The business, demolished in 1993, was situated south of Bridge Street where Bridge and Main Streets meet. (Both courtesy of the Cynthiana–Harrison County Museum.)

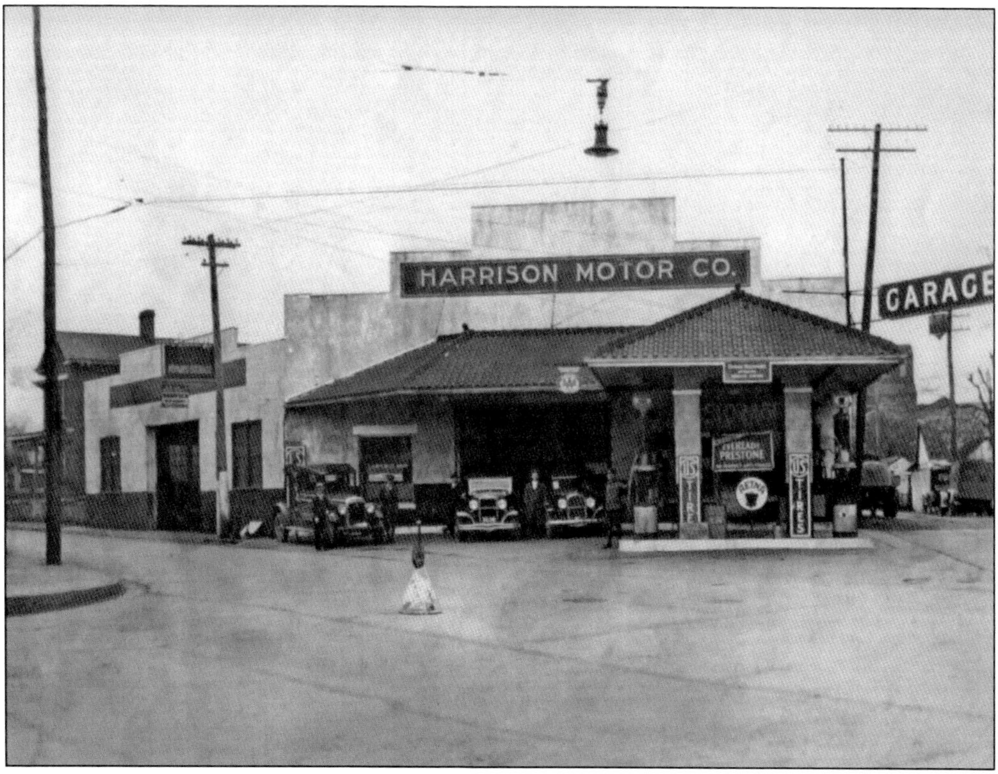

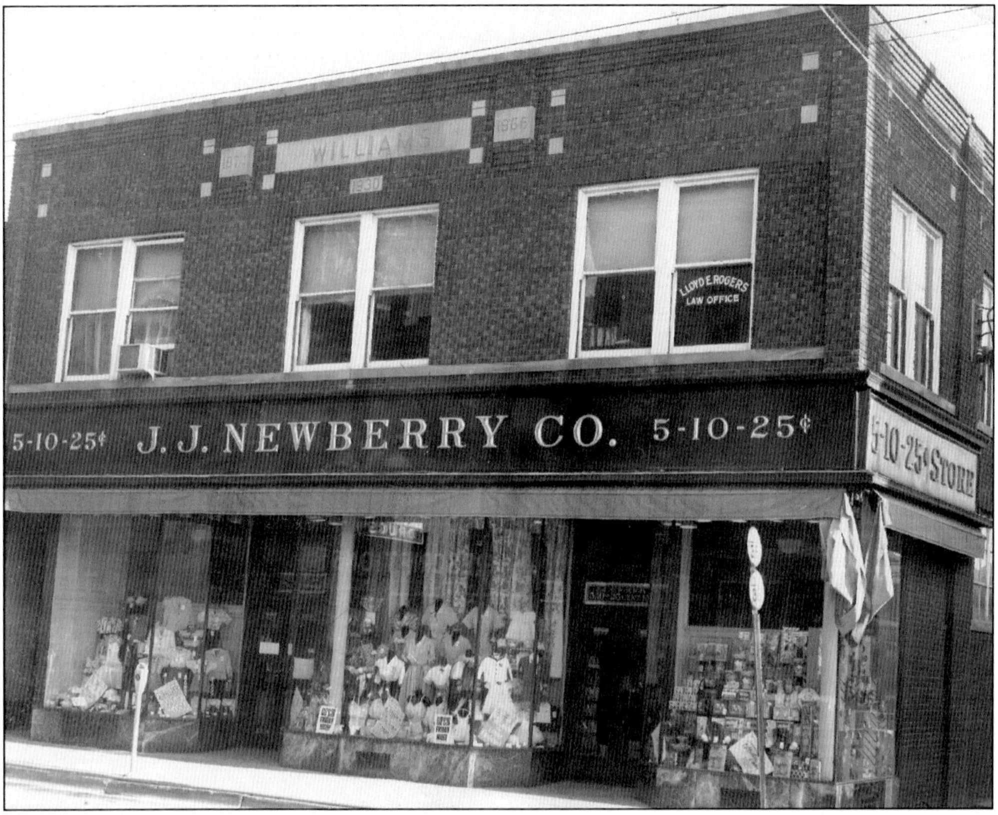

The J. J. Newberry store was part of the Pike Street scene in the early 1960s, housed in the Williams building along with the Lloyd E. Rogers law office. (Courtesy of the Cynthiana–Harrison County Public Library's James Saunders Whaley Collection.)

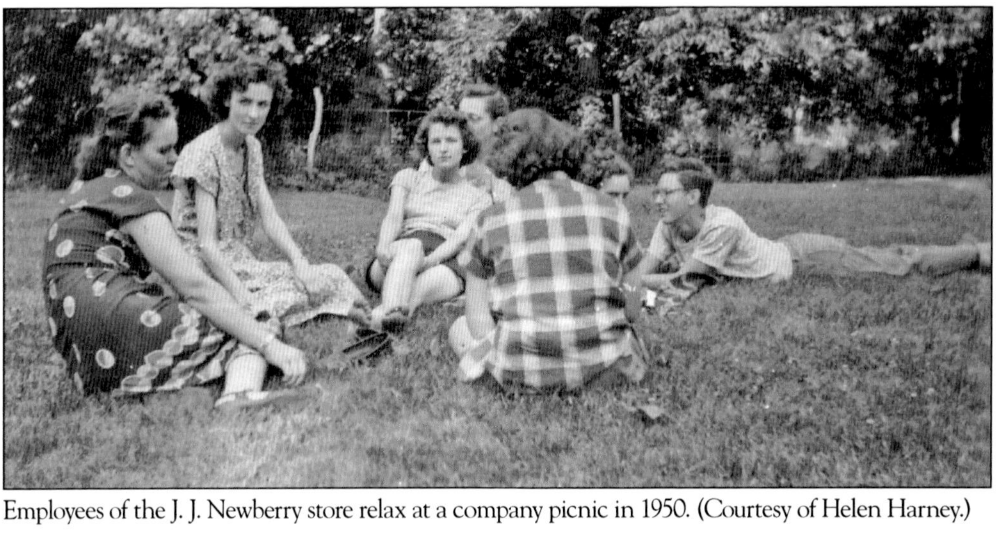

Employees of the J. J. Newberry store relax at a company picnic in 1950. (Courtesy of Helen Harney.)

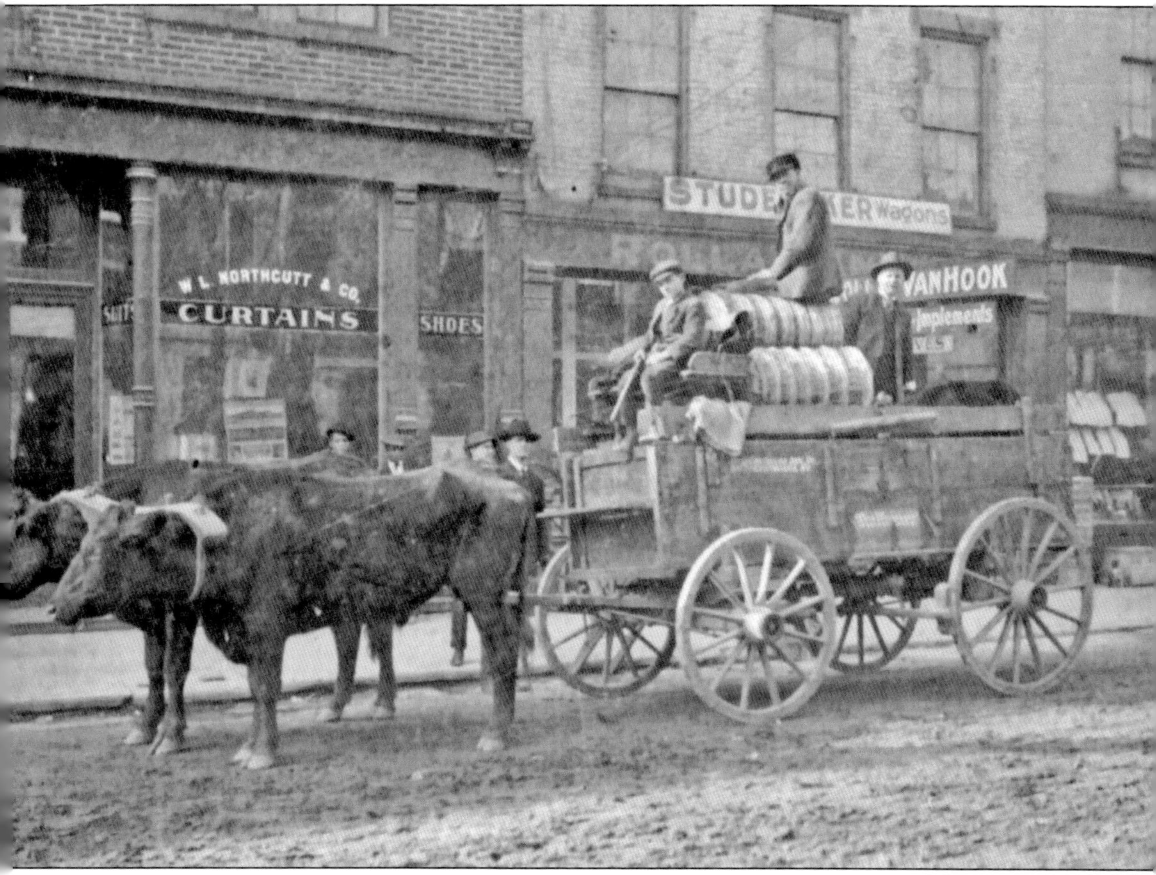

In 1903, Fred Jenkins and G. H. Watts opened a hardware store at 121 East Pike Street, in a building that had previously been used for whiskey storage and for two years as a grocery store. Two years later, Fred Jenkins bought out Watts; in 1908, Rolla VanHook and Elbert Smith bought out Jenkins. After Jenkins's death, VanHook bought the Smith interest and changed the name to VanHook and Son—the son being Edgar Smith. In 1918, Edgar went to war, and Will Jenkins and Taylor Cason (who came to the store as a clerk in 1906 at $5 per week) each bought a third interest in the operation. Since then, the store has been known as VanHook Hardware. Later Cason and Jenkins bought out VanHook, with Cason eventually owning the store with his son, Taylor Jr., and Charles Bland. Since 1958, the Cason family has owned the store. Here Reeves and his son are on the wagon with Rolla VanHook; Taylor Cason Sr. and Edgar VanHook are beside the wagon. (Courtesy of the Taylor Cason family.)

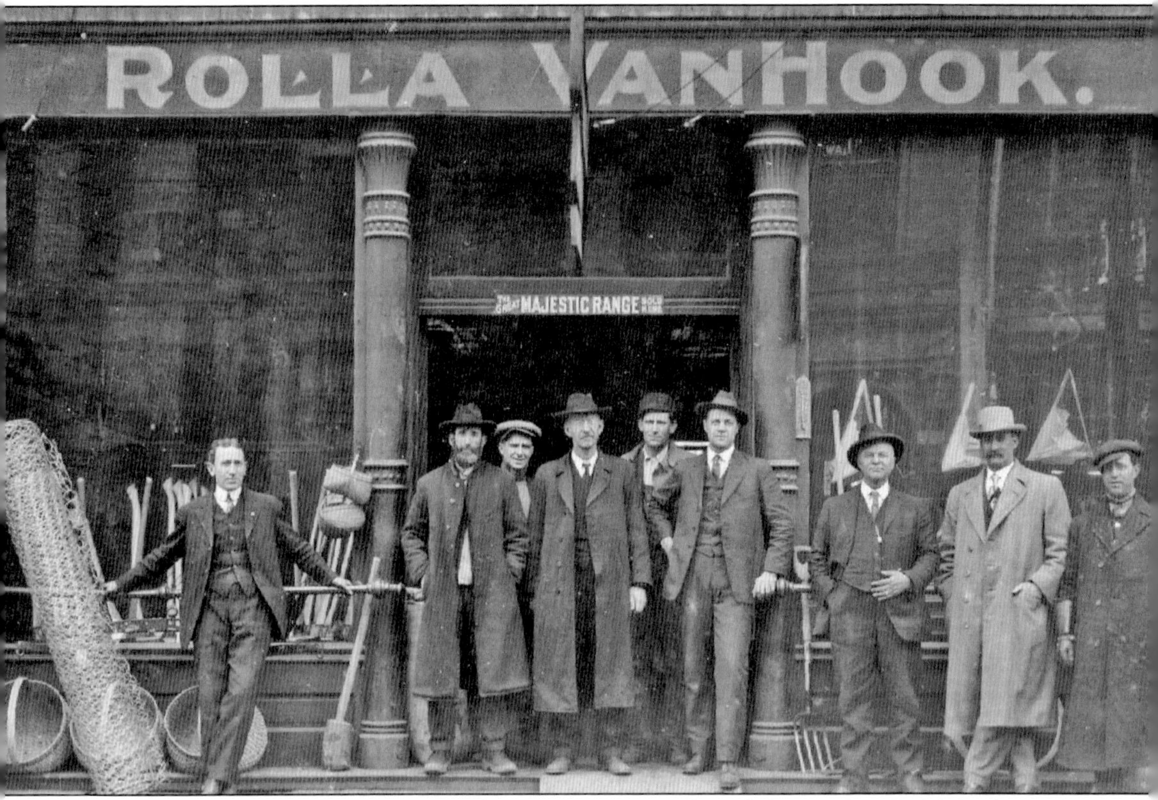

Pictured in front of VanHook Hardware in 1909 are, from left to right, W. H. Jenkins, Ace Williams, Edgar VanHook, J. S. Walden, Will McGee, Taylor Cason Sr., Rolla VanHook, George Baker, and an unidentified man. (Courtesy of the Taylor Cason family.)

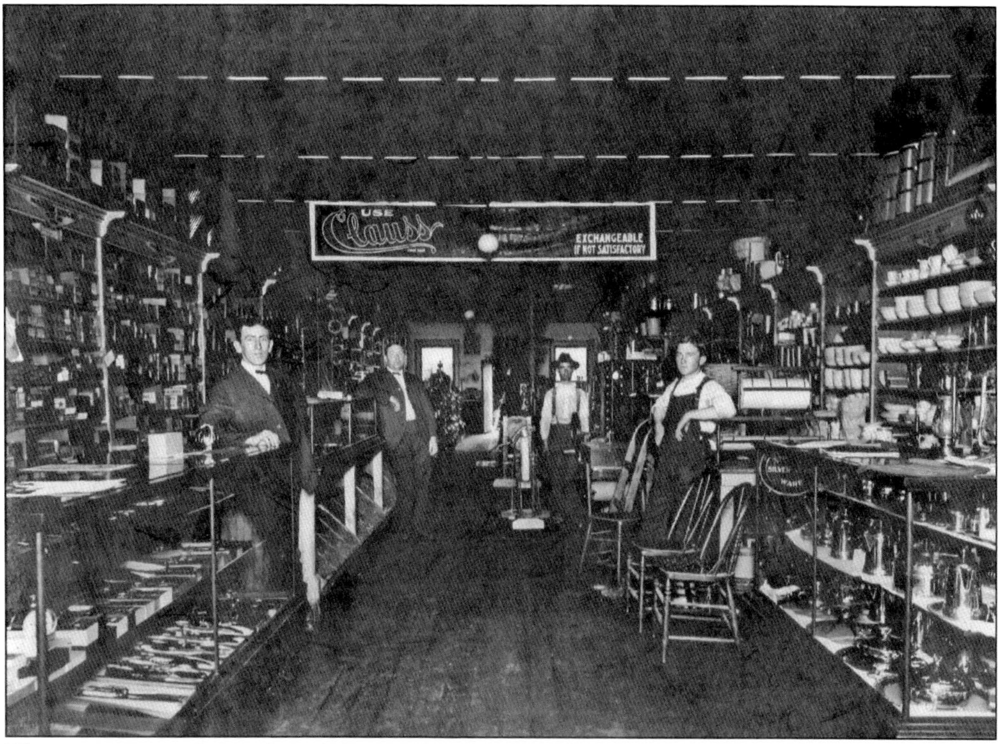

These men at work are, from left to right, W. H. Jenkins, an unidentified man, Taylor Cason Sr., and Fred G. Jenkins, who man the aisles in 1908 at the Pike Street landmark later renamed VanHook Hardware. (Courtesy of the Taylor Cason family.)

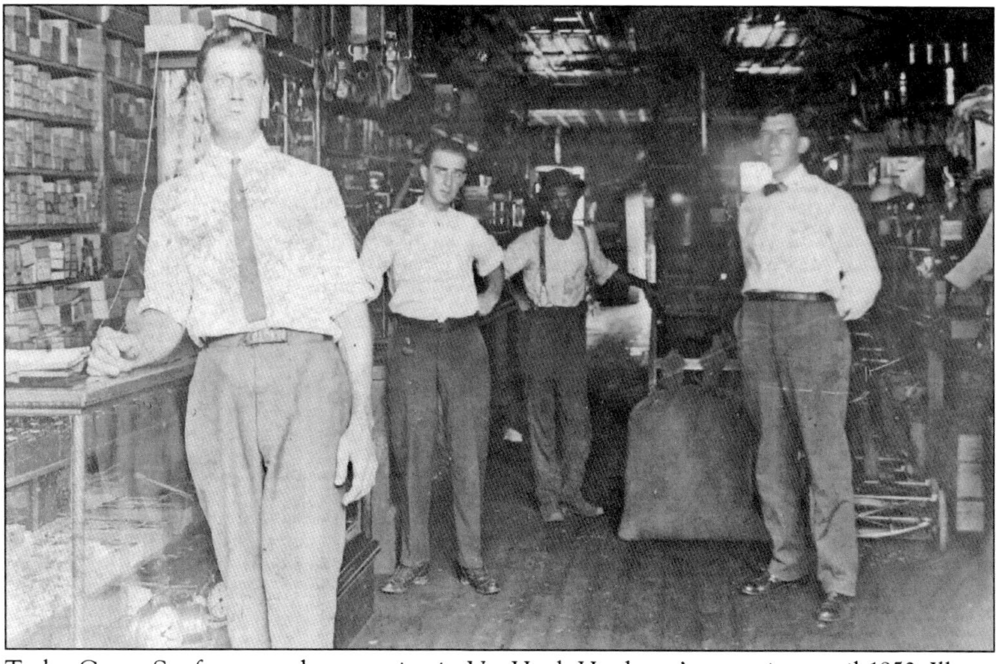

Taylor Cason Sr., foreground, was active in VanHook Hardware's operation until 1950. Illness forced him to turn the store over to his son, Taylor Jr. (Courtesy of the Taylor Cason family.)

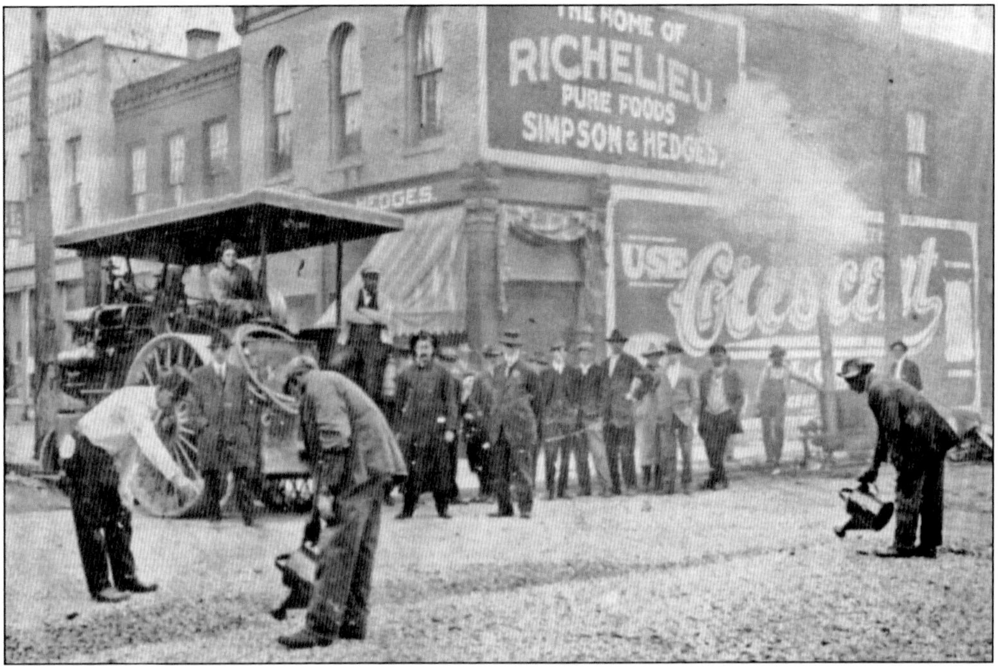

Poindexter Lumber Company has built a solid history over 100 years, personifying the phrase "keeping it in the family." Founded by James Robert "J. R." Poindexter in 1908 as J. R. Poindexter and Son, the company sold building materials from a building that still stands beside the railroad tracks at 208 East Pleasant Street. In this 1913 photograph, J. R., wearing a white shirt, helps pour oil on gravel at the corner of Pike and Walnut Streets. (Courtesy of Poindexter Lumber Company.)

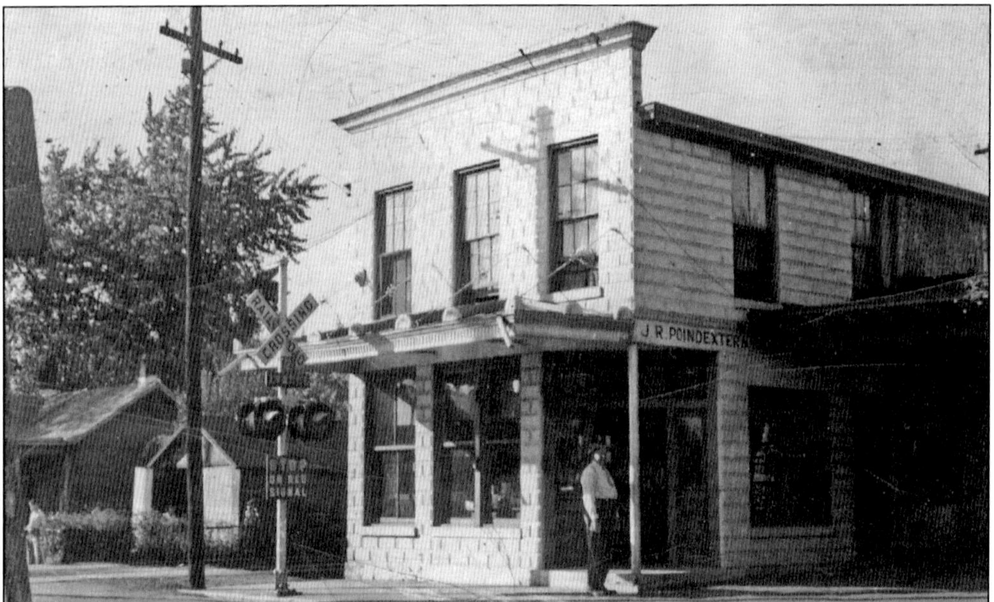

This pre-1950 photograph shows Poindexter Lumber Company when it was still known as J. R. Poindexter and Son. The "son" in the company name, Robert Harold Poindexter Sr., is seen in front of the store. (Courtesy of Poindexter Lumber Company.)

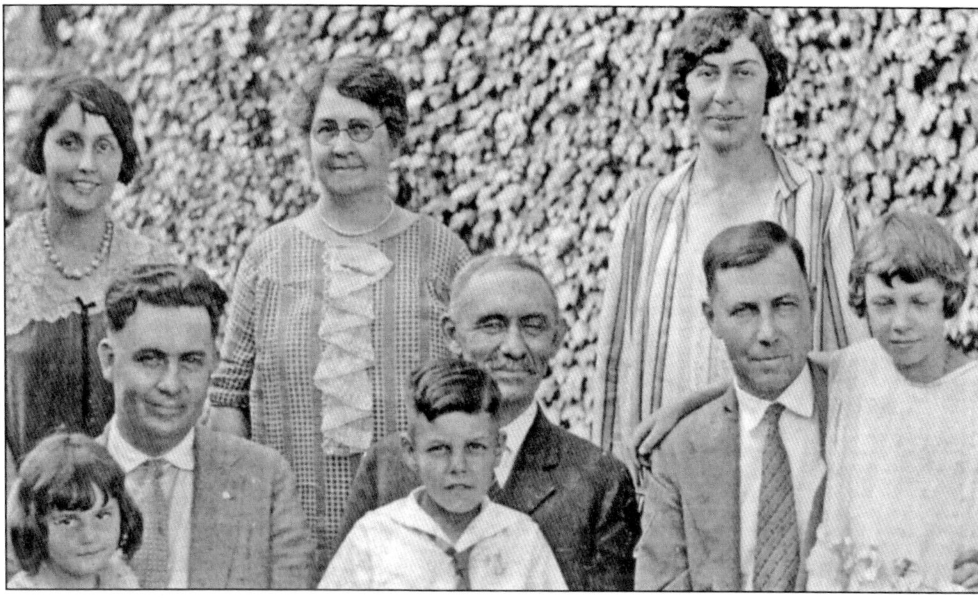

The Poindexter family gathers in 1925. Adults are, left to right, Sara Frances VanDeren, Robert H. Poindexter, Mary Lucy Ann Whiteker, James Robert Poindexter, Linda Elizabeth Poindexter, and John Thornton Gillig, who designed the University of Kentucky's Memorial Coliseum. Children, left to right, are Betty Ann Poindexter, John Robert Gillig, and Mary Elizabeth Gillig. (Courtesy of Poindexter Lumber Company.)

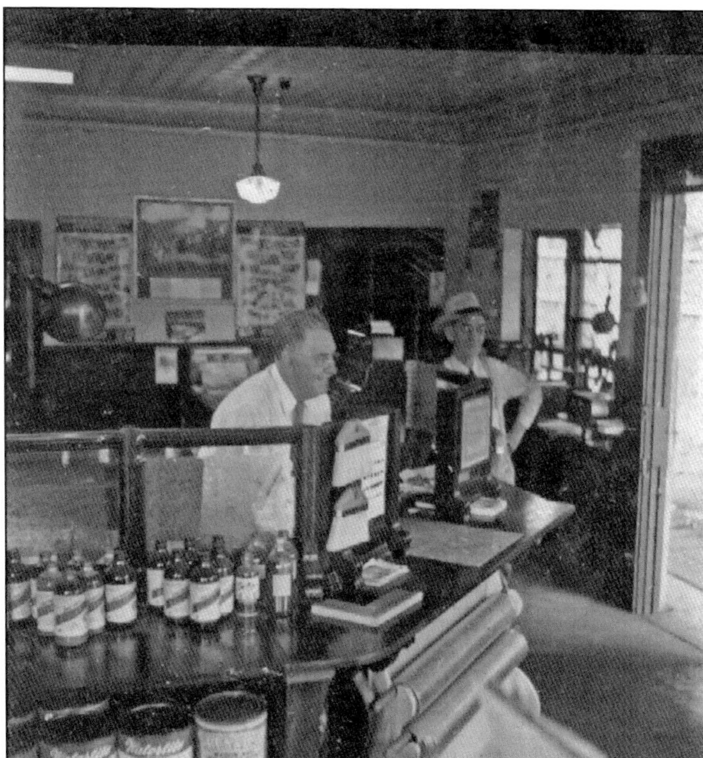

Robert Harold Poindexter Sr. works behind the counter at J. R. Poindexter and Son in this undated photograph. Today J. R. Poindexter's great-grandsons—Robert Poindexter Sr.'s grandsons, Bill Selin and Bobby Poindexter—run the business. (Courtesy of Poindexter Lumber Company.)

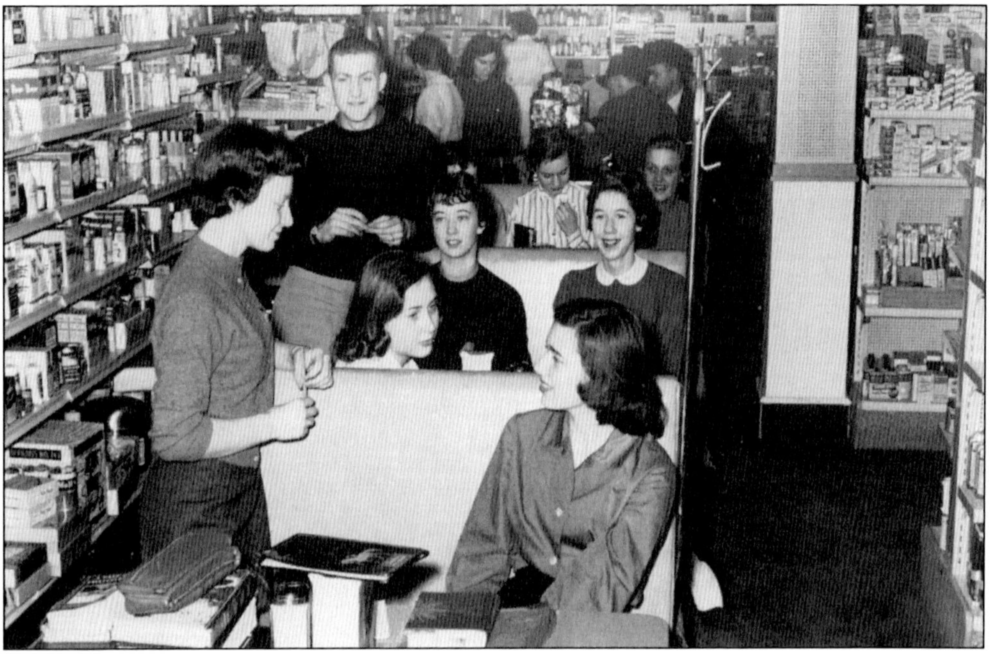

The Renaker Rexall drugstore on Cynthiana's Main Street, which served food and drink too, was a busy place for many years. This 1957 photograph shows the store's appeal as a hangout for teenagers. Cherry Coca-Colas were favorites for old and young alike. (Courtesy of the Cynthiana High School Alumni Association.)

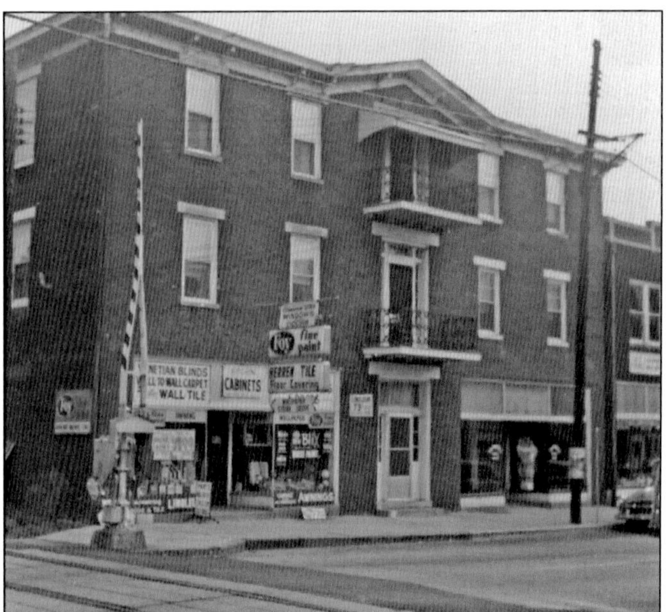

Long before those who worked on their own homes were called "do-it-yourselfers," the Herren store, west of the railroad track on Pike Street, offered tile, floor covering, and Foy paint. (Courtesy of William A. Penn.)

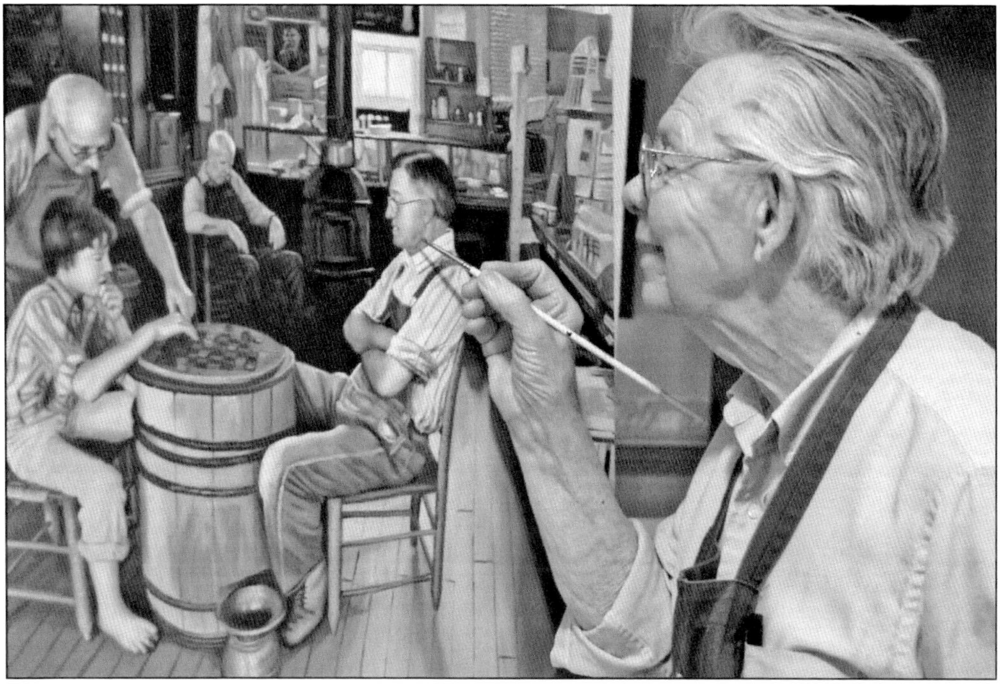

Artist Herbert Allen Moore works on a painting illustrating life inside a country store in this photograph. Moore, a Sunrise native, was born in 1930 to Herbert and Artie Bradford Moore. He was trained at the Cincinnati Art Academy and is a graduate of the University of Kentucky. In 1969, he opened the Mammoth Cave Wax Museum, which featured dozens of Moore-crafted wax figures of famous people. Moore sold the museum in 1982. Since then he has taught art in Cynthiana at the elementary and college level and continues to teach art in his home studio on Pleasant Street. (Courtesy of Kate Darnell.)

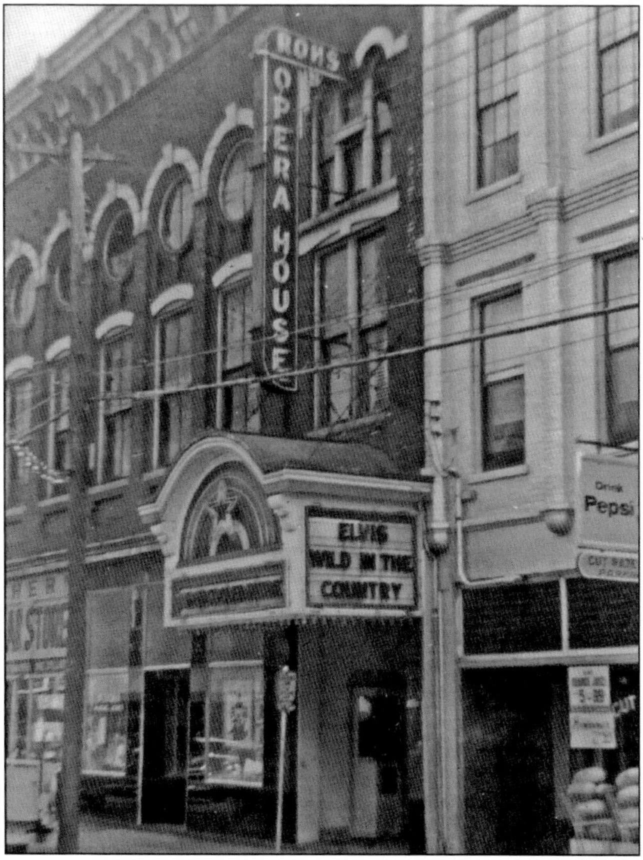

An Elvis Presley movie, *Wild in the Country*, was playing at the Rohs Theater when this photograph was taken in the early 1960s. (Courtesy of Roger and Shelley Slade.)

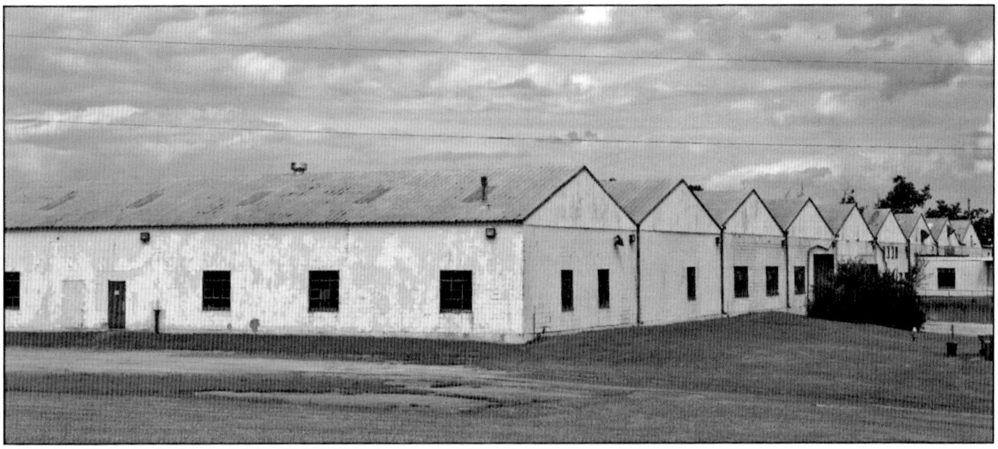

Writer Thelma Taylor noted in 1983 that Kawneer was the first large metal factory to make its home in Cynthiana, staying for 19 years before leaving in the early 1970s. Other factories in Cynthiana over the years have included Blake and Johnson, Cynthiana Screw Corporation, Blue Grass Industries, Bundy Tubing, Cynthiana Manufacturing (Cleveland Twist Drill), Eaton Corporation, Ladish, Safety Specialty (Bullard Manufacturing), and Taylor Farms, a meat processing plant. (Photograph by M. Britt Kennerly.)

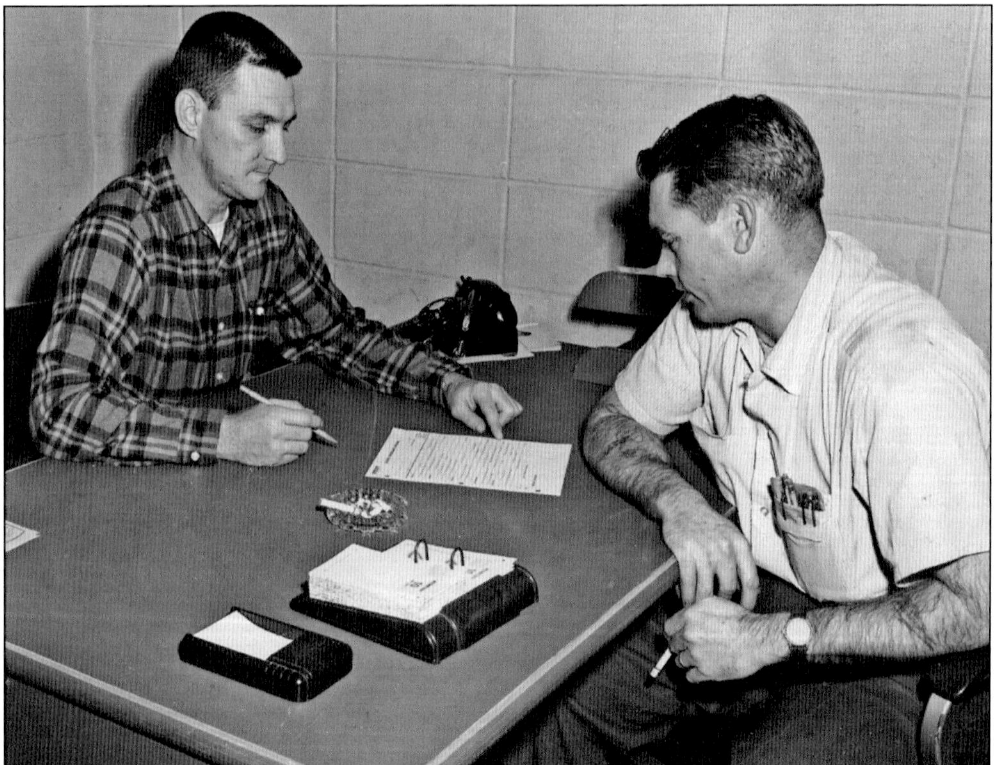

Earl Chasteen, a Kawneer supervisor, conducts an evaluation with employee Duke Beasley in this undated photograph, possibly taken in the 1960s. (Courtesy of Rose Chasteen.)

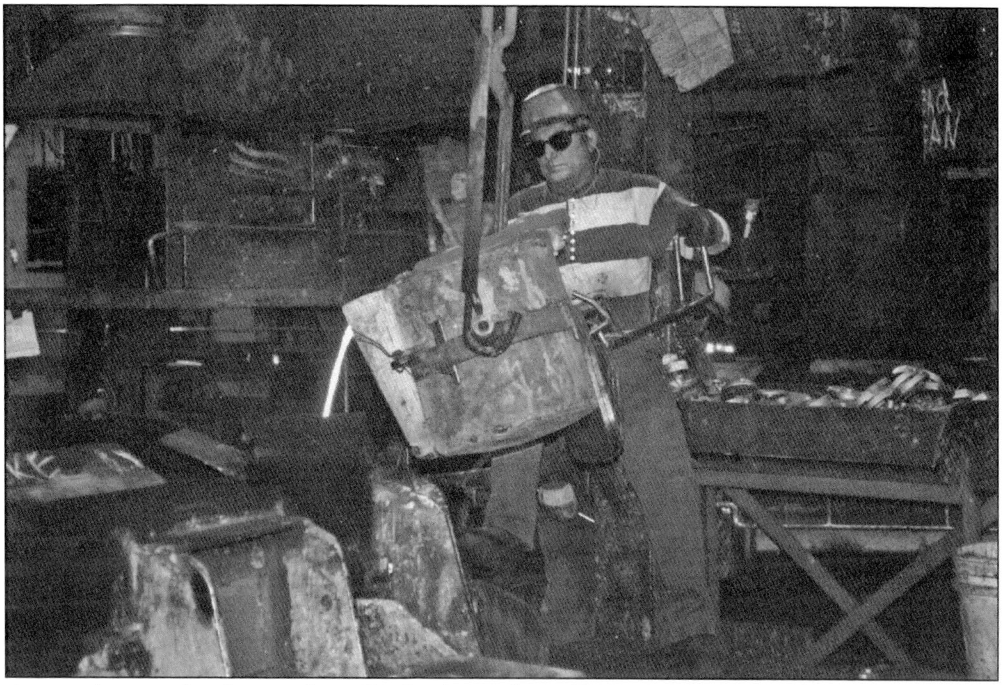

An employee is hard at work at Grede, formerly an Eaton Corporation plant, in the 1980s. (Photograph by Linda H. Moore.)

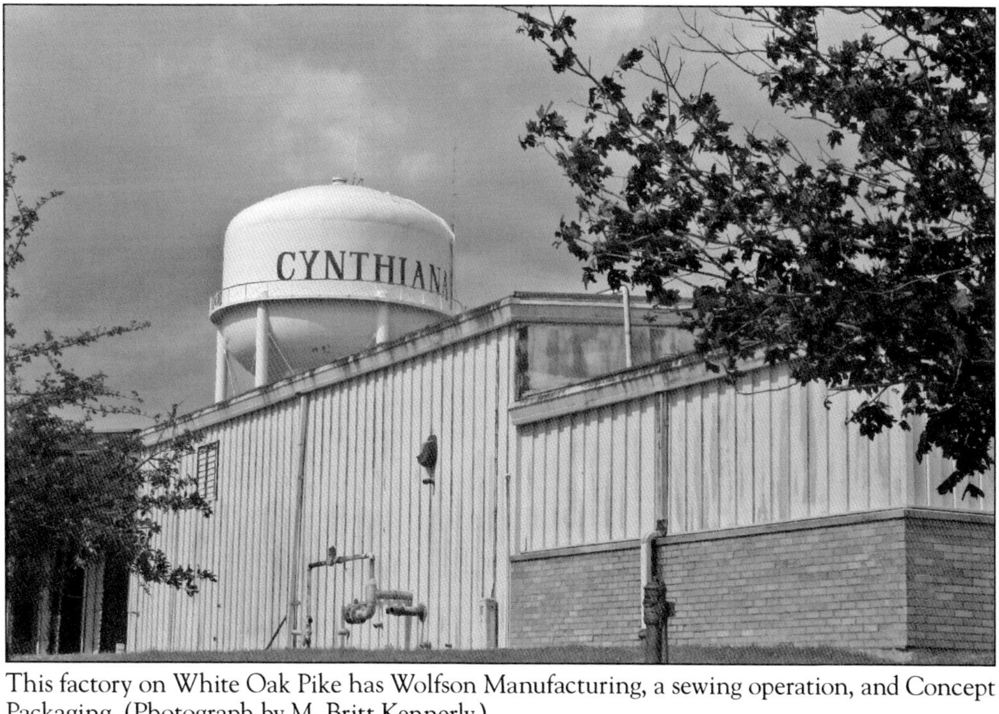

This factory on White Oak Pike has Wolfson Manufacturing, a sewing operation, and Concept Packaging. (Photograph by M. Britt Kennerly.)

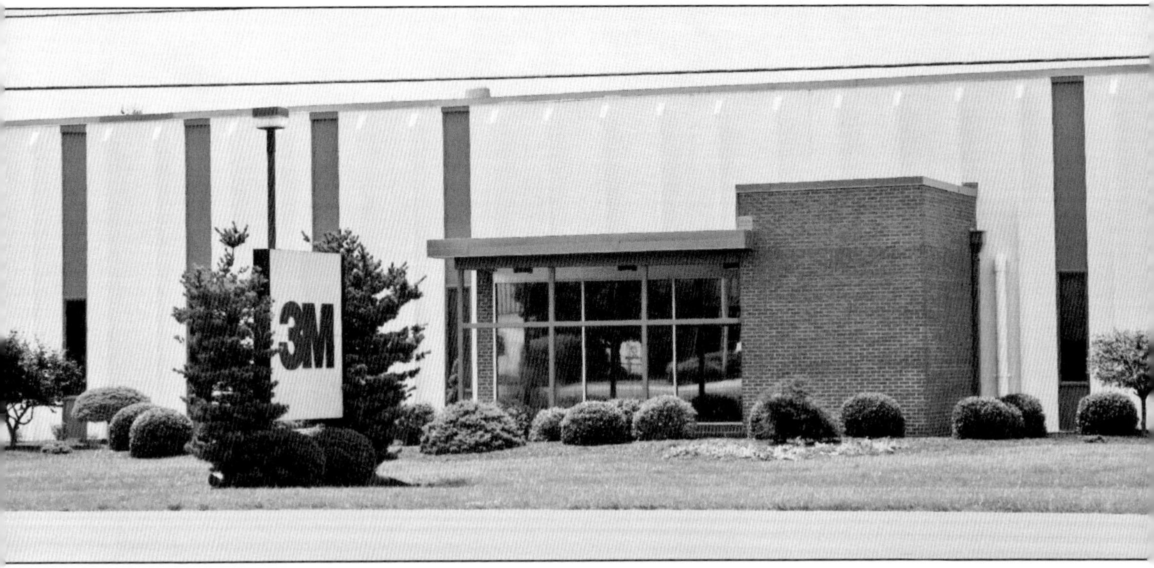

The arrival of 3M in 1969 stuck a new tag on the city's history: Cynthiana became the home of Post-it notes. Company records show that the first 3M operations began in a tobacco warehouse on Church Street in 1969. That was followed in the same year by the construction of a 200,000-square-foot plant on 52 acres on New Lair Road. At that time, the plant produced paper copiers and overhead projectors. In 1985, the plant was converted for local production of Post-it notes for the North American and Japanese markets. The plant, which is 250,000 square feet bigger in 2009 than when it came to town, employs hundreds of people. Take a note: back in 1985, the famous pads coming out of Cynthiana were available only in canary yellow and in just three sizes. (Photograph by Linda H. Moore.)

The man who made sausage synonymous with Cynthiana for meat lovers and who put jobs in the hands of hundreds of men and woman across central Kentucky came from a modest background. William A. Webber was born in an old log home at the corner of Hinton-Webber and Stringtown-Webber Roads. He built the multistate Webber Sausage Company (later Webber Farms) from a company he and his father, William Webber Jr., originally ran from the back of a station wagon. The two men started working together after William A. Webber's return from U.S. Navy service in World War II, cofounding the company with a GI loan obtained by the younger Webber. William Webber, a Sunday school teacher at the First United Methodist Church for 32 years and a former president of the Harrison Memorial Hospital board, died in 2007. (Courtesy of Jeanine Webber Lulich.)

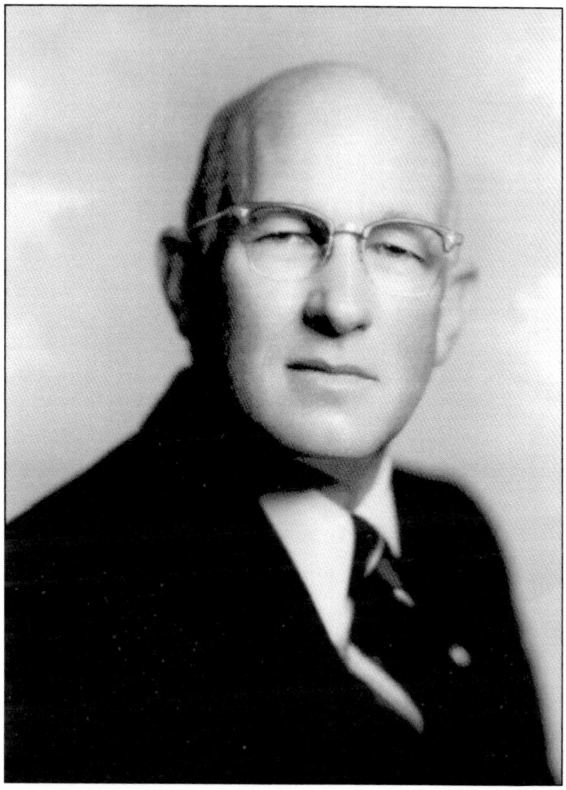

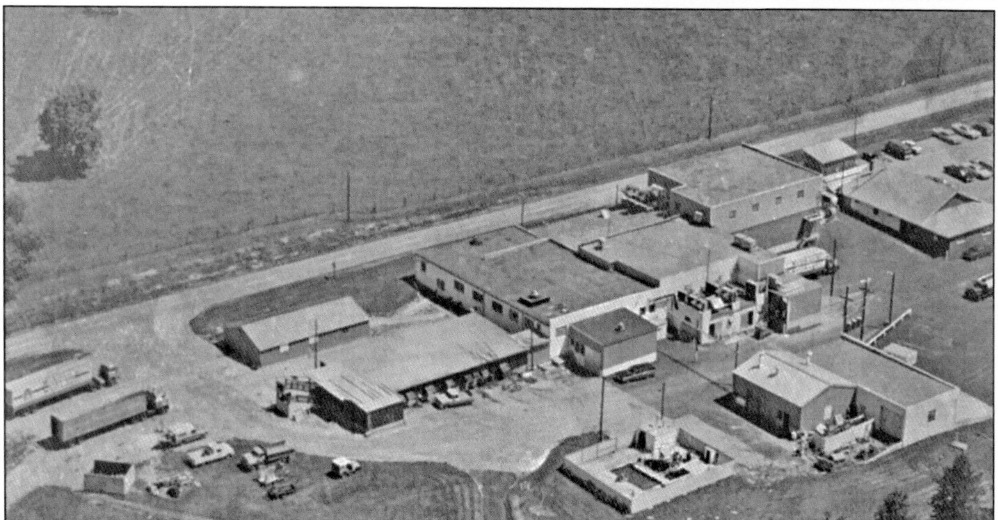

The Webber Sausage Company, first housed in a small building in Belmont and known to locals as "Webber's Sausage," was relocated to the corner of what is now Kentucky Highway 36 and Carl Stevens Road as the business grew. It was not unusual to be hired at Webber in one position and work one's way through the ranks into top jobs. Earl McNabb, for example, started as a truck loader, moving to a sales position in 1950 and eventually becoming vice president in charge of marketing and advertising. Millard Reynolds started as a salesman, moving into the plant manager position and later the company president's seat. (Courtesy of Jeanine Webber Lulich.)

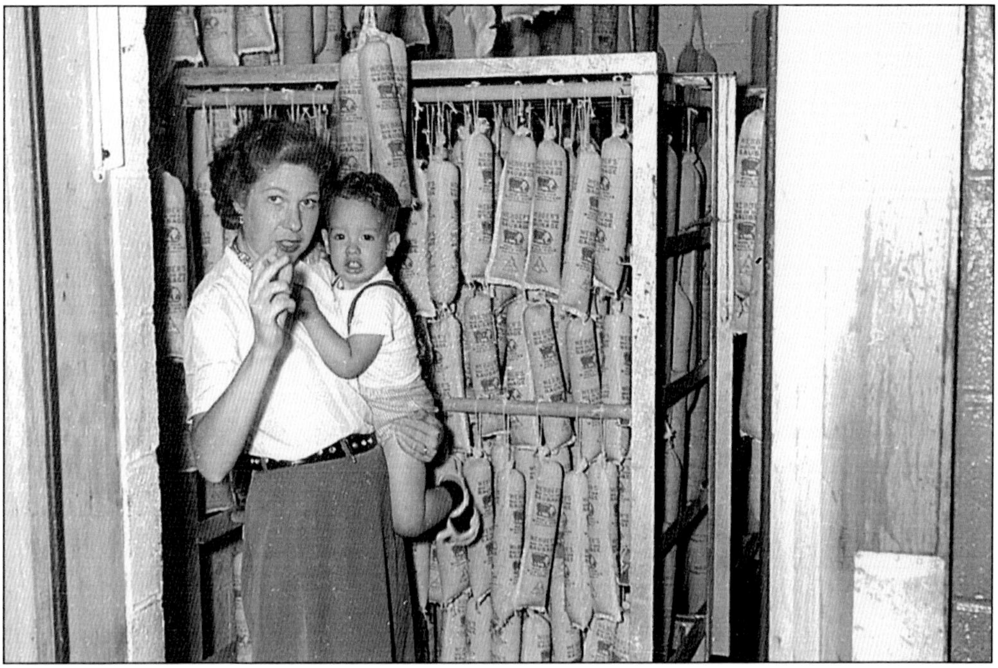

Martha Webber Rutherford, William A. Webber's sister, holds her son, Jack, in front of a sausage-filled refrigerator. Martha and her sisters, Jean and Elizabeth, stitched sausage bags for their father's business when they were growing up in Cynthiana. (Courtesy of Jeanine Webber Lulich.)

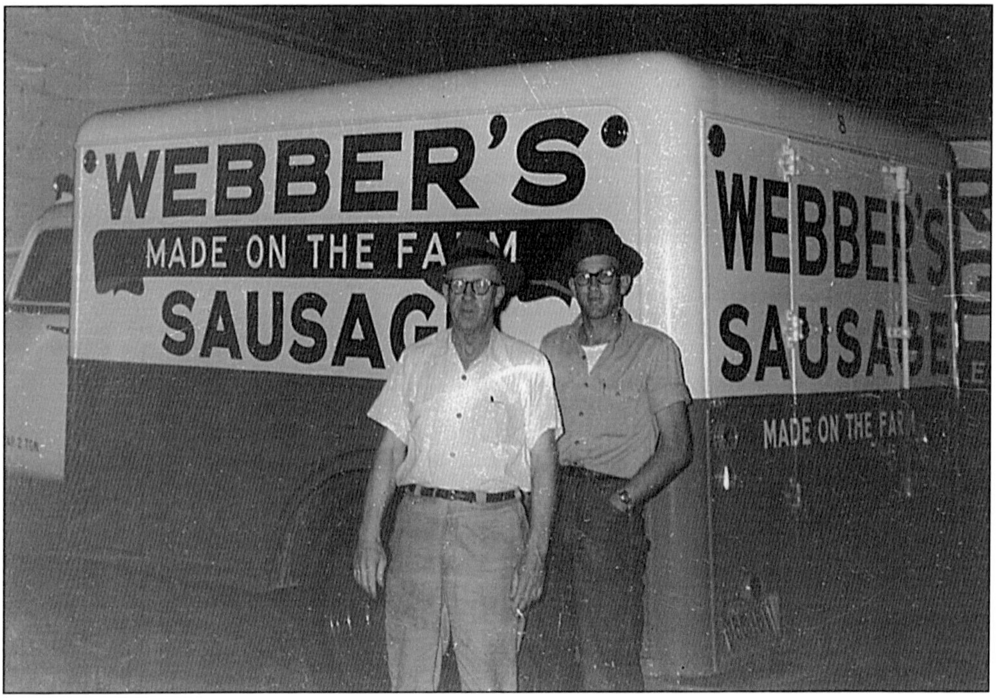

The Webber Sausage Company operated processing plants in Cynthiana and Lawrenceburg and sold meat products under the Webber and Edwards labels. The company was sold to Con-Agra in 1984. (Courtesy of Jeanine Webber Lulich.)

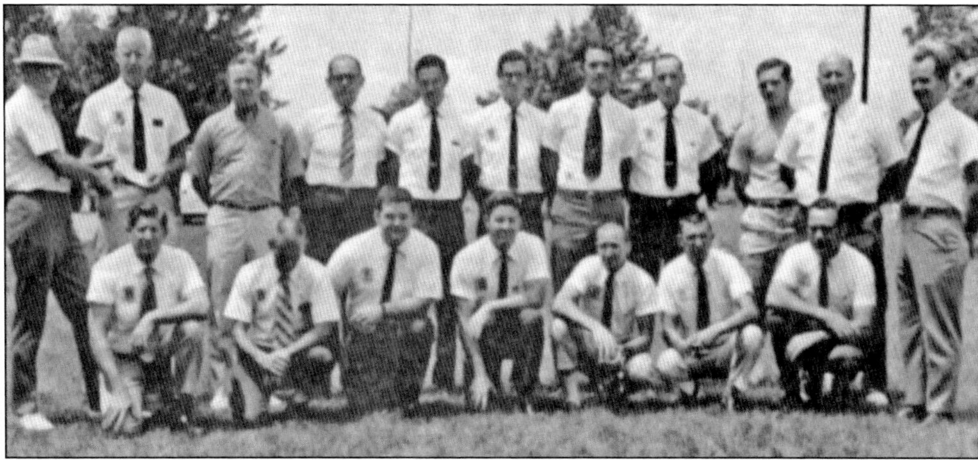

Webber Sausage Company drivers received safe driving honors as they gathered with their supervisors in 1971 at the company's annual picnic. Pictured are, from left to right (first row) James Snapp, Ohio supervisor; Ted Wright, Kentucky supervisor; Leroy Roberts; George Courtney; Lester Lawson; Carl Duncan; and Clay Morrison; (second row) William A. Webber, president; Clinton Haggard; Don Courtney, Ohio supervisor; Charlie Bowen, Indiana supervisor; Don Kenney; Jim Brooks; Jerry Anderson; Lovell Cloe; Bob Bockhorst; Donnie Gasser; and Larry Mattox. (Courtesy of Jeanine Webber Lulich.)

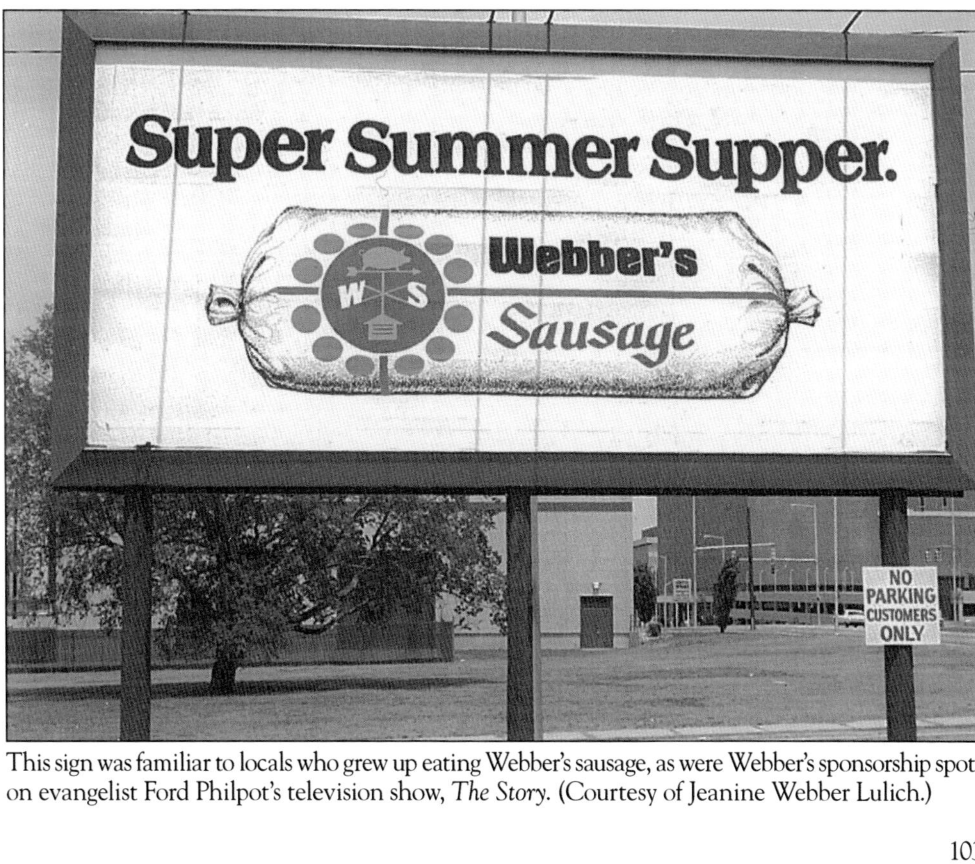

This sign was familiar to locals who grew up eating Webber's sausage, as were Webber's sponsorship spots on evangelist Ford Philpot's television show, *The Story*. (Courtesy of Jeanine Webber Lulich.)

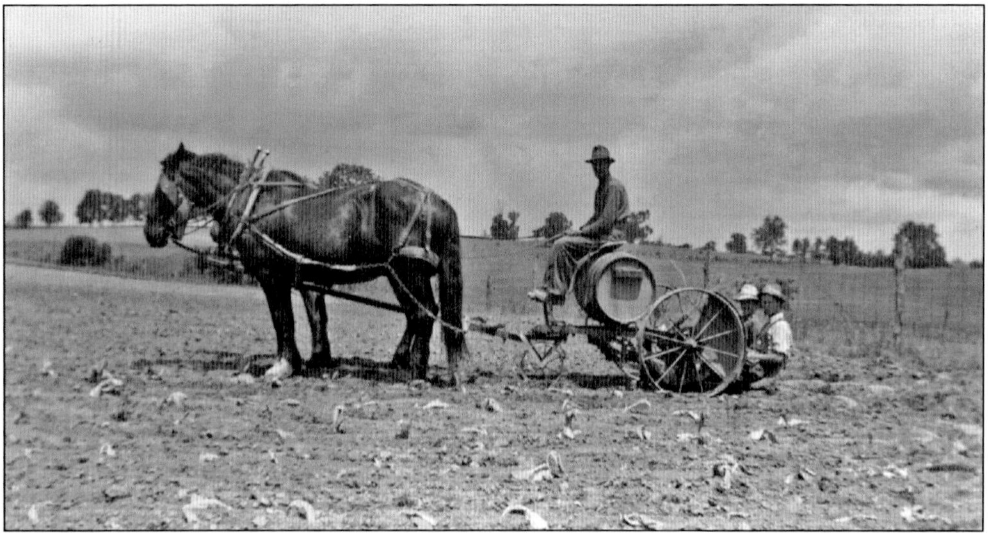

Agriculture is of longstanding importance in Cynthiana, shaping not only the landscape but also the livelihoods of thousands of farm families and related businesses countywide. In this 1938 photograph, Nelson Cordray of Salem sets tobacco with his sons, Harlan (center) and Swinford. (Courtesy of Jack and Nora McCauley.)

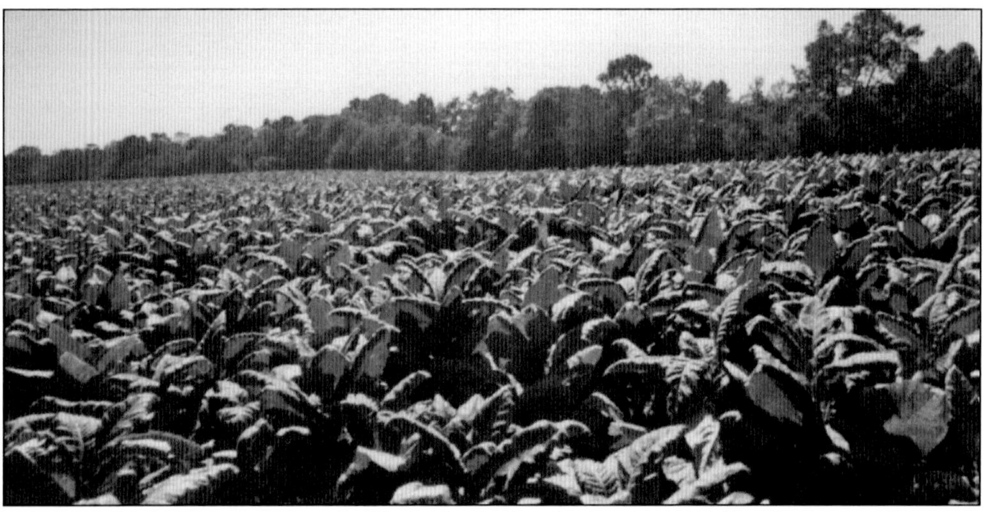

Tobacco—both the growing and selling of it—played a vital role in Cynthiana and Harrison County history, as it did in most of the commonwealth, for decades. A 1983 article by longtime *Cynthiana Democrat* writer Thelma Taylor said that for the 1982–1983 marketing year, "Cynthiana warehouses sold over 42 million pounds at an average of $187.11 . . . the highest of any town in the state except for two days of the marketing season." The first local sale of loose-leaf tobacco, Taylor wrote, was in 1900, conducted on South Church Street at the old Burley House. (Courtesy of Helen Harney.)

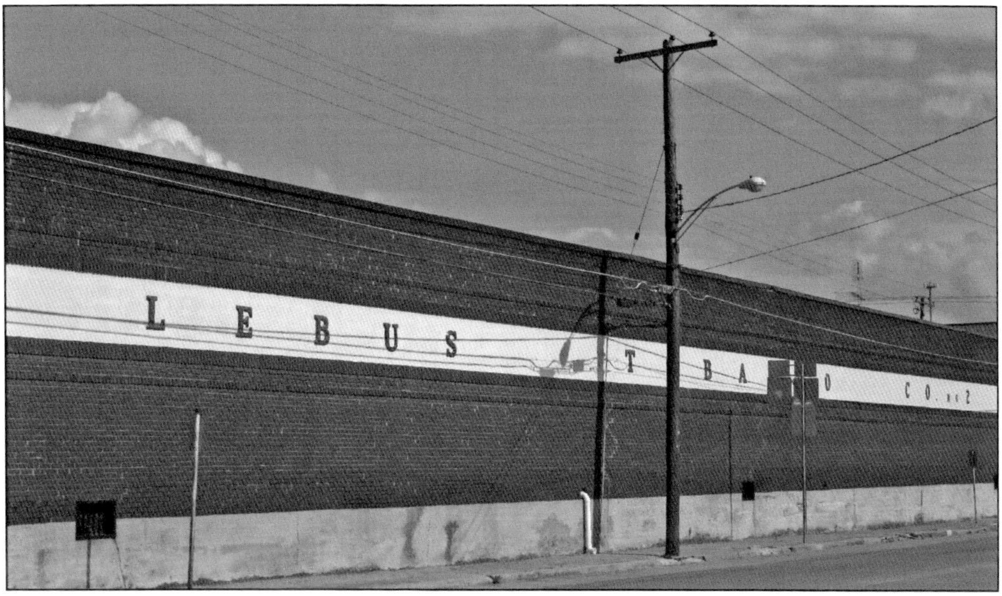

The former Lebus tobacco warehouse No. 2 still stands on Church Street. (Photograph by M. Britt Kennerly.)

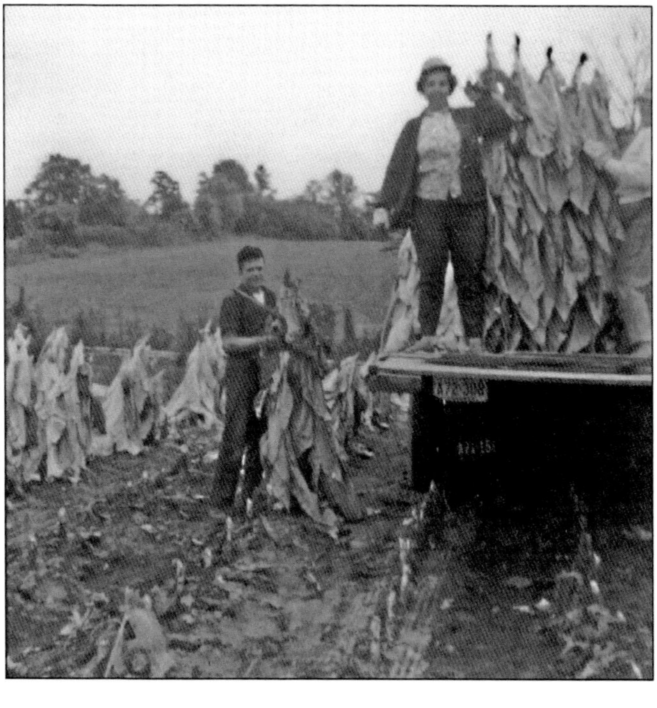

Cut it and load it: Louise Perraut, on the truck at left, and Ruth Ann Perraut hold up tobacco for viewing as they work with Butch Houston on Houston's farm in eastern Harrison County. (Courtesy of Ruth Ann Perraut.)

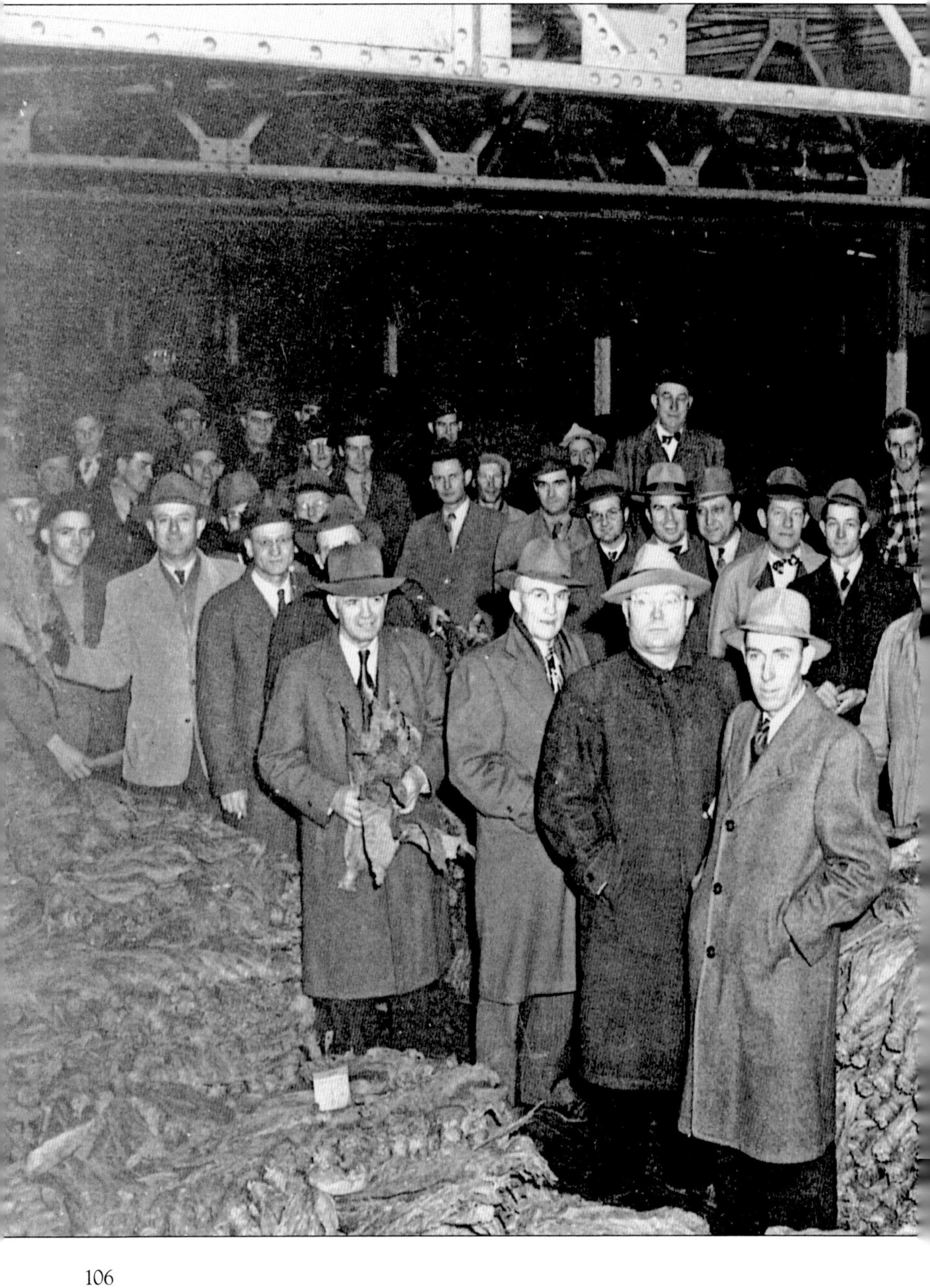

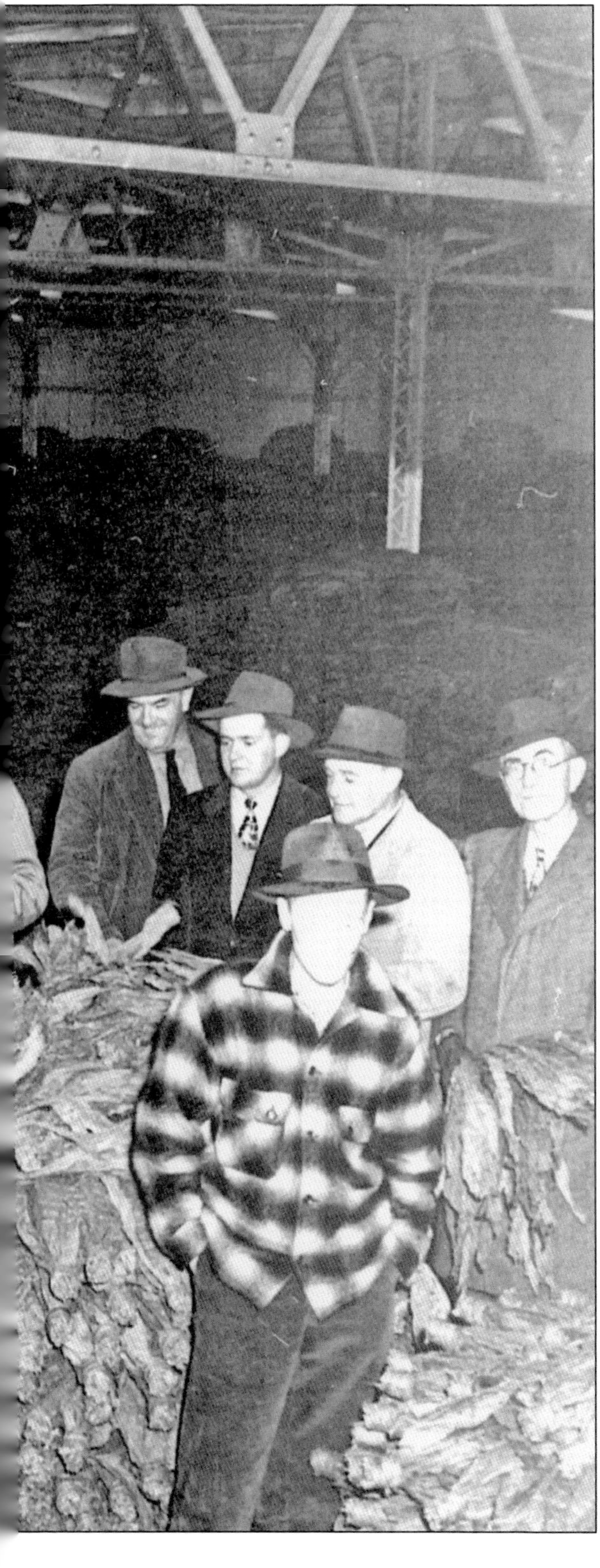

For decades, Harrison County ranked among the state's top tobacco producers. Here, at the Pepper, Peak, and Florence tobacco warehouse in the 1950s, John Roy Peak Sr. is pictured fifth from right on the first row, holding tobacco. To his left is Ross Pepper, and to Pepper's left is former Cynthiana mayor John Cummins. Peak's son, John Roy Peak Jr., is third from the right behind the tobacco on the right side of the photograph. (Courtesy of Dean Peak.)

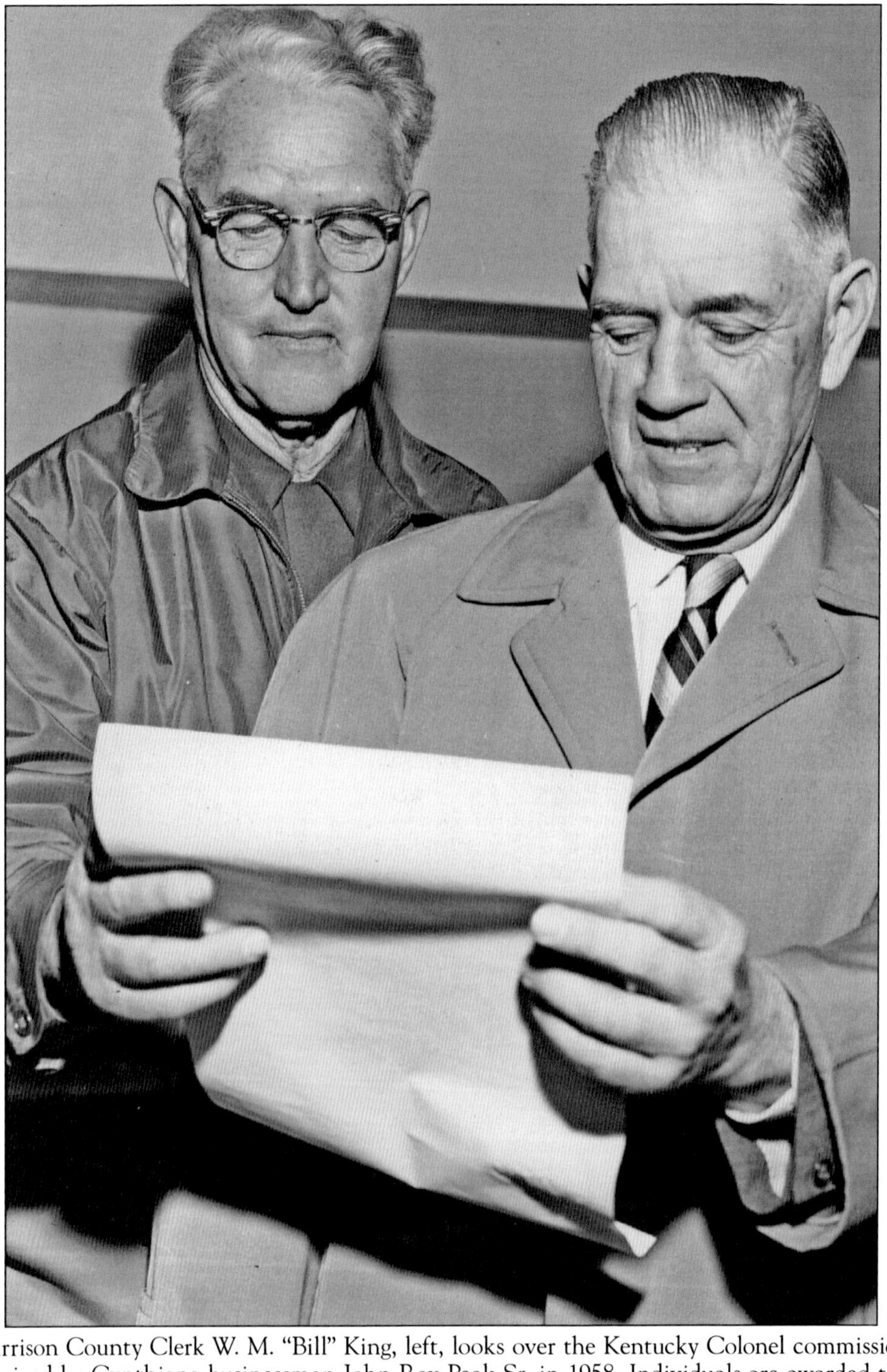

Harrison County Clerk W. M. "Bill" King, left, looks over the Kentucky Colonel commission received by Cynthiana businessman John Roy Peak Sr. in 1958. Individuals are awarded the Kentucky Colonel commissions by the governor and the secretary of state "in recognition of noteworthy accomplishments and outstanding service to a community, state or the nation." (Courtesy of Dean Peak.)

Seven

The Sports Pages

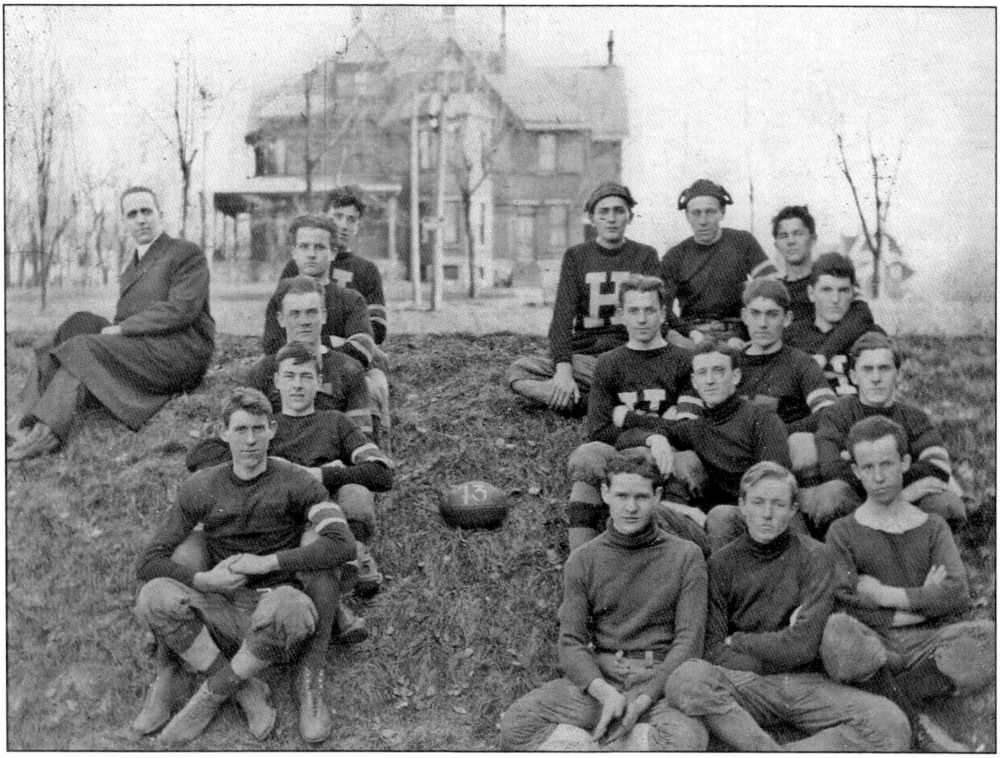

Since the city's earliest days, sports have played a vital role in building teamwork and buoying citizens' spirits. Across the decades, through war years, the Great Depression and beyond, football, baseball, and basketball teams each helped the city make the sports map in award-winning style. Here the 1913 Cynthiana High School football team is pictured in front of the Dedman house, which is still part of the local landscape. They form a "13" as they are seated on the hill where Cynthiana High School stood facing Bridge Street. At left is Superintendent R. I. Cord—the apostrophe in front of the "13." Forming the "1," from top to bottom, are Harold Ammerman, Clyde Bland, J. W. VanDeren, Forrest Wright, and McShane Shropshire. Shaping the "3" are, top to bottom, J. M. Durbin, H. D. Ingles, R. G. Poindexter, E. N. McIlvain, C. N. Rorer, Raymond Huffman, Herve McClellan, Alvin Rorer, LeRoy Bland, E. Y. VanDeren, and Roy McCracken. (Courtesy of the Cynthiana–Harrison County Museum.)

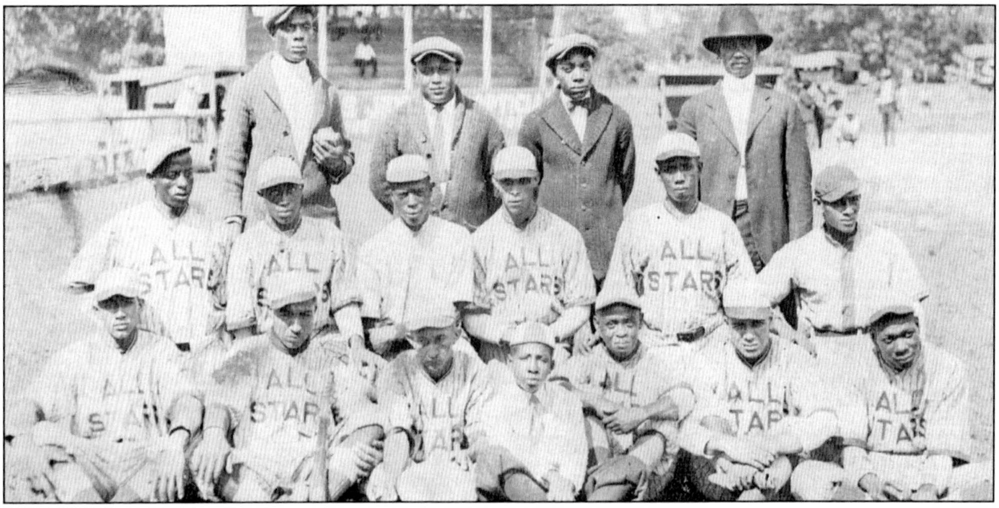

The Cynthiana All-Star baseball team suited up for this undated photograph. From left to right are (first row) Pythian Russ, McKinley Russ, Jake Lyons, Bert Russ, Arnett Lilly, George "Pete" Alexander, and Homer Henry; (second row) Remus Boyers, Raymond Conner, Pete Hayden, Jimmy Way, Henry Jacobs, and Herbert Rawls; (third row) Joe Campbell, Wallace Lilly, Bunk Coleman, and John Watson. (Courtesy of Alice Allen.)

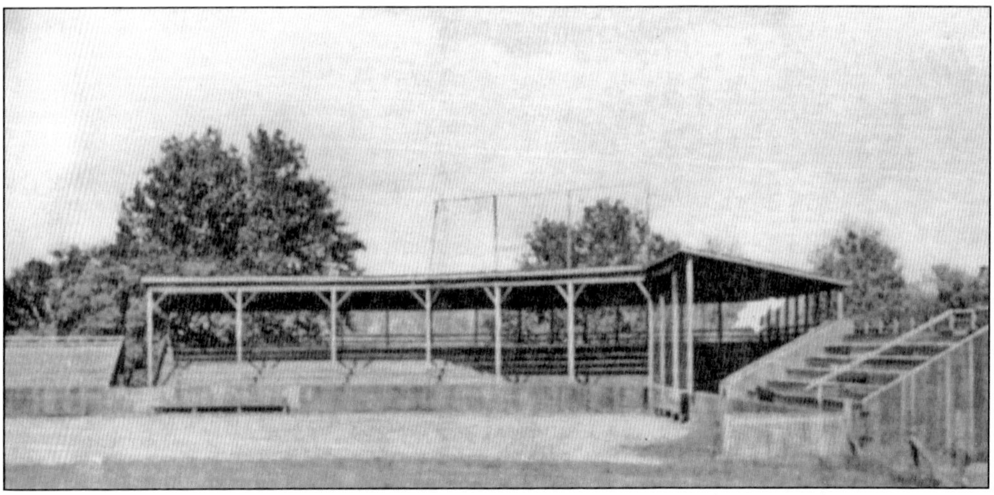

The Lebus ballpark, off U.S. Route 27 south of the city, is seen in the 1920s. (Courtesy of the Cynthiana–Harrison County Museum.)

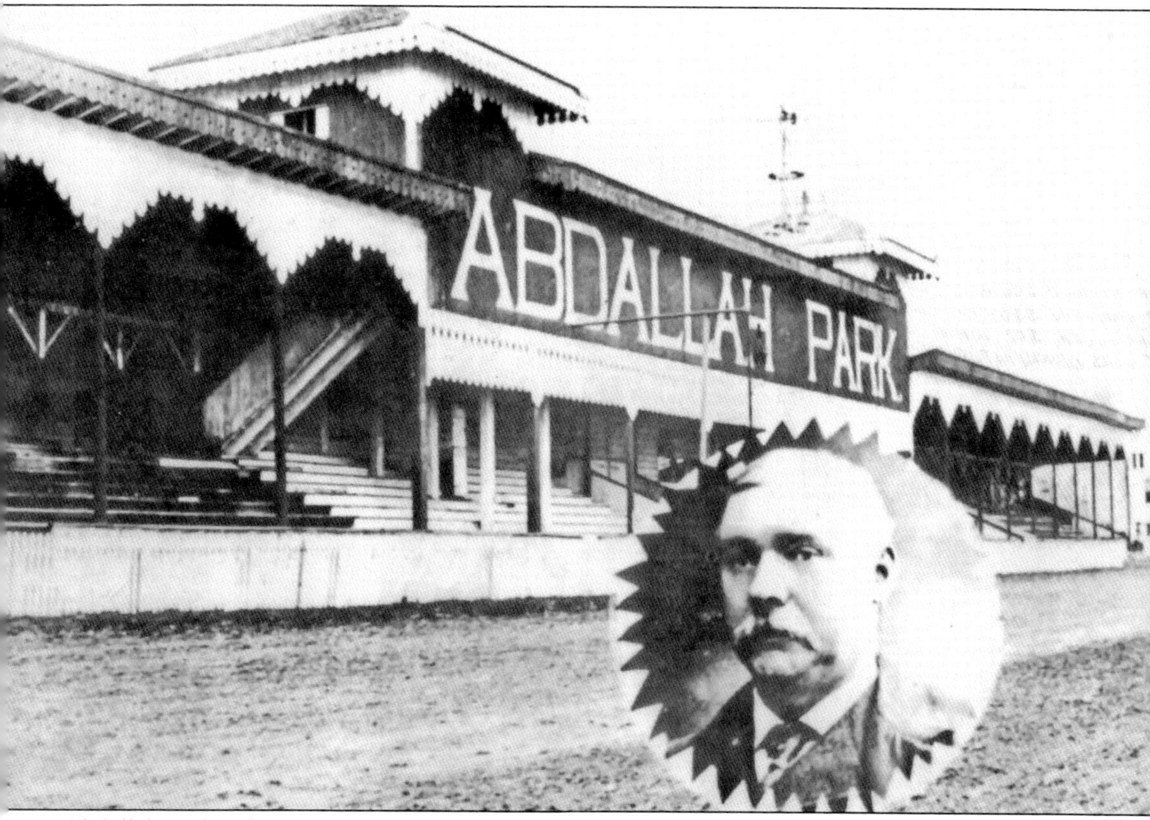

Abdallah Park, a horse racing venue, was established in 1875 by W. H. Wilson and named for one of Wilson's prized horses. On January 6, 1927, the *Log Cabin* newspaper reported that "the historic old grandstand at Abdallah Park was destroyed by fire on Monday, January 3, 1927. It was a conspicuous object from the Louisville and Nashville Railroad trains passing nearby, and many an old-timer recalled the days of its glory when the flowers of the trotting horse world would engage in speed contests over its fine mile track." In 1998, Abdallah Park Road's name was changed to Water Works Road. (Courtesy of the Cynthiana–Harrison County Museum.)

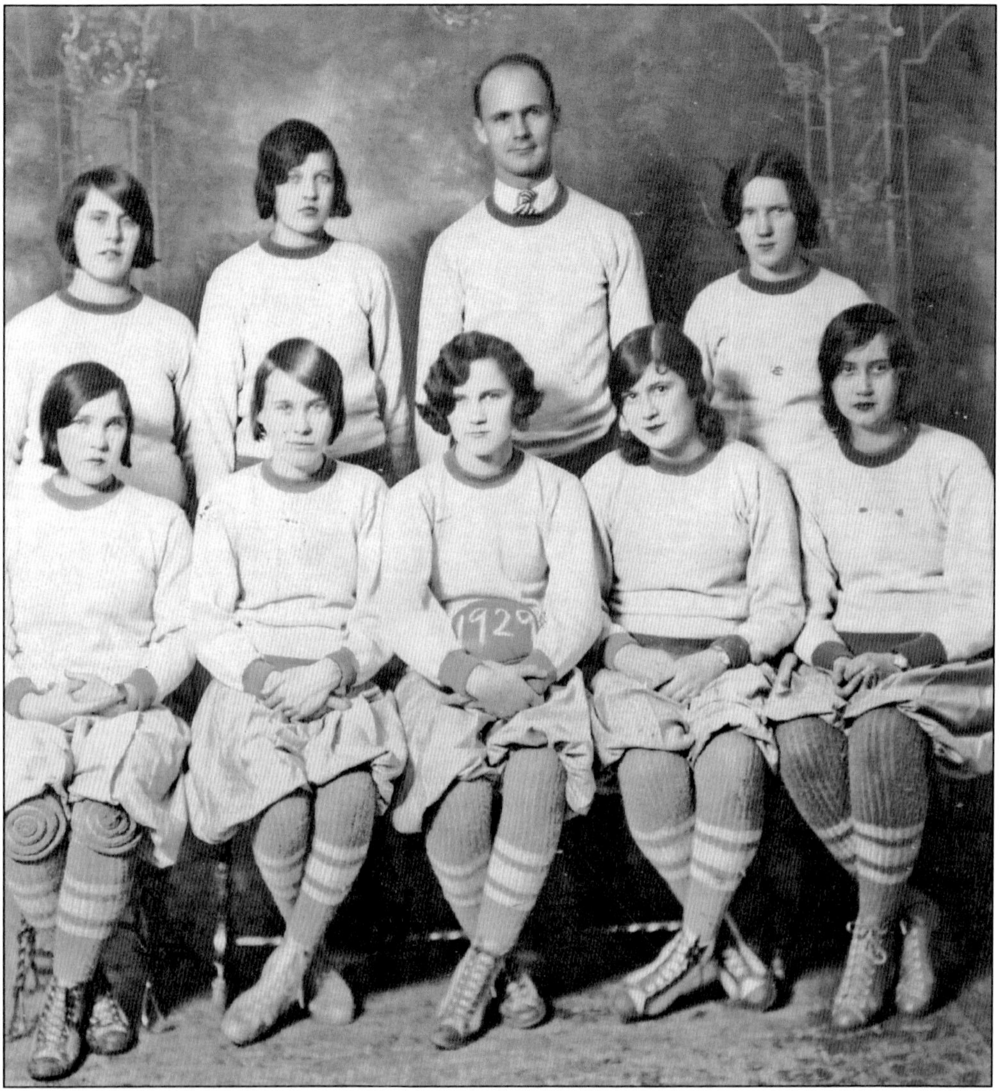

Members of the girls basketball team at Berry High School in 1929 were, from left to right, (first row) Elsie Buyer, Anna Myers Ross, Sara Whitaker, Orpah Swinford and Thelma Shadd; (second row) Florence Vanlandingham, Grace Chasteen, coach E. W. Richmond, and Nancy Whitaker. (Courtesy of the Cynthiana–Harrison County Museum.)

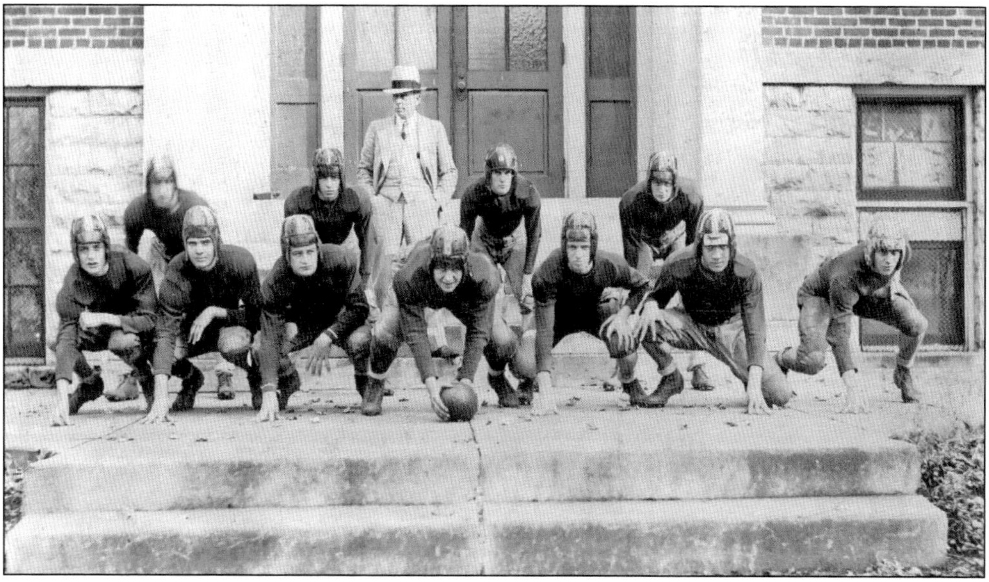

The 1933 Cynthiana High School football team featured, from left to right (first row) Paul Dorsey, Fithian Durbin, Hugh Ewalt, Terry Taylor, Floyd Russell, Bill Bauer, and Dave Ewalt; (second row) Eugene Fryman, Jack Wills, Stanley Schuler, and Joe Ammerman. Coach Buff Ingles backs the team. (Courtesy of the Cynthiana–Harrison County Museum.)

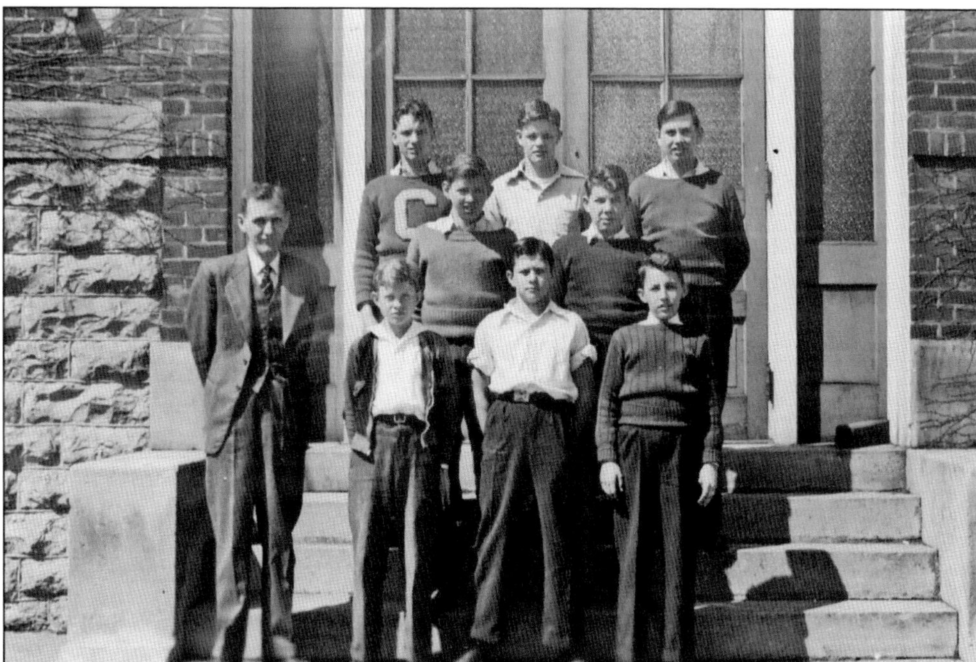

The 1940 Cynthiana Junior High basketball team members were, from left to right, (first row) James Cinnamon, Dewey Kuster, and Charles Cooper; (second row) Melvin Hampton and Eugene Turner; (third row) Royce Pulliam, Rufus Pulliam, and Oley Fightmaster. They were coached by Kelly Stanfield. (Courtesy of the Cynthiana High School Alumni Association.)

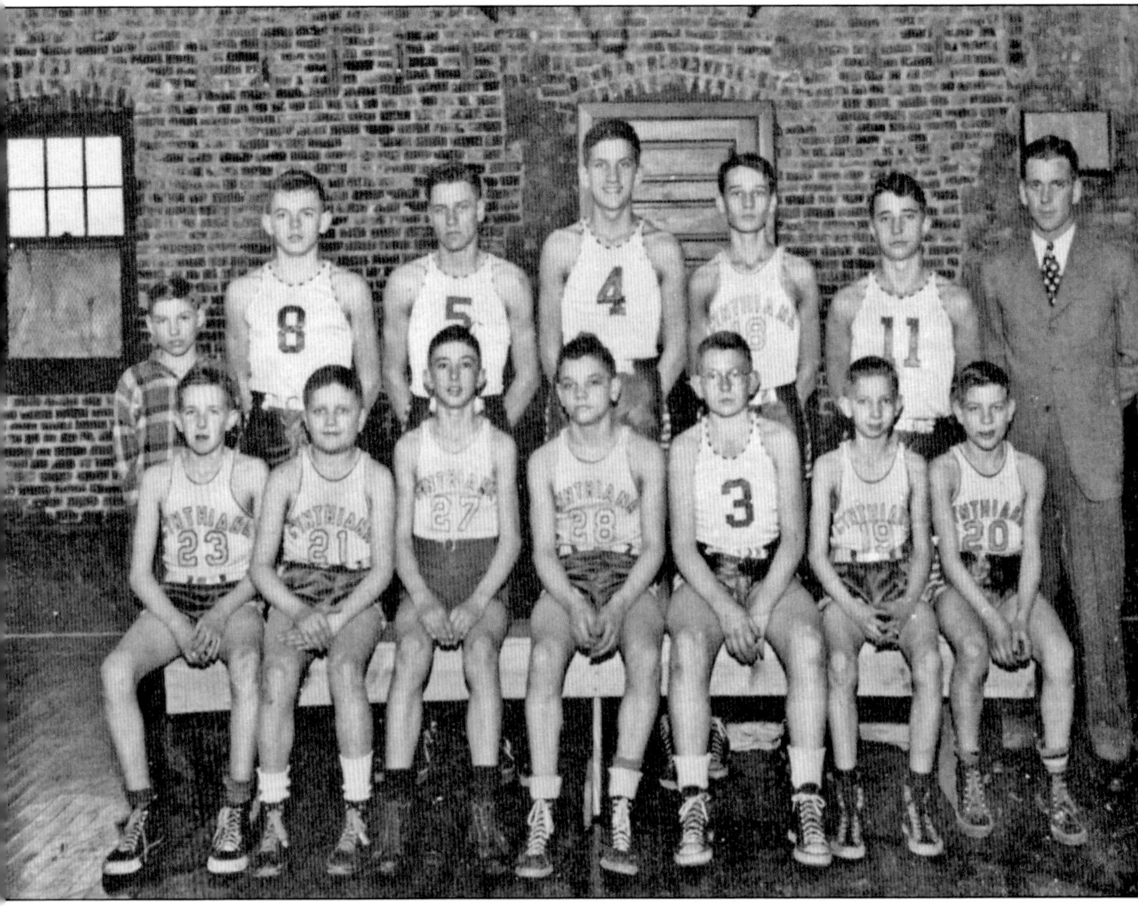

Junior basketball players at Cynthiana High School in 1948 were Clay Ashbrook, Kenneth Brumback, Richard Case, Gary Fields, James Florence, Jake Fowler, Marion Hardin, Arthur Hatterick, Richard Jacobs, Dwayne Moore, James Ritter, and Elbert Joe Smith. Their coach was "Larky" Box. (Courtesy of Helen McNees.)

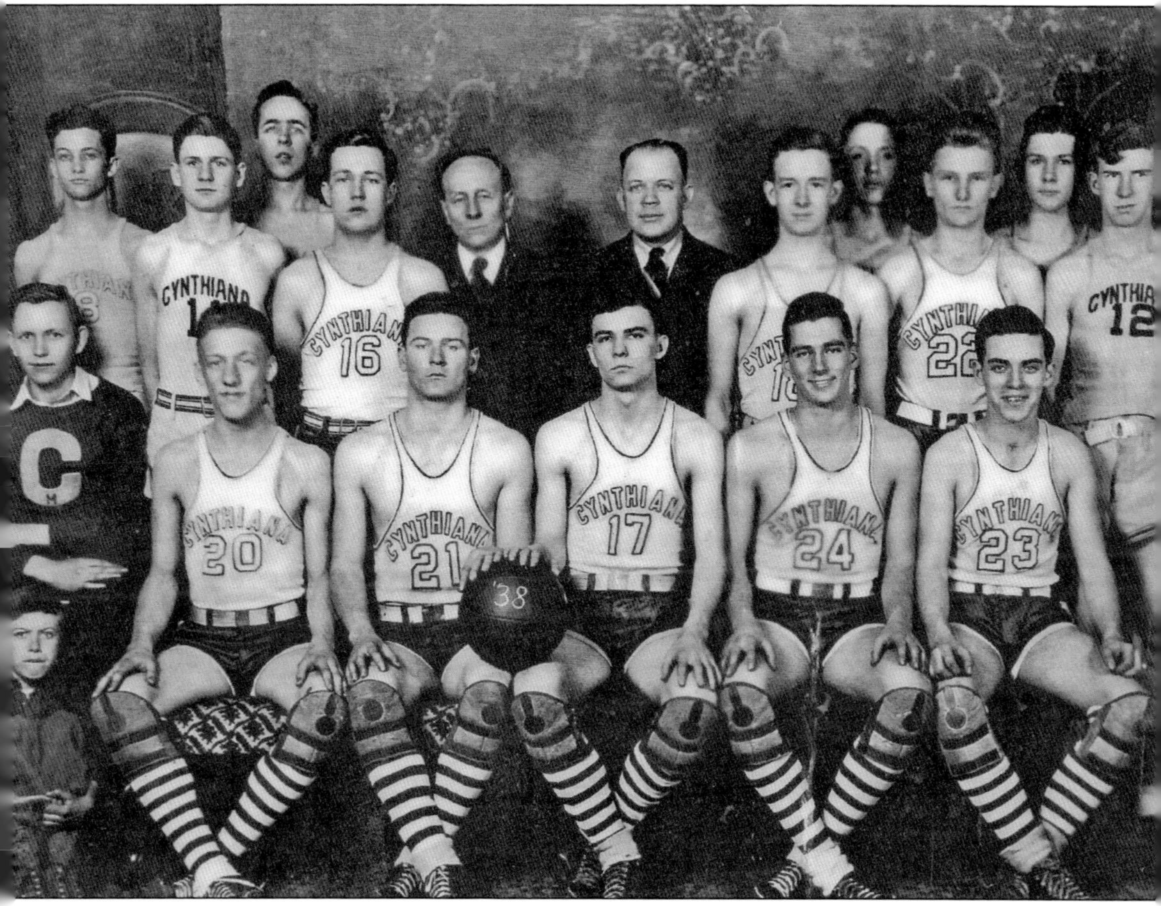

Members of the 1938 basketball team at Cynthiana High School, their coach, and principal were, from left to right, (first row) mascot "Cooter" Hill, Ralph Slade, Frazier Ravenscraft, Virgil Hatcher, Hershel "Huck" Turner, Harry Taylor, and Floyd Fightmaster; (second row) Carleton Eads, Paul Browning, Forrest Hill, Arthur Walsh, coach H. D. Ingles, principal Wendell Cason, Jack Taylor, Shearle Hicks, Emmett Whalen, Charles Kuster, and George Henson. (Courtesy of the Cynthiana–Harrison County Museum.)

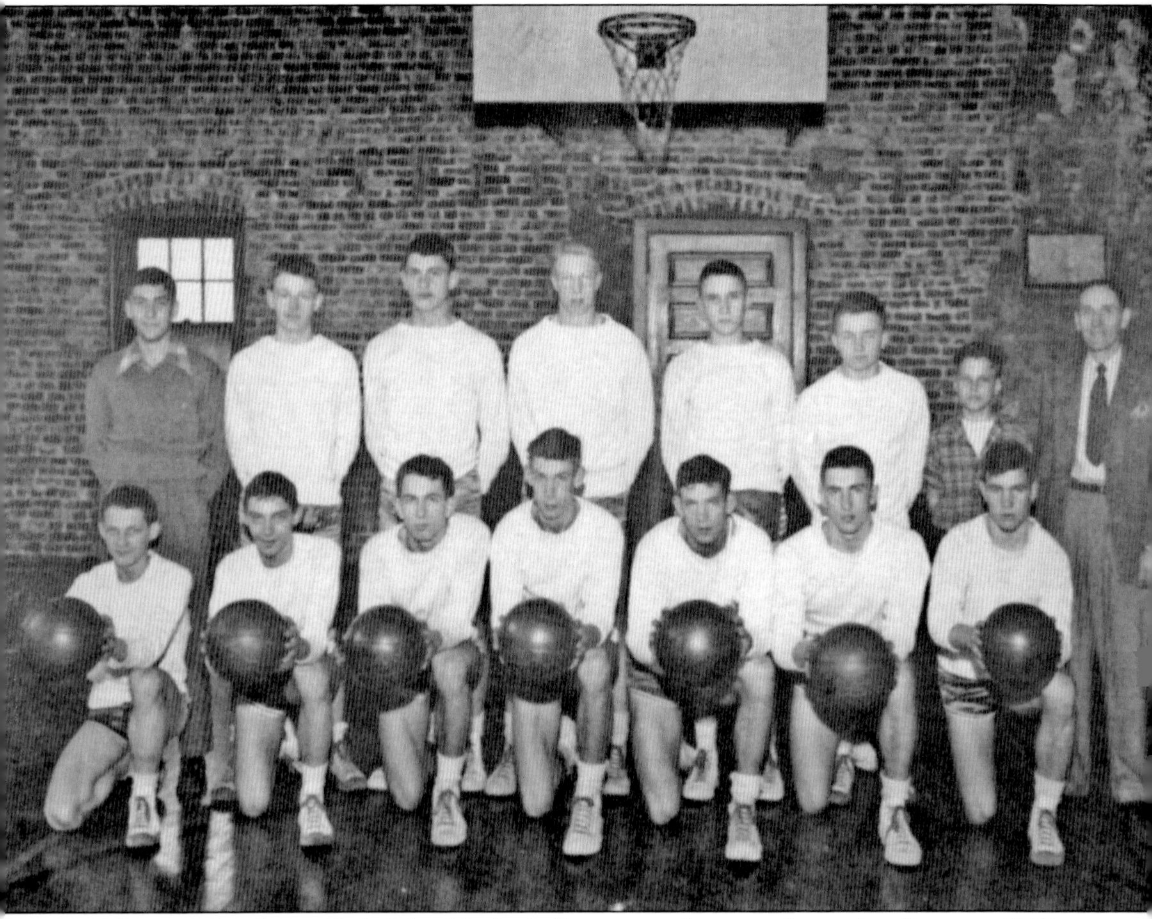

The 1948 Cynthiana High School basketball team members were Jimmy Lee Barnette, William Cook, Brown Feix, Billy Joe Hill, Myron Hill, Harold Kendall, Hall Kinney, Russell Richie, John Swinford, Lane Taylor, Charles Tolle, and Lewis Tolle. (Courtesy of Helen McNees.)

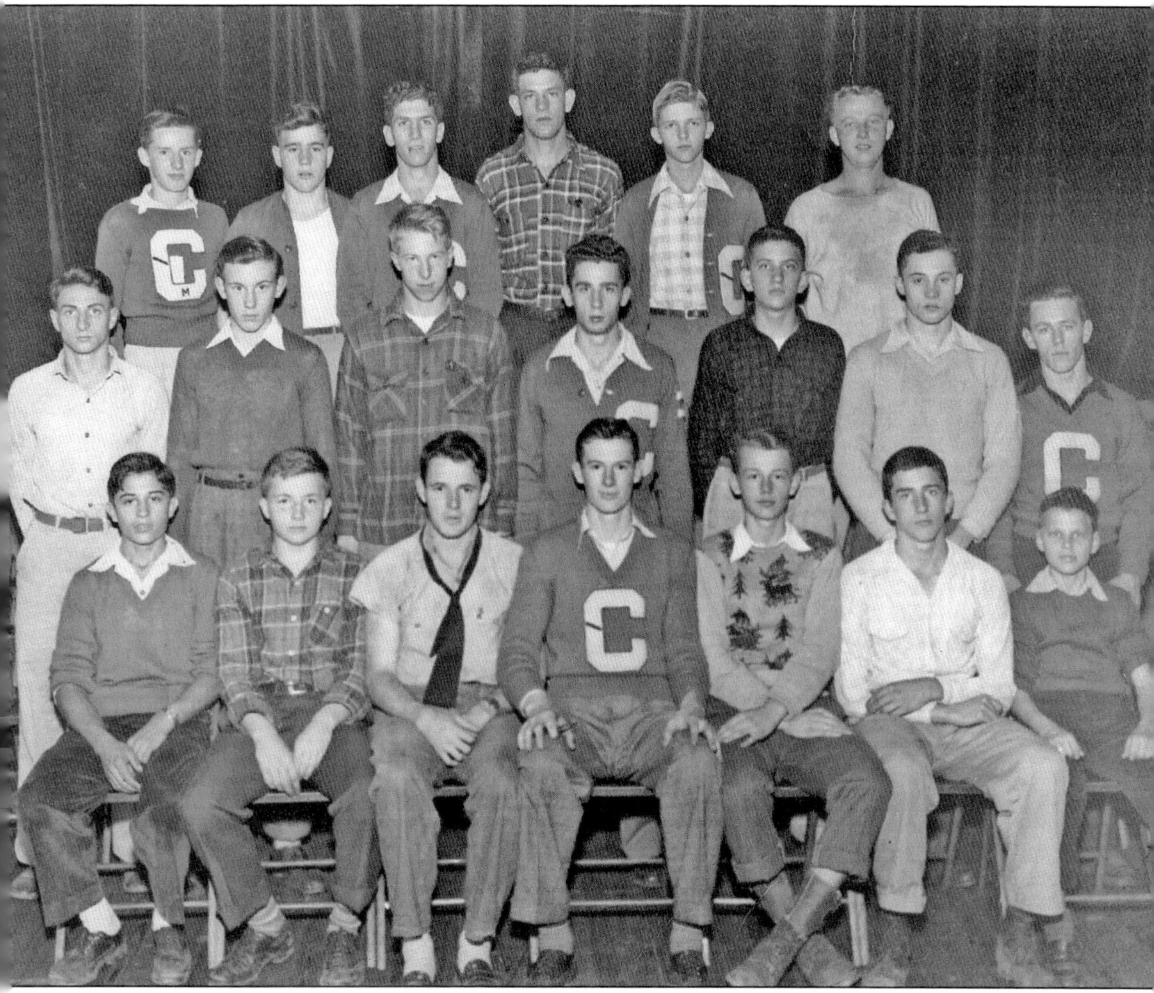

Members of the Cynthiana High School C Club in 1946–1947 were, from left to right, (first row) Raymond McNees Jr., Lane Taylor, Clarence Rankin, Joe B. Hall, Russell Richie, John Swinford, and David Withers; (second row) Larry Douglas, Albert Nutgrass Jr., William Cook, Robert Tussey, James "Mose" Florence, Clem Ritter, and Edward "Shorty" Ewalt; (third row) Gerald Fitzgerald, Brown Feix, Gayle Antle, Lewis Tolle, Allen Shirley, and David Ammerman. (Courtesy of the Cynthiana–Harrison County Museum.)

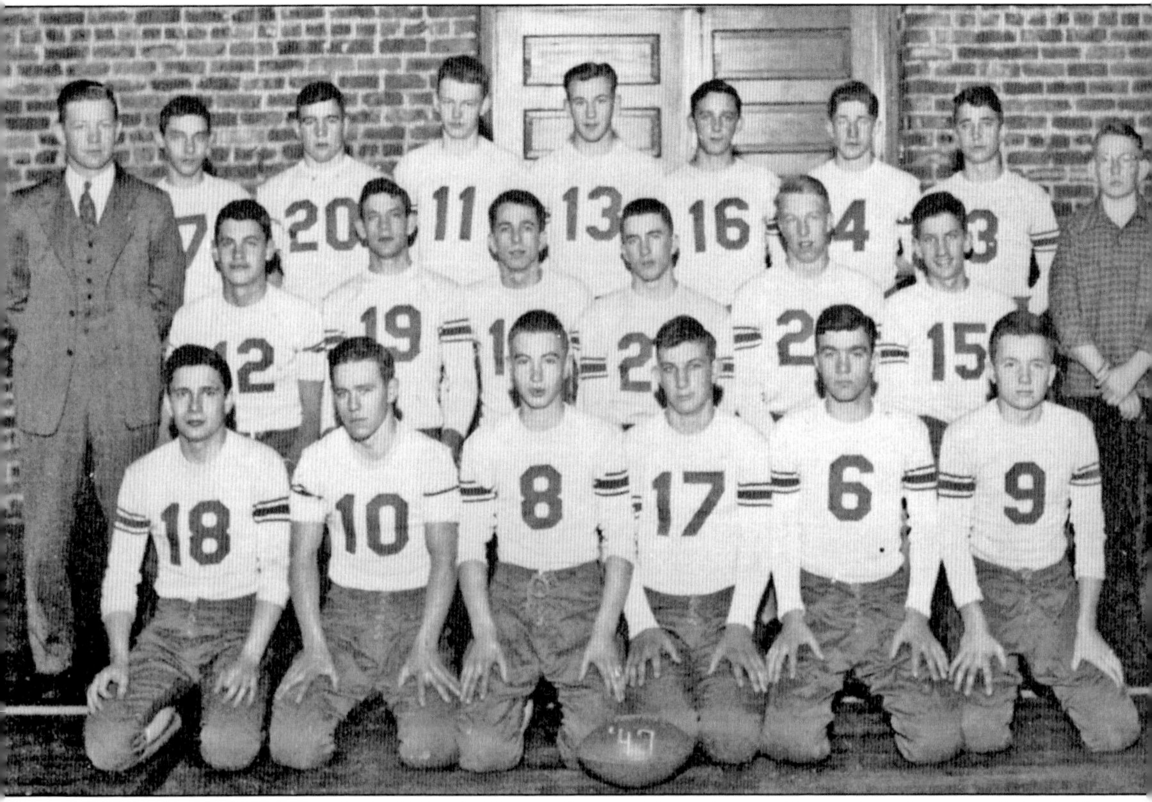

Cynthiana High School's 1948 football team featured the talents of James Lee Barnette, Mitchell Botts, Kenneth Brumback, William Cook, Edward Ewalt, John Feeback, Russell Feix, Wallace Feix, James Florence, Richard Gibson, Hall Kinney, Myron Hill, Albert Nutgrass, Richard Raymond, Russell Richie, John Henry Stivers, John Swinford, Lane Taylor, and Lewis Tolle. James Rocke coached the team. (Courtesy of Helen McNees.)

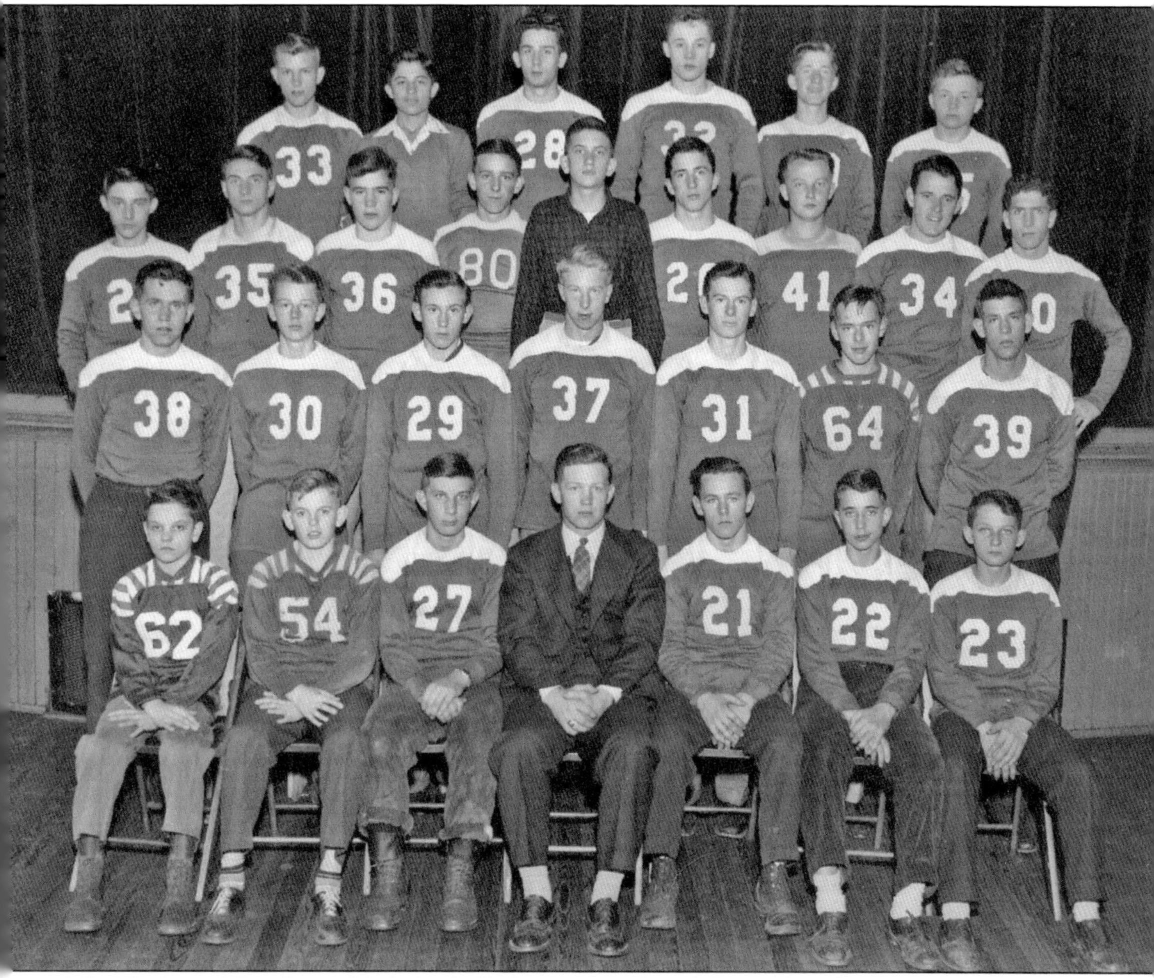

The 1946–1947 Cynthiana High football players were, from left to right, (first row) James Ritter, Clay Ashbrook, Mitchell Botts, Edward "Shorty" Ewalt, Kenneth Brumback, and Billy Joe Hill; (second row) Forest Gibson, Russell Richie, Albert Nutgrass Jr., William Cook, Joe B. Hall, Gayle Lawrence, and Lewis Tolle; (third row) Hall Kinney, Larry Douglas, Brown Feix, John Stivers, James "Mose" Florence, John Swinford, David Ammerman, Clarence Rankin Jr., and Gayle Antle; (fourth row) Tyrus Dailey, Raymond McNees, Robert Tussey, Clem Ritter, Richard Gibson, and Lane Taylor. (Courtesy of the Cynthiana–Harrison County Museum.)

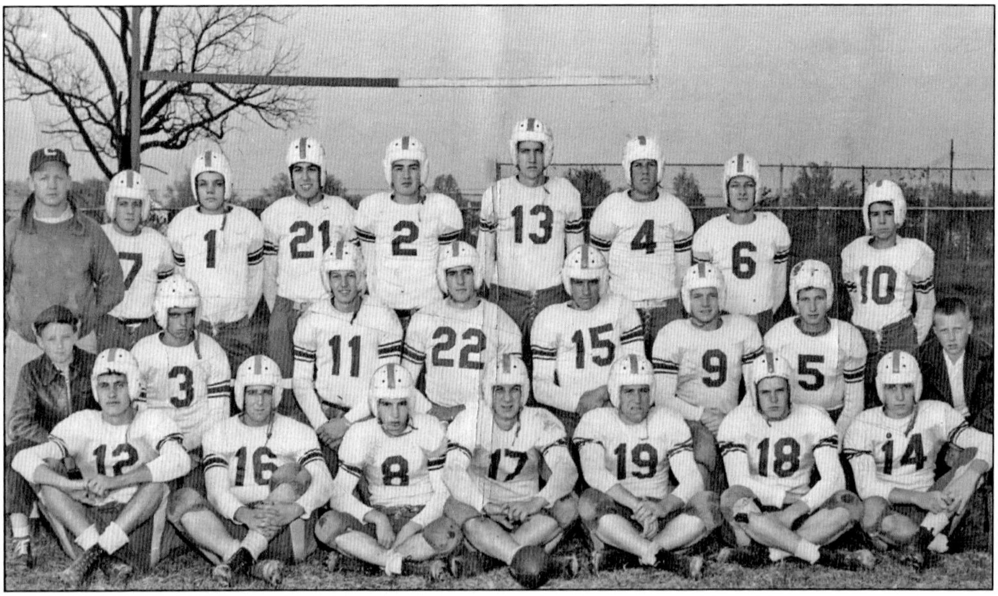

Members of the Cynthiana High School football team in 1949–1950 were, from left to right, (first row) James Barnett, John Stivers, Richard Raymond, Mitch Botts, Willie Wells, Clay Ashbrook, and Marion Hardin; (second row) Marion Glen, Bobby Wilson, Russell Richie, John Swinford, Orville "Jake" Fowler, Lane Taylor, David McCauley, and Walter Reed Ammerman; (third row) "Red" Rocke, Darrell Cooper, James Ritter, David Cole, Frazier Palmer, James "Mose" Florence, Norman Fowler, Billy Joe Hill, and Larry Shadd. (Courtesy of the Cynthiana–Harrison County Museum.)

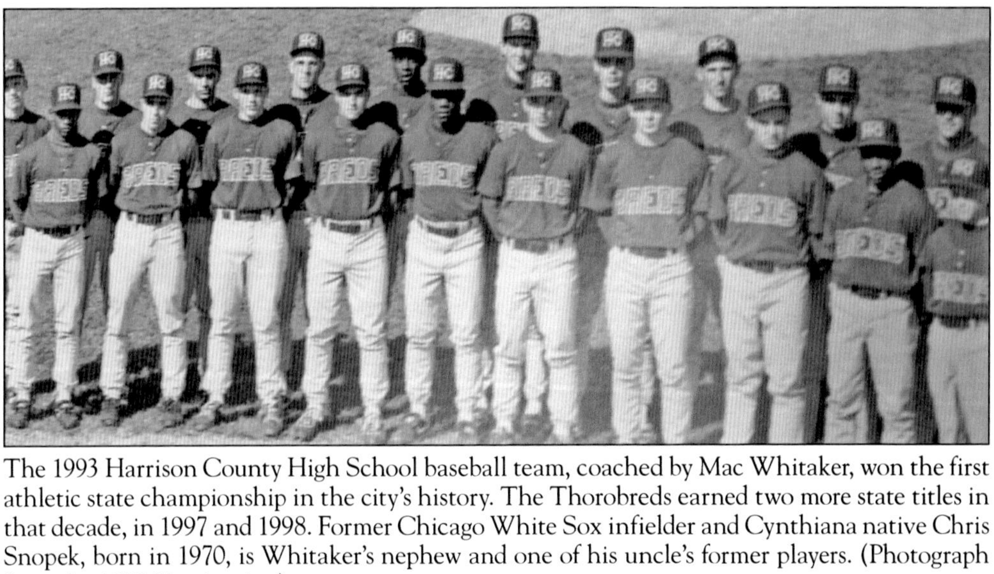

The 1993 Harrison County High School baseball team, coached by Mac Whitaker, won the first athletic state championship in the city's history. The Thorobreds earned two more state titles in that decade, in 1997 and 1998. Former Chicago White Sox infielder and Cynthiana native Chris Snopek, born in 1970, is Whitaker's nephew and one of his uncle's former players. (Photograph from the 1993 *Harrisonian*.)

Eight

Good Neighbors

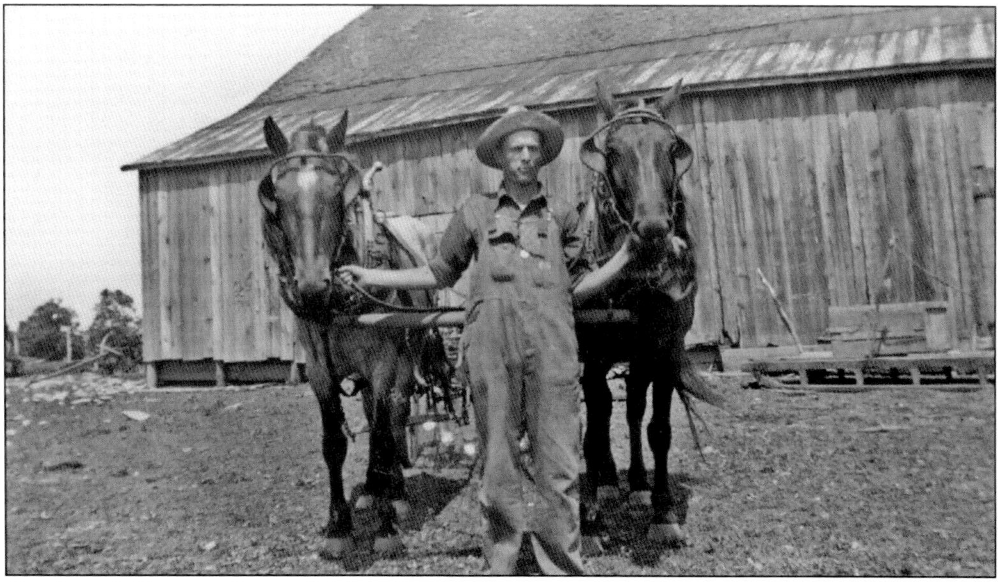

Cynthiana's Harrison County "siblings," past and present, are in most cases very small communities. Good neighbors and often Cynthiana residents hail from places with names that make reference to the people who founded them, places those folks had visited, or to physical surroundings. Some of those neighbors are Alberta, Antioch, Belmont, Berry, Boyd, Breckinridge, Broadwell, Buena Vista, Claysville, Colemansville, Colville, Connersville, Garnett, Hinton, Kelat, Lair, Lees Lick, Leesburg, Morning Glory, Oddville, Poindexter, Renaker, Robinson, Rutland, Salem, Sunrise, Sylvandell, and White Oak. Harlan Cordray of Salem is pictured in the 1930s with his horses, Mag and Bird, on the Clarence Martin farm south of Cynthiana. (Courtesy of Jack and Nora McCauley.)

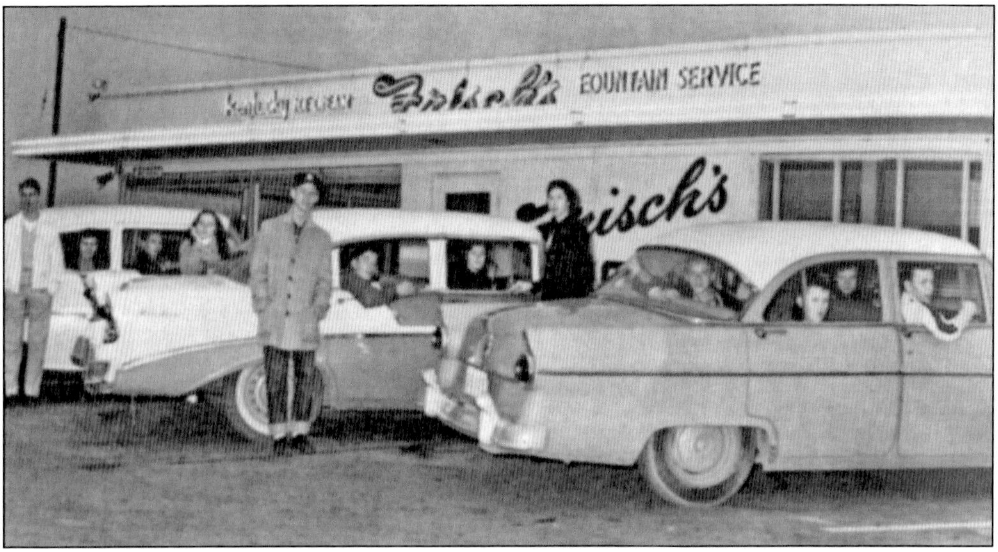

Young people and families from every part of the county made regular trips to Frisch's for Big Boy burgers. The restaurant was located a mile or so north of downtown off U.S. Route 27 in the 1950s. (Courtesy of the Cynthiana High School Alumni Association.)

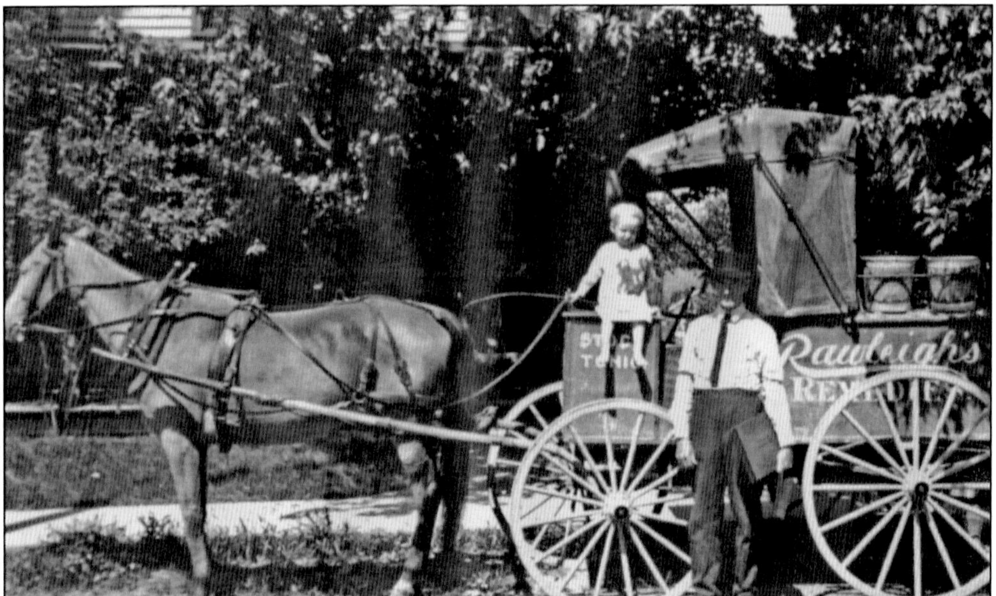

Lafayette "Lafe" Jackson Harney, a Harrison County native and the son of Willoughby Oscar Harney, moved to Scott County to establish a Rawleigh route, delivering salve, ointments, and other health care products. The child accompanying Lafe is Lafayette Jackson Harney Jr., the uncle of Jack McCauley of Salem. McCauley says that at one time, his grandfather Lafe had allergies so bad that he was forced to wear his wife's dresses until his sores healed, quit farming, and buy into the Rawleigh business, securing the Scott County route because the Harrison County one was taken. (Courtesy of Jack and Nora McCauley.)

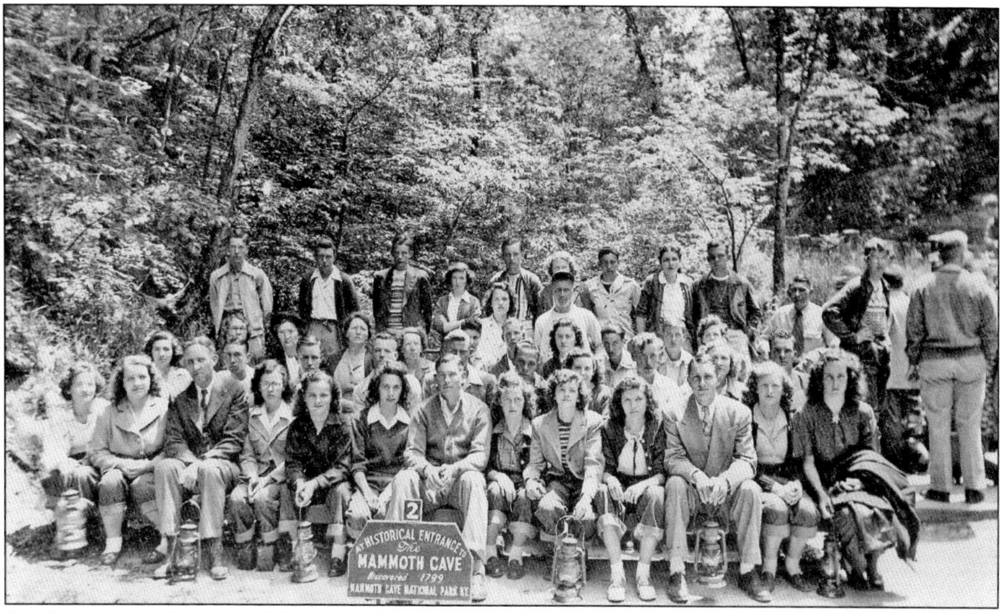

Students from Renaker School took a field trip to Mammoth Cave in 1949. (Courtesy of the Cynthiana–Harrison County Museum.)

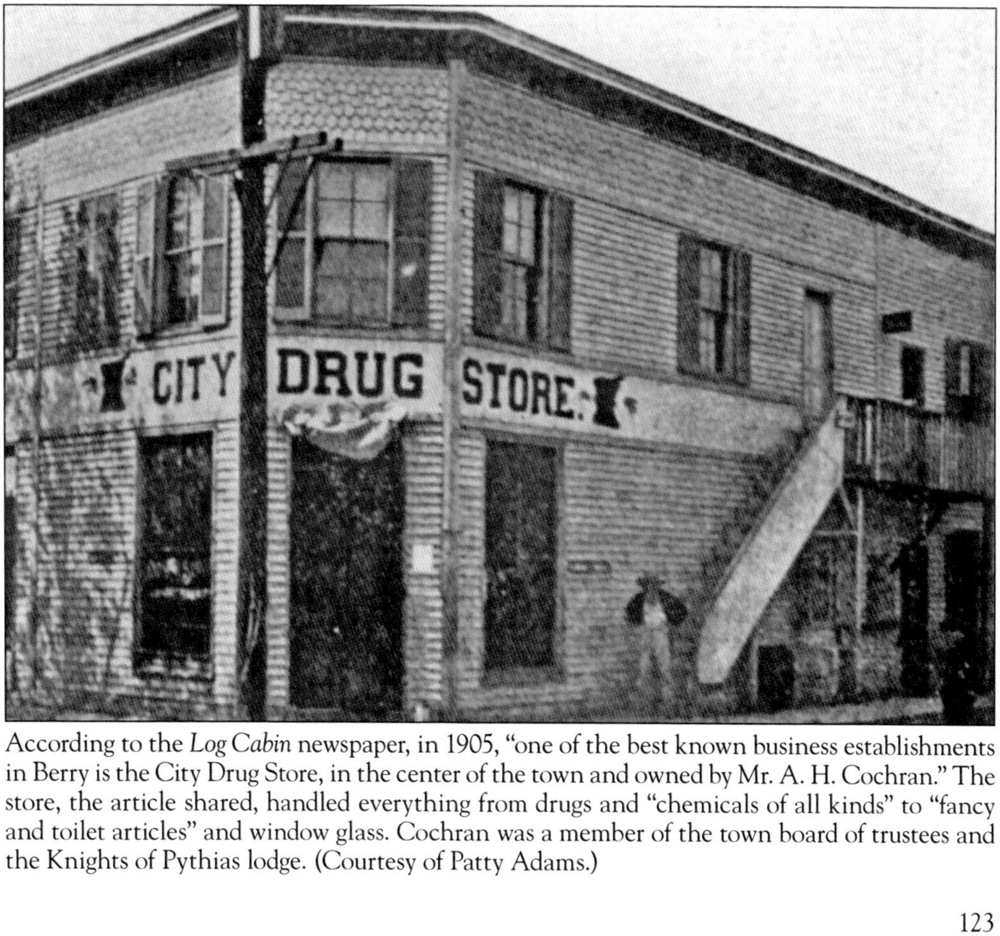

According to the *Log Cabin* newspaper, in 1905, "one of the best known business establishments in Berry is the City Drug Store, in the center of the town and owned by Mr. A. H. Cochran." The store, the article shared, handled everything from drugs and "chemicals of all kinds" to "fancy and toilet articles" and window glass. Cochran was a member of the town board of trustees and the Knights of Pythias lodge. (Courtesy of Patty Adams.)

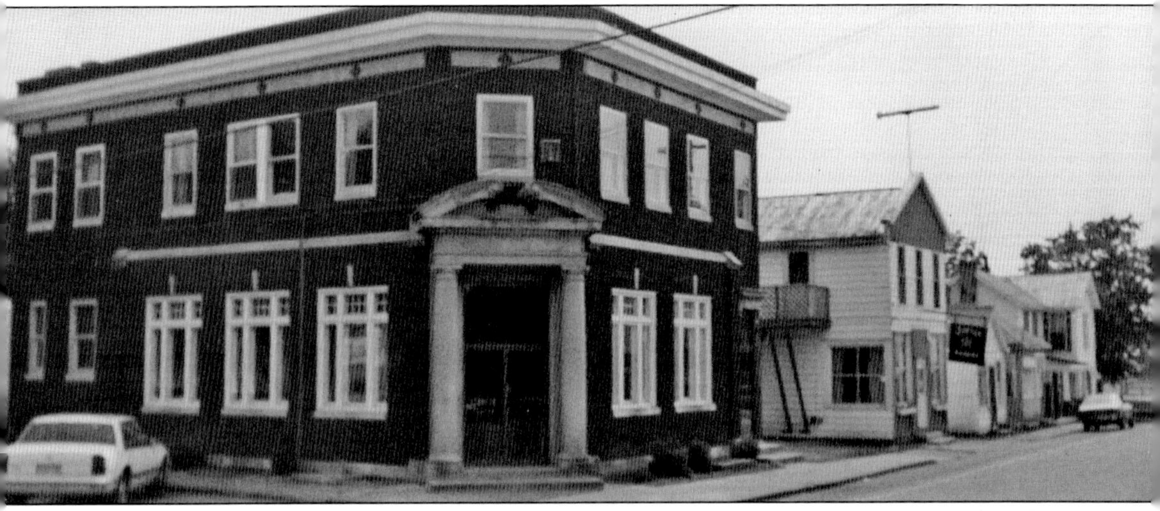

The old Berry Bank would later be used as the Blake building. (Courtesy of Patty Adams.)

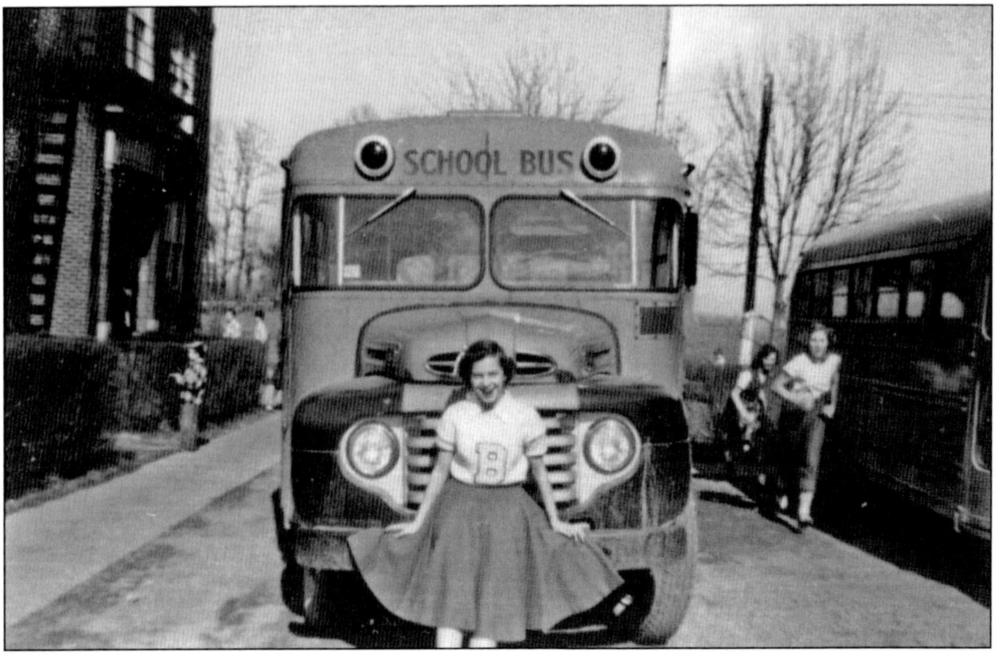

An unidentified cheerleader flashes a grin near the old Berry school. (Courtesy of Patty Adams.)

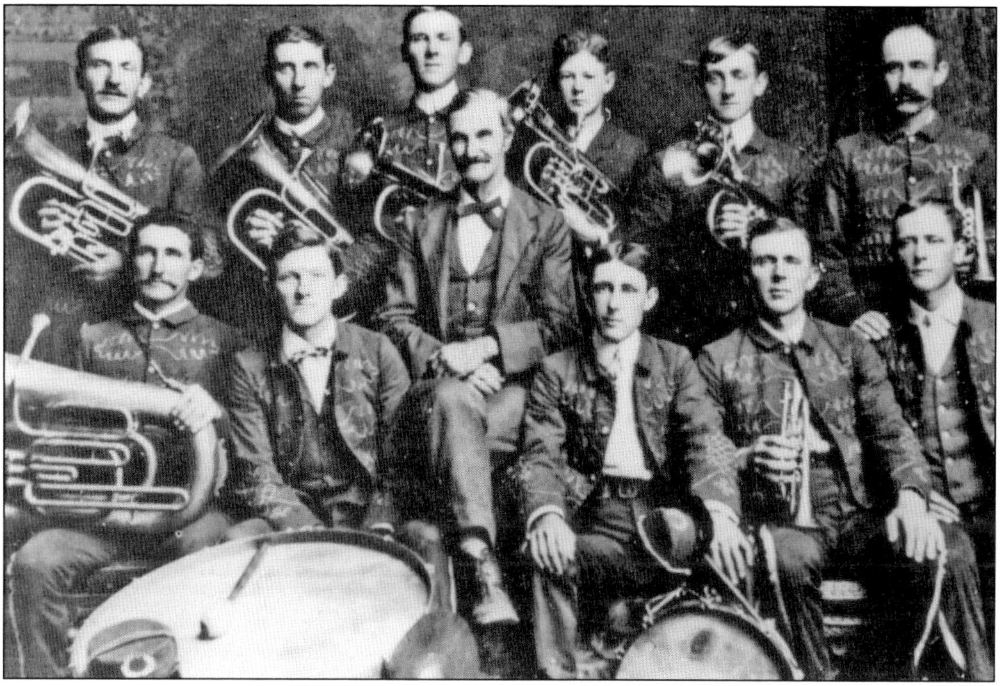

Cynthiana resident Dorothy Slade's grandfather, Robert E. Florence Sr., was a member of the Sylvandell-based Henry Band. Florence is at left, joined by Luther Mastin, Alexandria I. "Doc" Pope, Harry McCauley, Virgil Judy, Dow McCauley, Ed Judy, Fred Florence, Jim Judy, Bowen Smith, Orie Peddicord, and Tom Peddicord. (Courtesy of the Cynthiana–Harrison County Public Library's James Saunders Whaley Collection.)

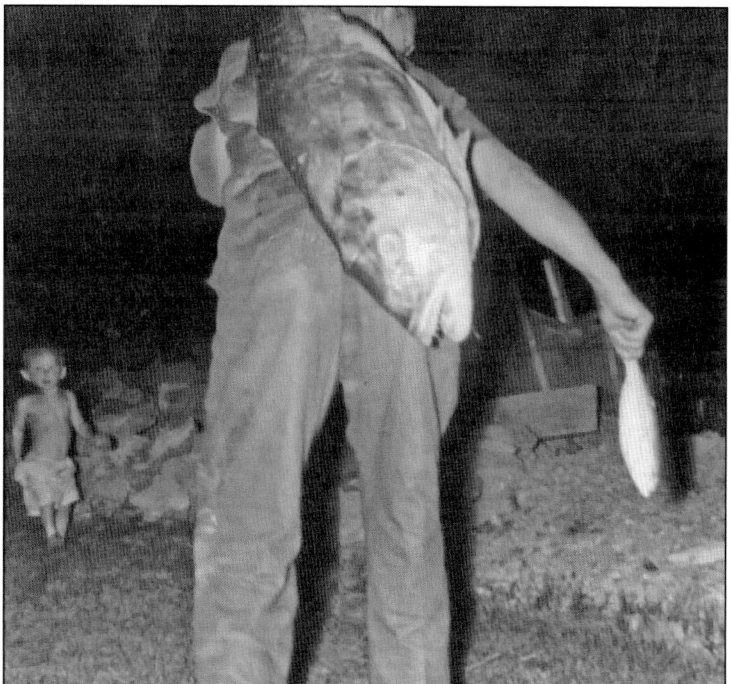

Fishing has long lured area residents. Greeted by a young neighbor, Roy Ecklar lugs his large (and small) catch after a trip to a Harrison County fishing hole. (Courtesy of Helen Harney.)

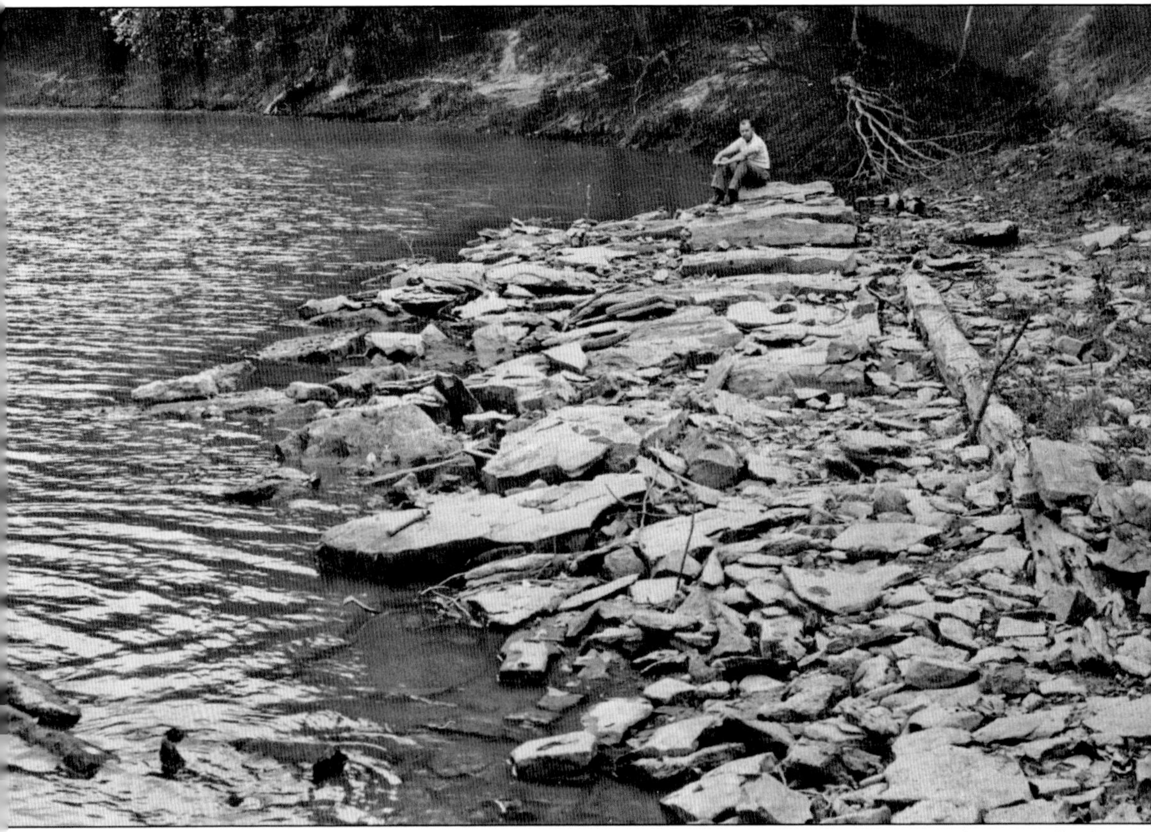

William O. Penn, former manager of the Harrison Rural Electric Cooperative, was photographed in the 1960s on the banks of the Licking River near Claysville after the river sank due to drought. When the water level fell, pieces of a long-sunken barge were visible. The *Falmouth Outlook* reported that the barge sank about 3 miles northeast of Buena Vista, near a farm owned by Judge Mac Swinford. (Courtesy of William A. Penn.)

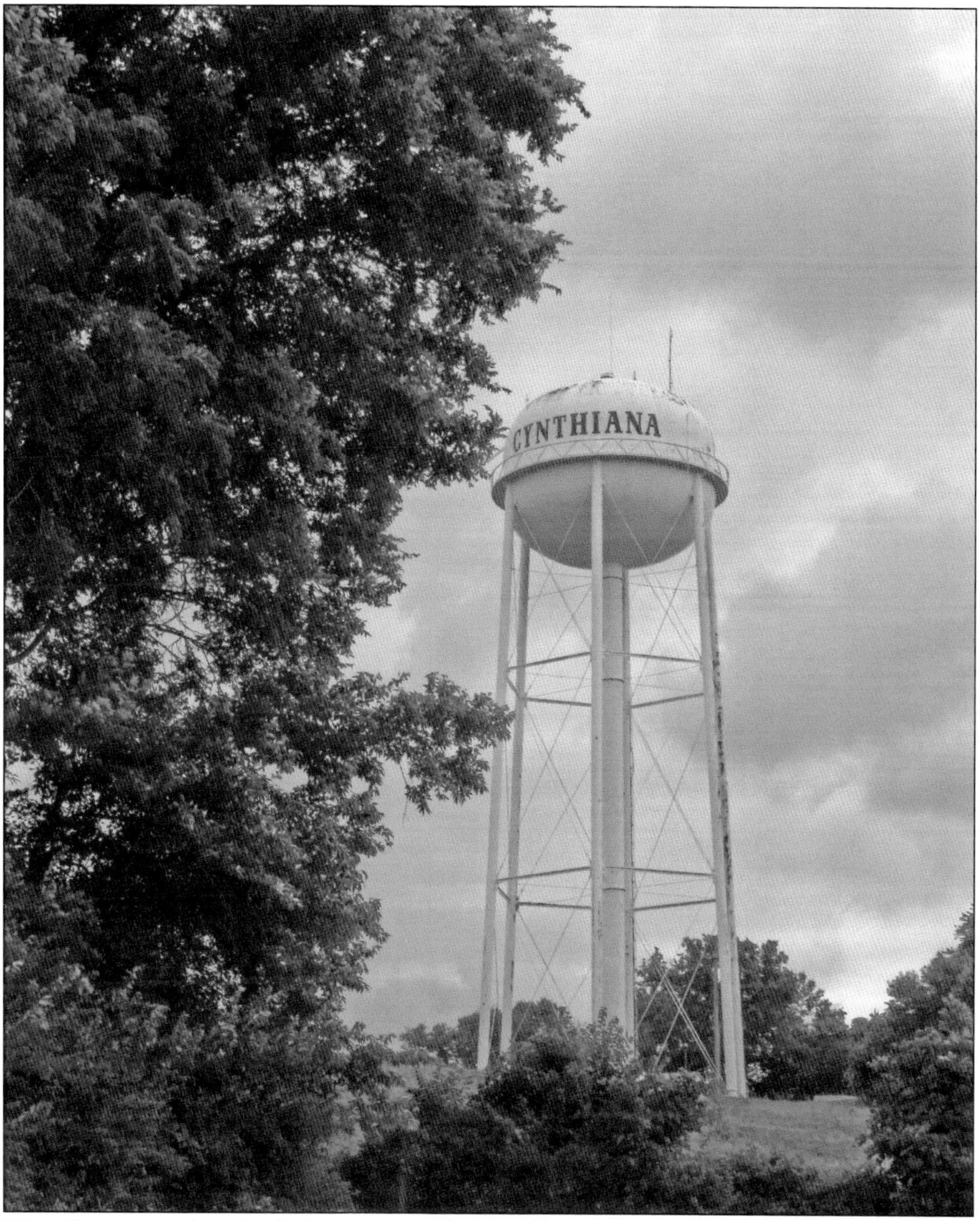

We call it home: this plainly lettered local landmark on a water tower near the Lebus Field off U.S. Route 27 is visible to drivers leaving and entering Cynthiana from the city's north side. (Photograph by M. Britt Kennerly.)